Wilderness Empire
A Story of the Iroquois Confederacy

Michael L. Hart

Wilderness Empire

Copyright © 2017 by Michael L. Hart

No part of this publication may be reproduced, distributed, or transmitted in any form or by any means, including photocopying, recording, or other electronic or mechanical methods, without the prior written permission of the author, except in the case of brief quotations embodied in critical reviews and certain other non-commercial uses permitted by copyright law.

Tellwell Talent
www.tellwell.ca

ISBN
000-0-00000-000-0 (Hardcover)
000-0-00000-000-0 (Paperback)
000-0-00000-000-0 (eBook)

This book is dedicated to my grandchildren
Gabrielle, Benjamin, Jacob, and Henry.

*"Another generation and there will be no custom;
still another generation and there will be no memory."*

Seneca Nation Chief John *Ganio'dai'io* Gibson (1850-1912),
on the importance of keeping traditional knowledge
and Haudenosaunee history alive.

Table of Contents

Prologue: The Iroquois Confederacy Building an Empire....................xv

Chapter 1: Early history of the Iroquois...1
    The Constitution of the Iroquois Nations
    Gayanashagowa, the Great Binding Law ... 5
    Awakening to the Concept of Economic Advantage ... 9
    Ancestral Homeland of the Five Nations of
    the Haudenosaunee Confederacy ... 15

Chapter 2: First Contact...17
    Champlain's Campaign to Defeat the Iroquois ... 26
    Old Enemies and New Alliances ... 30
    Iroquois ... 31
    Tuscarora Alliance Wampum ... 39
    Women's Nomination Wampum ... 40
    Algonquin Nation ... 41
    Wendat Nation ... 43
    Petun Nation ... 46
    Neutral Nation ... 46
    Mahican Nation ... 47
    Susquehannock Nation ... 49

Anishinaabe and Mississaugas ... 53
In the Beginning: ... 54
The Council of Three Fires: ... 56
Mississaugas: ... 59
Indigenous People of eastern North America, 1600 ... 61
Summary ... 62
Friendship Wampum ... 63

Chapter 3: The Fur Trade ... 65
Foundations for a Wilderness Empire ... 65

Chapter 4: The Covenant Chain ... 73
A Coalition of Tribes ... 73
Friendship Treaty Wampum ... 73
Two Row Wampum ... 78

The French Period, 1615-1763

Chapter 5: The French Period 1615-1763 ... 81
Kiotsaeton's Treachery ... 85
Mohawk truce with the French, Algonquin and Huron ... 87
The Iroquois Destruction of the Huron Begins. ... 88

Chapter 6: The Beaver Wars, 1640-1701 ... 91

Chapter 7: Seizing an Empire ... 101
The Great Pursuit and Dispersal of the Huron ... 101
The Great Pursuit ... 104
The Huron-Wendat Dispersal, 1653-1667
A Diaspora of Epic Proportion ... 108

Chapter 8: The Battle of Long Sault ... 113

Chapter 9: Victors and Vanquished ... 117
Aftermath of War ... 117
Iroquois du Nord ... 118

Chapter 10: Campaigns of the Eastern Iroquois..................121
   The French Offensive ... 121
   The French Offensive ... 124

Chapter 11: The Iroquois Confederacy and Aftermath of the Beaver Wars 129
   Victors and Vanquished ... 131
   Iroquois Empire, 1667 ... 134

Chapter 12: Second Phase of the Beaver War Begins..................135
   Denonville's Treachery ... 140
   The Grand Settlement of 1701 ... 148
   The Nanfan Council: ... 149
   The Montreal Council: ... 150
   Little Stays the Same Forever.
   The Resumption of Hostilities.
   Queen Anne's War, 1702-13 ... 153
   The Assassination of Alexander Montour
   and Samuel Vetch's Plans for the Invasion of Canada ... 155
   Iroquois Strategy of Economic Warfare
   against the French ... 157
   Iroquois Beaver Hunting Grounds ... 160
   Iroquois Empire, 1701 ... 161

Chapter 13: The Jesuit Influence..................163

Chapter 14: Religious tensions among the Iroquois..................173
   A fracturing of the Great Binding Law ... 173

Chapter 15: The Western Campaign..................179
   Shifting Iroquois Fortunes in the Ohio Valley ... 179
   War on Many Fronts
   The Continuing Struggle for Alliance and Advantage ... 185

Chapter 16: The French and Indian War, 1755-1763..................189
   New England and the Ohio Valley
   Changing Iroquois Alliances ... 189

The English Period, 1763-1783

Chapter 17: The English Period, 1763-1783
Unravelling of the Iroquois Empire 201
    Pontiac's Rebellion, 1763-1766 ... 203
    The Covenant Chain is Broken ... 206
    Treaty of Fort Stanwix, 1768 ... 208
    Lord Dunmore's War, 1774 ... 210

Chapter 18: The Beginning of the End of the Iroquois Empire 213
    The Iroquois Confederacy – From Princes of
    Empire to Refugee; the Council Fire of the
    Iroquois Confederacy is extinguished. ... 213
    The Western Campaign ... 216
    Seven Nations of Canada ... 227
    The Sullivan Expedition, 1779
    Scorched Earth and Refugees ... 227
    Civil War Among the Iroquois ... 230
    The Iroquois Confederacy
    From Empire to Refugee ... 231

The American Treaty Period, 1783-1830

Chapter 19: The American Treaty Period 1783-1830
Struggle for the Ohio Valley, an undeclared War 235
    The Ohio Valley Region, 1783 ... 236
    Anishinaabe
    Council of Three Fires ... 238
    Illinois Confederacy ... 239
    Western Confederacy (Post 1776) ... 240
    Northwest Indian War, 1785-1795 ... 241
    Little Turtle's War ... 245
    Northwest Territory, 1785 ... 248

Chapter 20: A Time for Treaties 249
    Treaty of Canandaigua, 1794; Jay Treaty, 1794;
    Greenville Treaty, 1795; Treaty of Big Tree, 1797 ... 249
    Jay Treaty, 1794 ... 250
    Greenville Treaty, 1795 ... 253
    Treaty of Big Tree, 1797 ... 255

Chapter 21: A Broken Chain 257
    The Iroquois Confederacy and the War of 1812 ... 257
    Battle of Queenston Heights ... 260
    Battle of Fort George
    and the Battle of Beaver Dams ... 262
    Tecumseh's Confederacy ... 265

Chapter 22: Haudenosaunee Reconciliation 269
    William Claus Wampum Belt ... 269
    William Claus Wampum Belt ... 270
    Pledge of the Crown Wampum ... 272

Chapter 23: A Defeated People From Princes of Empire to Refugee 273
    The Winter of an Empire
    From Princes of Wilderness Empire to Refugee ... 273
    Lands Lost to Treaty ... 277
    The Seven Nations of Canada
    Relinquished Land Claims in New York State ... 278
    The Indian Removal Act, 1830 ... 279
    Iroquois Communities (Cdn.) and
    Reservations (U.S.), 2016 ... 281

The Iroquois in Recent Times

Chapter 24: The Iroquois in Recent Times 285
    The influence of the Seneca prophet Handsome
    Ganiodaiio Lake and the Good Message;
    Suppression of Traditional Governance ... 287

Chapter 25: The Great Binding Law in Contemporary Times 291
    Interpretation of the Great Binding Law
    Differences and Division ... 293
    Louis Karoniaktajeh Hall and the Warrior Society ... 297

Chapter 26: Political Positions of the Mohawk
Haudenosaunee; a Contemporary View 303
    Tragedy of Societal Dilution ... 305
    Language - the Keeper of Culture ... 306
    Steadfast Iroquois Nationalism ... 308

Chapter 27: Wandering from the Path 311

Epilogue 315

Acknowledgements 319

About the Author 321

Bibliography 323
    Primary Sources ... 323
    Secondary Sources ... 330

Wilderness Empire

Prologue
The Iroquois Confederacy
Building an Empire

This is a story of the rise and fall of the wilderness empire of the Iroquois Confederacy.

This book is not an academic work of cultural anthropology or history. Rather, it is a collection of stories that capture the intrigue, treachery, victories and defeat across three centuries in a vast wilderness landscape. This is a story of Indigenous confederacies and alliances, and the struggles for territory and domination by the empirical powers of the Netherlands, France, and England in Eastern North America.

The story captures the intrigue and treachery associated with a clash of European and Indigenous cultures from first encounter in the 16th Century to the early years of the 19th Century. The story explores a complex web of far-flung wilderness alliances and exposes betrayal and duplicity of friend and foe. The story follows bold statesmanship and diplomacy of Indigenous leaders backed by brilliant military strategy that altered the history of empires.

Foremost, this is the story of the Haudenosaunee Confederacy and its ascent to regional dominance through military and political prowess. This is also the story of a proud people with a distinct culture who, in the face of overwhelming pressure from European encroachment, became refugees in their ancestral lands.

Central to this story are the five tribes whose ancestral lands lay in present-day upper New York State. The five tribes were unified by Dekanawida, the Peacemaker. The Peacemaker satisfied the royaner (hereditary leaders) of the five tribes that accepting the armistice and unity of the Great Binding Law was to their advantage.

Around 1142 CE, the royaner of the five tribes - Mohawk, Oneida, Onondaga, Cayuga, and Seneca - accepted the armistice proposed by the Peacemaker and a confederacy of five tribes was established. The Great Binding Law's message of peace, unity, and justice is the constitution of the Confederacy.

The followers of the Great Binding Law called themselves Haudenosaunee, meaning *followers of the longhouse teaching*. And so, the five united tribes became known as the Haudenosaunee Confederacy. Later, when the French arrived in the St. Lawrence River region, they called the Haudenosaunee *Iroquois*. The five tribes became known as the Iroquois Confederacy. The French, noting that each tribe functioned within civil and political parameters, recognized the tribes as *nations*.

When the Dutch, Swedish, and English adventurers began to settle in the Hudson River region and the Manhattan Island region, they called the five tribes the League of Five Nations, or simply the Five Nations. In 1722, the Oneida sponsored the British persecuted Tuscarora and they were adopted by the Confederacy. Now, the British began to call the Haudenosaunee the Six Nations.

Today, the Five Nations confederacy is commonly referred to as the Iroquois Confederacy. Perhaps, in a historical sense, Haudenosaunee Confederacy is most appropriate. After all, not all Iroquois are Haudenosaunee, but all Haudenosaunee are Iroquois.

And so, now begins the epic story of the rise and fall of the Haudenosaunee Confederacy.

Chapter 1

Early history of the Iroquois
Not so very long ago

In the beginning, not so very long ago, across the unspoiled wilderness of eastern North America, a rich and diverse tapestry of human cultures existed in harmony with nature. The various cultures were grouped as tribes, each distinct yet similar, to the other.

Some of the tribes were nomadic. They hunted and fished and moved through the four seasons in sync with the seasonal patterns of the fish and wildlife they depended upon. Other tribes became strong agrarian societies and grew the three sisters - corn, squash, and beans - on land cleared by fire. The social center for the agrarian society was a village consisting of long houses built of poles and bark. A longhouse would provide shelter for a number of families. A village was usually surrounded by a palisade of upright logs. The walled villages, built on high ground, would later be called *castles* by the Europeans.

An agricultural settlement would thrive until soil fertility was depleted. Sometimes this would take twenty or more years. When the need to find new, fertile soil arose, the village would relocate and begin the cycle of slash and burn agriculture. The agrarian tribes had greater food security than the nomadic hunters and gatherers. Food security allowed time to establish complex social and political systems and a process for civil governance. The Creator was celebrated in a cycle of ceremonies that recognized and honored all the gifts bestowed upon man. Spirituality flourished among the people.

A few tribal groups, brutalized by intertribal warfare, established armistices and formed durable confederacies. The confederacies produced statesmen who articulated diplomacy to achieve the policies of complex systems of governance. Military power integral to powerful confederacies was unleashed when threats to member tribes or allies could not be resolved through diplomacy and consensual agreement. Trade ebbed and flowed across vast regions comprising lands between the Great Lakes Region and the eastern Atlantic coast.

The land was seldom at peace. Intertribal warfare was a fact of life. Before the arrival of the Europeans, intertribal warfare consisted of sporadic raiding and random skirmishes resulting in a few dead, some captured and killed, and others adopted into the victorious tribe. Grief for war losses fed fear and hatred ensuring that revenge warfare would be passed from generation to generation. Raiding to capture prisoners to replace persons lost in warfare became known as *mourning-wars*. The mourning-war was a principal cultural component of the Mohawk, Oneida, Onondaga, Cayuga and Seneca.

The Creator grew tired of the warfare between the five tribes, and was saddened by the endless grief of the people. He gave Dekanawida, the Peacemaker, a mission. The Peacemaker, a Wendat [Huron], traveled across Lake Ontario in a stone canoe and arrived on the shore of the ancestral tribal lands of the Mohawk, Oneida, Onondaga, Cayuga, and Seneca. The Peacemaker's mission was to bring the five tribes together in peace.

Within Haudenosaunee culture it is considered rude and disrespectful to speak the Peacemaker's name. Some Haudenosaunee prefer that his name not be written down at all, and if it must be, then as infrequently as possible. Acknowledging this preference, the writer has used *Peacemaker* as often as the occasion will allow.

The Peacemaker, using his powers of diplomacy, shared the message of the *Kaianerenko:wa* [Mohawk language] - the Great Binding Law - to convince the *royaner* [hereditary lords, clan chiefs] of the five tribes that replacing warfare with an armistice and the unity of confederacy would bring peace and power to the five tribes.

The five tribes gave their allegiance to the Great Binding Law. The five unified tribes include: Mohawk, *People Possessors of the Flint*; Oneida, *Granite People*; Onondaga, *People of the Hills*; Cayuga, *People at the Mucky Land*; Seneca, *Great Hill People*.

It was a challenge to convince the five tribes that an armistice would be in their interest. The Peacemaker allied himself with a Mohawk royaner named Hahyonhwatha [Hiawatha]. Hahyonhwatha translates as *he who has misplaced something, but knows where to find it*.

The Peacemaker, in a deciding moment, broke a single arrow across his knee. Then, passing a bundle of five arrows to a royaner, the Peacemaker asked him to break the arrows. The royaner could not do it. In this way, the Peacemaker satisfied the leaders of the five tribes that, standing alone they were weak and vulnerable, but together, as a confederacy of five nations, they would be strong.

After much resistance, the Peacemaker had persuaded the difficult holdout, the cannibal Adodarhoh, an Onondaga royaner, to accept the message of *Kaianereenko:wa*, the Great Binding Law. The epic story of the contest of wills between the Peacemaker and Adodarhoh, the troublesome royaner of the Onondaga, is a magnificent story by itself.

By the year 1142 CE, the Peacemaker's negotiations with the royaner of the five tribes had achieved an armistice. The armistice became the Haudenosaunee Confederacy.

The Great Binding Law of the Haudenosaunee Confederacy is the Constitution of the five tribes. The Constitution is a cultural document with 177 articles. The articles set out rules of civil society and provide policy and procedure for governance. The Constitution provided the foundation for unity among the five founding tribes. The Peacemaker's message is also the basis for a strong Haudenosaunee nationalism which continues to this day.

For generations, the Great Binding Law has been passed down orally through the generations. Today, we have several written translations for the Great Binding Law. Actually, there are five versions.

Beginning in the 1870s, Onondaga Chief Seth *Dayodekane* Newhouse (1842-1921) began to collect and record the oral narrative of the Great Binding Law. *Dayodekane's* transcription of the traditional oral narrative described the founding of the Iroquois Confederacy. The work was *Dayodekane's* defence of the original intent of the Great Binding Law.

Dayodekane tried several times to have the Six Nations Council of Chiefs approve his rendition of the Great Binding law. His last attempt was in 1899. The reason for the Council rejections may rest with their interpretation that *Dayodekane* had given too much emphasis to the importance of the Mohawk role within the Confederacy. *Dayodekane*, in the Council's opinion, also gave more importance to the work of Hiawatha then to the Peacemaker. This did not please the Council.

Seneca Nation Chief John Arthur *Ganio'dai'io* Gibson (1850-1912) is the author of the *Chief's Version*. Gibson is also known by his traditional Seneca royaner name *Skanyadehehyoh*. Gibson's version of the Great Binding Law was approved by the Council of Chiefs of Six Nations in 1900. Hence the name *Chief's Version*. The *Chiefs Version* is considered the authoritative record of the founding of the Iroquois Confederacy and the Great Binding Law.

In 1910, the Confederacy Chiefs sent *Dayodekane's* manuscript to Arthur C. *Gawaso Wanneh* Parker (1881-1955). Parker was an accomplished Seneca citizen, archeologist and historian with the New York State Museum. Parker combined *Dayodekane's* manuscript with the transcription of Seneca writer John *Ganio'dai'io* Gibson. Parker's version was published in 1916 by the New York Sate Museum as a bulletin titled *The Constitution of the Five Nations or the Iroquois Book of the Great Law*.

To provide a flavour for the influence and power of the Peacemaker's oratory rhyme and purpose, the opening seven sections of the *Great Binding Law* are shared below.

The version provided was translated by Arthur C. Parker from the work of Seneca Nation Chief John *Ganio'dai'io* Gibson

The Constitution of the Iroquois Nations
Gayanashagowa, the Great Binding Law

1. "*I am Dekanawidah and with the Five Nation's Confederate Lords I plant the Tree of Great Peace. I plant it in your territory, Adodarhoh, and the Onondaga Nation, in the territory of you who are Firekeepers.*

   I name the tree the Tree of the Great Long Leaves. Under the shade of this Tree of the Great Peace we spread the soft white feathery down of the globe thistle as seats for you, Adodarhoh, and your cousin Lords.

   We place you upon those seats, spread soft with the feathery down of the globe thistle, there beneath the shade of the spreading branches of the Tree of Peace. There you shall sit and watch the Council Fire of the Confederacy of Five Nations, and all the affairs of the Five Nations shall be transacted at this place before you, Adodarhoh, and your cousin Lords, by the Confederate Lords of the Five Nations.

2. *Roots have spread out from the Tree of Great Peace, one to the north, one to the east, one to the south and one to the west. The name of these roots is the Great White Roots and their nature is Peace and Strength.*

   If any man or any nation outside the Five Nations shall obey the laws of the Great Peace and make known their disposition to the Lords of the Confederacy, they may trace the Roots to the Tree and if their minds are clean and they are obedient and promise to obey the wishes of the Confederate Council, they shall be welcomed to take shelter beneath the Tree of the Long Leaves.

   We place at the top of the Tree of the Long Leaves an Eagle who is able to see afar. If he sees in the distance any evil approaching or any danger threatening, he will at once warn the people of the Confederacy.

3.   To you Adodarhoh, the Onondaga cousin Lords, I and the other Confederate Lords have entrusted the caretaking and watching of the Five Nations Council Fire.

    When there is any business to be transacted and the Confederate Council is not in session, a messenger shall be dispatched to either Adodarhoh, Hononwirehtonh or Skanawatih, Fire Keepers, or to their War Chiefs with a full statement of the case desired to be considered. Then shall Adodarhoh call his cousin (associate) Lords together and consider whether or not the case is of sufficient importance to demand the attention of the Confederate Council. If so, Adodarhoh shall dispatch messengers to summon all the Confederate Lords to assemble beneath the tree of the Long Leaves.

    When the Lords are assembled the Council Fire shall be kindled, but not with chestnut wood, I, and Adodarhoh shall formerly open the Council.

    Then shall Adodarhoh and his cousin Lords, the Fire Keepers, announce the subject for discussion.

    The Smoke of the Confederate Council Fire shall ever ascend and pierce the sky so that other nations who may be allies may see the Council Fire of the Great Peace.

    Adodarhoh and his cousin Lords are entrusted with the Keeping of the Council Fire.

4.   You, Adodarhoh, and your thirteen cousin Lords, shall faithfully keep the space about the Council Fire clean and you shall allow neither dust nor dirt to accumulate. I lay a Long Wing before you as a broom. As a weapon against a crawling creature I lay a staff with you so that you may thrust it away from the Council Fire. If you fail to cast it out, then call the rest of the United Lords to your aid.

5.   The Council of the Mohawk shall be divided into three parties as follows: Tekarihoken, Ayonhwhathah and Shadekariwade are the first party; Sharenhowaneh, Deyoenhegwenh and Oghrenghrehgowah are the second party, and Dehennakrineh, Aghstawenserenthah and Shoskoharowaneh are the third party. The third party is to listen only to the discussion of the first and second parties and if an error is made or the proceeding is irregular they

are to call attention to it, and when the case is right and properly decided by the two parties they shall confirm the decision of the two parties and refer the case to the Seneca Lords for their decision. When the Seneca Lords have decided in accord with the Mohawk Lords, the case or question shall be referred to the Cayuga and Oneida Lords on the opposite side of the house.

6. I, Dekanawidah, appoint the Mohawk Lords the heads of the leaders of the Five Nations Confederacy. The Mohawk Lords are the foundation of the Great Peace and it shall, therefore, be against the Great Binding Law to pass measures in the Confederate Council after the Mohawk Lords have protested against them.

    No council of the Confederate Lords shall be legal unless all the Mohawk Lords are present.

7. Whenever the Confederate Lords shall assemble for the purpose of holding a council, the Onondaga Lords shall open it by expressing their gratitude to their cousin Lords and greeting them, and they shall make an address and offer thanks to the earth where men dwell, to the steams of water, the pools, the springs and the lakes, to the maize and the fruits, to the medicinal herbs and trees, to the forest trees for their usefulness, to the animals that serve as food and give their pelts for clothing, to the great winds and the lesser winds, to the Thunderers, to the sun, the mighty warrior, to the moon, to the messengers of the Creator who reveal his wishes and to the Great Creator who dwells in the heavens above, who gives all the things useful to men, and who is the source and the ruler of health and life.

    Then shall the Onondaga Lords declare the council open.

    The council shall not sit after darkness has set in."

In the preceding narrative, the *Tree of Great Peace* and the *Tree of the Long Leaves* refers to the White Pine tree. Direction is given that chestnut wood not be burned in the council fire. Chestnut wood burns with frequent loud sparking which would be a distraction for the Council Lords.

Article 4 makes reference to Adodarhoh and his thirteen Onondaga cousin lords. When negotiating with the five tribes to find consensual agreement for an armistice, the Peacemaker allocated a number of lords for each of the five tribes.

Of the five tribes, the Onondaga had the least population. Their primary lord, Adodarhoh, offered the fiercest resistance to any agreement for unity of the five tribes. In his effort to pacify Adodarhoh, the Peacemaker offered to allocate thirteen lords to the Onondaga and assign the Onondaga the responsibility of *Keepers of the Confederacy Fire*. Adodarhoh recognized that he was being given increased responsibility and authority. Adodarhoh was pleased. He accepted the messages of the Peacemaker and agreed that the Onondaga would join the other four tribes in armistice and a unity of five nations.

As the *American Revolutionary War, 1765-1783*, drew to a close, the founding fathers of the new United States of America found themselves challenged to find an existing document that provided a satisfactory example for their view of a democracy in a modern world. Benjamin Franklin, a founding father of the new United States of America, was impressed by the inclusive civil process and consensus seeking laid out in the Great Binding Law. The founding fathers of the new United States found much in the Constitution of the Haudenosaunee they were pleased with. The Constitution of the United States includes ideas and process borrowed from the Constitution of the Haudenosaunee Confederacy.

Ideas and imagery adopted by the Americans can be seen on the United States one-dollar bill. The eagle, atop the Tree of Peace and always alert for danger to the Confederacy, is shown clutching a bundle of thirteen arrows representing the Thirteen Colonies. The Peacemaker used a bundle of five arrows to demonstrate the strength of unity of the five tribes of the Haudenosaunee Confederacy.

The Peacemaker had succeeded in bringing an end to the brutal conflict between the five tribes. The armistice was sealed when the lords agreed to accept the message of the Great Binding Law. The followers of the Great Binding Law of the Confederacy are known as Haudenosaunee which means *followers of the longhouse teaching*.

The Great Binding Law is often referred to as the Great Law of Peace. In theory, this is true. However, in practice it was not a law intended for universal peace. The Great Binding Law forbid the five unified tribes from fighting among themselves. There is nothing in the Great Law that ensured peace with tribes outside the Confederacy was a requirement of the Great Binding Law. The Confederacy was free to wage war on any tribe or nation that was a threat to the Confederacy. War was sanctioned against any tribe or tribal confederacy that was seen as an impediment to territorial expansion or Haudenosaunee control over territory and trade.

Awakening to the Concept of Economic Advantage

With European contact and the introduction of the fur trade, the Haudenosaunee soon became dependant on metal trade goods and firearms. European trade goods were first available from the Dutch who established trading posts in the Hudson River Region. Later, the French traded European goods for furs at their trading posts along the St. Lawrence River and throughout Great Lakes Region.

The availability of European trade goods was a game changer. Tribes quickly recognized the concept of economic advantage and trade competition. The Haudenosaunee began to strategize in terms of territorial expansion for all the same reasons as European nations: the management of external threats; acquisition of territory and resources; economic dominance in trade; building alliances; and securing stability within an expanded territory for the primary well-being and future security for the group winning power.

The Haudenosaunee were exceptional diplomats. Using their unity, strong political organization, and military power, the Haudenosaunee built strategic alliances over a vast territory. If diplomacy failed to win Haudenosaunee objectives, then military power was unleashed with devastating effect.

The Five Nation unity solidified by the Great Binding Law, and the establishment of a superior political organization, enabled the Haudenosaunee to formulate a sense of purpose. This sense of purpose was strategic – economic superiority through domination of trade and the expansion of Confederacy territory. Certainly, the unity of the Great Binding Law created a strong and unwavering nationalistic ideology among the Five Nation citizenry. The people identified themselves as *onkwehonwe – the people*. The Mohawk Haudenosaunee saw themselves as *ongwi honior - the superior people*.

The Confederacy armistice established the foundation of unity on which the Haudenosaunee built military skills and organization to achieve their strategic goals of territorial expansion and trade domination. After territory and trade alliances had been secured by force of arms, the Haudenosaunee excelled in the application of diplomacy to secure and sustain their growing empire.

The Confederacy used two strategies to manage the people and tribes they defeated.

The first strategy was the cultural practice of the mourning-war. Although the mourning-wars provided an opportunity for young men to experience war and prove their courage, the primary function of the mourning-wars was to secure captives. The importance of securing captives was paramount.

Captives seized during mourning-war raids were valued. In the majority of instances, captives would be adopted and assimilated into the Confederacy. In time, the adopted person would acquire all the privileges, duties, and responsibility of a Confederacy citizen. Adoption was a way to address family and community grief by replacing lost loved ones. In the broad sense, adoption and assimilation replenished population and replaced warriors lost in battle. Adoption had a social function in terms of sustaining families and clans in both a physical and spiritual sense. Adoption ensured the balance of influence and power was maintained within clans and tribal society. On the side of least forgiveness, a vengeful grieving mother would demand the torture and death of a captive as retribution for her loss.

The second Haudenosaunee strategy, extending the rafters of the longhouse, was to build alliances and coalitions among tribes. Two methods were used to build allegiance to the Confederacy and establish tribal alliances. First, when it served their purpose, the Haudenosaunee would bring an accepting and defeated opponent under the shelter of the Great Tree of Peace. Later, with the arrival of the Dutch, the Covenant Chain was established. If the Haudenosaunee extended Covenant Chain status to a tribe, that tribe became part of a coalition of tribes with principal allegiance to the Haudenosaunee Confederacy.

Accepting the duties and responsibilities of the Covenant Chain was essentially an act of tribal submission to the Haudenosaunee Confederacy. Covenant Chain tribes were assured of the protection of the Haudenosaunee Confederacy. In theory, the Confederacy would represent and consult with Covenant Chain members for mutual advantage in the important matters of treaty and coexistence with other tribes and nations. In practice, the Confederacy more often initiated decisions that served the Confederacy first, sometimes at the expense of Covenant Chain members.

Covent Chain alliances were managed through the threat of Haudenosaunee Confederacy military power and reprisal should compliance not be forthcoming. The Confederacy knew that if a defeated and vengeful enemy was not watched closely, there was always the danger of insurrection from within.

From a political perspective, the Haudenosaunee used their policy *extending the rafters of the longhouse* to force alliances. *Extending the rafters of the longhouse* was the opportunity and means to advance the Confederacy goal of territorial expansion.

For generations to come, the civil and military strength of the Haudenosaunee Confederacy ensured the Haudenosaunee could manage their affairs as an equal with the arriving Europeans. The Europeans and the Five Nations of the Haudenosaunee Confederacy recognized each other as distinct nations. At the same time, each had their own aspirations for wilderness empire.

During the years of the fur trade, the Haudenosaunee Confederacy built an empire. Their empire was vast in terms of territory. The Haudenosaunee empire was immensely diverse in terms of tribal identities the Confederacy had either subjugated or absorbed through adoption and assimilation.

Over time, history has shown that all empires peak and retract. As we shall learn, the empire built by the Haudenosaunee Confederacy is not an exception to the history of empires.

The Haudenosaunee Confederacy built an empire founded on skillful diplomacy, force of arms, and strategic coalitions. In time, the overwhelming pressures of a culturally devastating European population reduced the Haudenosaunee empire to a fractured and dysfunctional tribal alliance whose people fell from a position of influence and power and into civil war.

Near the end of their empire, the Haudenosaunee became refugees in their own ancestral lands. By then, the Haudenosaunee Confederacy was referred to as the *Iroquois Confederacy* or the *Six Nations*. The members of the five original tribes – Mohawk, Oneida, Onondaga, Cayuga, Seneca – were lumped together as *Iroquois*.

The Haudenosaunee history is an amazing, but rather short lived, passage in time.

FIREKEEPER'S WAMPUM OF THE ONONDAGA NATION

This wampum belt records that Adodarhoh and his thirteen Onondaga cousin Lords have responsibility to protect the Confederacy fire, to keep it clean and bright, and ensure that it is never extinguished.

Source: pers. comm. Darren Bonaparte

GREAT TREE OF PEACE WAMPUM

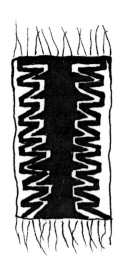

The roots of the tree represent peace and strength. The roots spread out – one to the north; one to the east; one to the south; and one to the west. A person or tribe wishing to accept and obey the Great Binding Law may follow one of the roots to the tree, and take shelter there. Purple wampum centre and white wampum border. Source: pers. comm. Darren Bonaparte

Haienwatha' Wampum

Often called Five Nations Territorial Belt, this wampum tells the holder that the Haudenosaunee are united and the land and its bounty is in the trust of all Five Nations equally.

The first square on the left is the Mohawk Nation and its territory; next on the right is the Oneida Nation and its territory. Central is the Great Tree of Peace representing the Onondaga Nation and its territory. The Great Tree of Peace, sometimes visually interpreted as the heart of the Confederacy, signifies that the Onondaga are the Keepers of the Confederacy Fire. Next is the Cayuga Nation and its territory, then the Seneca Nation and its territory. The background wampum is purple; the lines are white wampum. Source: pers. comm. Darren Bonaparte

Dish with One Spoon Wampum

This wampum belt, purple figure on white background, records the Haudenosaunee agreement that the hunting grounds of the Five Nations are considered common ground and meant to be shared among the Five Nations. The central figure is a dish with a beaver tail on it. Source: pers. comm. Darren Bonaparte

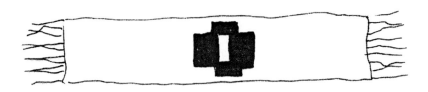

The 70th Wampum of the Great Binding Law

The wampum showing the 50 lords of the Haudenosaunee Confederacy unified together in one body. Source: pers. comm. Darren Bonaparte

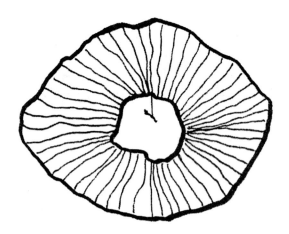

Ancestral Homeland of the Five Nations of the Haudenosaunee Confederacy

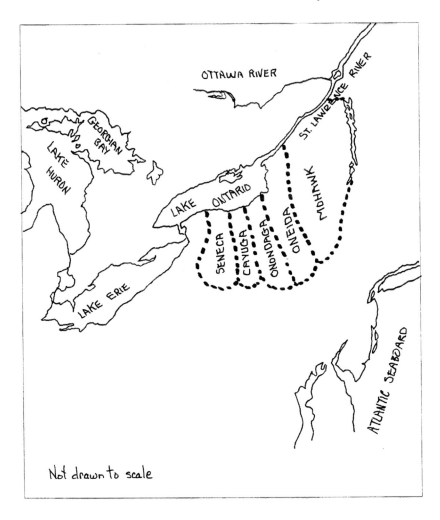

Chapter 2

First Contact
Old Enemies and New Alliances

In the not too distant past, in the time before the Europeans arrived, Indigenous tribes and confederacies in the vast wilderness of Eastern North America had achieved significant political and military accomplishment and influence.

The anthropologic calendar refers to the *Terminal Woodland Period* (1000 CE to first European contact) as the emergence of the historic *Wendat (Huron), Petun (Tobacco), and Neutral* cultures now referred to as the *Ontario Iroquois Tradition*. In the St. Lawrence River Region consisting of southern Quebec and a part of eastern Ontario, a separate development led to the emergence of the *St. Lawrence Iroquoians*.

The Iroquoian linguistic group and Algonkian linguistic group comprised the major linguistic groups of the Great Lakes Region and the St. Lawrence River Region. Although the two linguistic groups were similar in their culture and spirituality, enmity flourished between tribes.

The first historic descriptions of the Canadian Iroquoians are given to us by Jacques Cartier. Cartier kept careful records of his 1534, 1535, and 1541 voyages to the lower St. Lawrence River Region.

To have an understanding for the terms Stadacona Indian, Hochelaga Indian, and St. Lawrence Iroquois, explanation is helpful.

The Stadacona and Hochelaga Indians are believed to be people of the St. Lawrence Iroquoian group. The Stadacona were the first people encountered by Cartier. He named the people *Stadacona* after the name of their principal village Stadacona, present-day Quebec City. The upstream St. Lawrence River fortified village was called Hochelaga, present-day Montreal City. Cartier referred to the people who lived in this vicinity as the Hochelaga. Chief Donnacona, whose principal village was Stadacona, also had influence over the people of Hochelaga.

The St. Lawrence Iroquoian were a different people than the Iroquois, whose ancestral homeland is in present-day upper New York State. The St. Lawrence Iroquoian and the Iroquois are two distinct Indigenous groups. While the St. Lawrence Iroquoian group is extinct, the Iroquois continue to be a vibrant culture and a dynamic part of the social fabric of New York State and the Canadian Province of Ontario, Canada.

Cartier's journals tell us the Stadacona people lived in fortified villages. Cartier's observations also tell us the people were an agrarian society. The Hochelaga settlement was surrounded by extensive fields of cultivated corn.

Cartier provided a record of an ongoing war between Stadaconans and another group he referred to as *Toudaman*. Cartier wrote that the Toudaman had raided and destroyed a Stadacona village, killing two hundred people.

Cartier's first voyage in 1534 was commissioned by the French King, Francis I. The royal charter was to find precious metals and a route to the Orient. Instead of finding a new passage to the Orient, Cartier found himself sailing in present-day Gulf of St. Lawrence. In time, after getting his bearings, Cartier sailed upstream on the mighty river we know today as the St. Lawrence River.

Sailing along the Gaspe shore, Cartier came upon a group of Indigenous fishermen belonging to the St. Lawrence Iroquoian group. During this first encounter,

Cartier enticed two of the fishermen to board his ship. The fishermen were Domagaya and Taignoagny. The two young men were the sons of the Stadacona chief Donnacona.

In late summer, Cartier - with Domagaya and Taignoagny aboard his ship - began the return journey to France, arriving there in September, 1534. (Hakluyt, 1600)

Cartier's second voyage left France on May 19, 1535. Domagaya and Taignoagny set sail from France with Cartier, and served as valuable guides to bring Cartier to the village called Stadacona. The French, after establishing a settlement at Stadacona, renamed the site *Habitation*, present-day Quebec City.

The people Cartier called Stadacona, were determined to secure an alliance with the French. The Stadacona were in awe of the power of French firearms. An exchange of people was offered as a sign of good faith and trust. If the alliance was accepted, the Stadacona would provide guides to take Cartier upriver to Hochelaga. Cartier showed no interest in such an alliance. However, he was not to be discouraged from continuing his explorations upstream on the St. Lawrence River.

Accompanied by Domagaya and Taignoagny, Cartier continued his journey upstream. He arrived at Hochelaga, present-day Montreal City, on October 2, 1535. The appearance of Cartier with Stadacona guides created distrust in the village. No amount of gift giving by Cartier could overcome a simmering animosity.

Cartier writes that upon arrival, he walked through fields of corn to visit the village of *Hochelaga*, present-day Montreal, referred to in Cartier's writing as *Ville des Savages*. After arriving at the village, Cartier read to the people from his bible. Cartier climbed the mountain near the village, naming the mountain Mount Royal for his sovereign, King Francis I of France. From the vantage point at the top, Cartier viewed vast fields of corn, the expanse of St. Lawrence River, and present-day Lachine Rapids. (Trudel, 1966)

The village of Hochelaga consisted of 50 longhouses and a population Cartier estimated to be 1,500 persons. Downstream of Hochelaga, in the vicinity of present-day Lac St. Pierre of the St. Lawrence River, Cartier found several small, unfortified villages with a combined population estimated to be 3,000 persons. Cartier named this area *Kanada* – using the Indigenous word for *village*.

The French began to call the Indigenous inhabitants of Kanada *Stadaconans* after their large fortified and best known village at present-day Quebec City. Cartier believed that all of the St. Lawrence River villages were under the authority of Chief Donnacona.

The Hochelaga and the Stadacona groups appeared to be at peace with each other. However, both were at war with neighboring tribes. The Hochelaga were at war with the Agojuda - named *Mauvais Gens* by the French. This group raided from their western homeland. At the same time, the Stadacona warred with the Toudaman whose homeland was southwest of Stadacona, in the interior of the region known today as the Richelieu River.

The French wintered at Hochelaga. During that first 1536 winter in the wilderness, the French grew sick and began to die of scurvy. Cartier lost 25 of his people before the Hochelaga shared healing herbal medicines with the French. Relations between the French and their Hochelaga hosts deteriorated.

Over the winter the French listened, with growing excitement, to stories about the vast unexplored wilderness. A land the Indigenous people called the Kingdom of Saguenay. The French began to envision an undiscovered land full of gold, rubies, and other treasures. Cartier wanted to believe he was on the doorstep of the golden fleece.

By early May of 1536, the great growling mass of broken St. Lawrence River ice had moved off into the Gulf of St. Lawrence. Cartier was excited about the stories of the wealth to be taken from the unexplored region. At the same time, Cartier was skeptical that the stories were being used as a ploy by the Hochelaga to use the French as allies in their war against their neighbour enemies.

Cartier acted. He kidnapped Donnacona, his sons Domagaya and Taignoagny, and seven others. Knowing that he would require leverage to secure funds for a return voyage and extended exploration of the region, Cartier needed the Hochelaga with him in France as witnesses for the wealth waiting to be taken. With his involuntary guests, Cartier sailed for France in May, 1536. Cartier arrived in Saint-Malo, France, on July 15, 1536, ending his second voyage to the New World.

Donnacona and his fellows were certainly a novelty in France. They were treated well at the King's expense. Cartier promised Donnacona that he would return him to Hochelaga within 12 moons. The long war between France and Spain delayed Cartier's return to Hochelaga until 1541.

The physical presence of the Indigenous people and their stories of the golden Kingdom of Saguenay, excited the French and encouraged investment in further exploration of the New World. Cartier's kidnapping and transport of his Indigenous hosts to France achieved his goal of securing financing and a royal charter for a third voyage.

Sadly, during their time in France, all but one of the Indigenous people Cartier had taken to France died. Donnacona died in France in 1539. The only survivor was a small girl whose ultimate fate is unknown.

Jacques Cartier set sail for the New World on his third and final voyage, arriving in May of 1541. Not one of the Indigenous people he had kidnapped in 1536 returned with him.

After another brutal winter along the St. Lawrence River with his Hochelaga hosts, Cartier packed up and set sail for France in May of 1542. In the hold of his ship he carried a cargo of gold and diamonds. Upon arrival in France, this precious cargo was discovered to be pyrites and quartz. (Burrage, 1906)

This occasion must have been humiliating for Cartier. Certainly, Cartier's error in treasure would not have earned the confidence of French King Francis I. Cartier's credibility to win financing for another voyage was severely damaged. The event would have been an awkward entry on any explorer's resume. Cartier would never again return to the St. Lawrence Region.

The next French adventurer to visit the St. Lawrence Region was Samuel de Champlain. Returning 61 years after Jacques Cartier's last visit, Champlain could find no evidence of the St. Lawrence Iroquoian people. Where villages flourished, Champlain found only brush covered openings in the forest. Champlain anchored his ship at Stadacona, put a ship's boat over the side, portaged around the Stadacona rapids, and with a part of his ship's crew, began his upriver journey. Champlain arrived at Hochelaga in the summer of 1603.

At Hochelaga, once rich with great fields of corn, Champlain found only uncultivated fields reverting to scrub brush. Champlain had found no trace of the Stadacona or the Hochelaga. What he did find was a terrorized region travelled by war parties he began to refer to as *Iroquois*. At the time of Cartier's arrival, Iroquois and Algonquin war parties were fighting for control of the St. Lawrence River.

The St. Lawrence Iroquoian people had vanished. Early 17th century opinion held that people were destroyed by intertribal warfare in the late 16th century. The Algonquin blamed the Wendat [Huron] for the destruction of Hochelaga. French missionaries Marc Lescarbut in 1610, and Recollect priest Denis Jamet in 1615, blamed the disappearance on the Iroquois. Reference is made in the Jesuit Relations of a war between the Mohawk and the Susquehannock and Algonquin alliance sometime during the period 1580 and 1600. Some anthropologists and historians, using the scarce information of political and economic conditions for that time, suggest the Mohawk could indeed have been the aggressor. (Johansen, 1995; 2006)

The cause of the St. Lawrence Iroquoian disappearance may have been largely due to the savagery of unrelenting inter-tribal warfare. However, an unanswered question is whether European disease imported to the Stadacona and Hochelaga by the voyages of Jacque Cartier may have been a factor in the extinction of the St. Lawrence Iroquoian. But this is mere conjecture. The true cause for the disappearance of the St. Lawrence Iroquoian people remains a mystery.

In time, Champlain founded the town of Habitation at the site of the Stadacona village. At the Stadacona site the St. Lawrence River narrows considerably on its way upstream from the Gulf of St. Lawrence. In the years to come, the town of Habitation would be named Quebec. The name Quebec is derived from Stadacona word *kebec*, which means *narrows*.

Champlain was befriended by the Montagnais who lived close to the new settlement of Habitation. The French called this group *Montagnais* because of their mountain homeland.

Continual warfare simmered throughout the region. During the period 1570 - 1600, the eastern tribes of Mohawk and Oneida campaigned to drive the Algonkin tribes from the Adirondack Mountain region and the upper St. Lawrence River region. Around 1600, the wampum trade had attracted the attention of the Iroquois. Skirmishes between the Iroquois and the powerful Mahican Confederacy began to intensify.

The wampum trade was an important element of the Indigenous economy of the time. Wampum beads are made from the Atlantic coast shells of the Channeled Welk and Quahog. For the Haudenosaunee, wampum provided a record of a person's credentials and certificate of authority. Wampum was used extensively in ceremonies and for official purposes. Wampum belts recorded important events and agreements between tribes. Attempting to win influence in the wampum trade, the eastern Iroquois, campaigning far south of their ancestral lands, skirmished with the powerful Mahican Confederacy.

The Mahican, an eastern Algonquian people, were themselves a confederacy occupying an area we know today as the Hudson River Valley Region and western New England. The Mahican Confederacy consisted of five tribes living in as many as forty villages. The tribes included the Mahican; Mechkentowoon; Wawyachtonoc; Westenhuck; and Wiekagjoc tribes.

In 1609, when Englishman Henry Hudson, under Dutch charter, sailed up the Hudson River, the Mahican Confederacy was the first indigenous group to begin trading with the Dutch. Having traded successfully with the Mahican, Hudson returned to the Netherlands with a rich cargo of fur.

A year later, 1610, Dutch traders arrived to begin the fur trade. This event was the catalyst that in the decades to come would bring about the displacement and destruction of many Indigenous groups. The arrival of Dutch traders was also the beginning of the struggle between European nations to win the New World territory for King and country. (Starna, 2013)

By 1609, the value of the pelts of North American furbearers had become the momentum which fueled financing for French voyages and exploration of the St. Lawrence River and Great Lakes Regions.

In the beginning, French voyages to the New World were not about settlement, as it later became for the British. The French purpose was the pursuit of wealth available from the furs of this new-found wilderness. The French goal was to establish a fur trade industry and to secure and sustain themselves as the dominant player in the fur trade. In order to achieve this goal, the French needed alliances with Indigenous tribes to ensure a supply of furs, establish trading partners, and secure and defend territory.

In the summer of 1609, the Wendat, Algonquin, Montagnais, and Etchemin (Malecite), sought an alliance with Samuel de Champlain. Their intent was to persuade Champlain to give aid in their war with the Iroquois. The people called Champlain *the man with the iron breast*. The name referred to the iron cuirass soldiers wore for upper body protection.

Later that same summer, Samuel Champlain saw an opportunity to show French unity with the Native alliance. Learning of a planned incursion into Iroquois territory by the Wendat, Montagnais, and Algonquin; Champlain agreed to demands that French soldiers accompany the raiding party. The raiding party, made up of three hundred Natives and nine French soldiers, set out to explore the Riviere des Iroquois, present-day Richelieu River. The party reached Lake Champlain without incident and Champlain began to map the lake. Growing confident in the absence of Iroquois contact, a part of Champlain's group began their return journey. Champlain now had two French soldiers and sixty Natives in his command.

On July 29th, somewhere near present-day Ticonderoga and Crown Point, Lake Champlain, New York State, the French survey party encountered a group of Iroquois. Skirmishing broke out. The next day a group of some two hundred Iroquois approached Champlain`s band. One of Champlain's Natives identified three of the advancing Iroquois as sachems [Algonquin word for chief].

Champlain took aim with his harquebus (matchlock firearm), fired, and when the powder smoke had cleared, two of the Iroquois chiefs lay dead. The third chief was shot down by one of Champlain's soldiers. The Iroquois fled in shock and disarray at this display of European firepower. (Hessel, 1993, pgs. 42-43)

This short and decisive action would set the tone for French and Iroquois relations for the next two centuries. The fearful damage inflicted by Champlain's matchlock weapons also changed how the Iroquois would fight. They learned that their long shields of tightly woven cornstalks offered no defence to powder and ball. Neither did their wooden helmets, and body armor made of wooden slats woven together to provide a flexible protection for chest, upper arms and thighs. As word spread among the Iroquois and Wendat of the power of French firearms, the realization spread that shields and wooden body armour would soon be obsolete. The powerful bow, similar in size and power to the English longbow, would be gradually replaced by firearms, powder, and ball, acquired, at first, through trade with the Dutch. Traditional close quarter melee weapons such as the formidable bone breaking club would remain in the Iroquois arsenal for centuries.

The French, following Champlain's hostile engagement with the Iroquois on July 29, 1609, were now, willingly or not, entangled in the Wendat, Montagnais, and Algonquin war with the Iroquois. The Wendat alliance, seeking an early advantage in the emerging fur trade, began to forge strong relations with the French. Following Champlain's decisive action against the Iroquois, the Wendat realized a military alliance with the French was fundamental to their success as the dominant players in the lucrative fur trade. As part of the bonding initiative, the Wendat accepted a French request that missionaries be allowed to move among the villages of their confederacy.

The following year, 1610, Champlain, with his Algonquin, Montagnais, and Wendat allies, again fought the Iroquois. The skirmish was fought at Cap de la Victoire, on the Richelieu River. The French matchlocks again took their toll in causalities. The Iroquois were forced to retreat. Champlain was wounded, but his reputation as a warrior was now established among the Natives. (ibid, pg. 44)

During this skirmish, fifteen Iroquois were captured. This could be a fate worse than death on the battlefield. Torture of prisoners was not uncommon. Champlain recorded the torture and death of a captured Iroquois warrior after the Battle of Cap de la Victoire.

" *Meanwhile our Indians kindled a fire, and when it was well lighted, each took a brand and burned this poor wretch a little at a time in order to make him suffer the greater torment. Sometimes they would leave off, throwing water on his back. then they tore out his nails and applied fire to his membrum virile. Afterwards they scalped* him and caused a certain kind of gum to drip very hot upon the crown of his head. Then they pierced his arms near the wrists and with sticks pulled and tore out his sinews by main force, when they saw they could not get them out, they cut them off. This poor wretch uttered strange cries, and I felt pity at seeing him treated in this way. Still he bore it so firmly that sometimes one would have said he felt scarcely any pain. They begged me repeatedly to take fire and do like them ……. when they saw that I was not pleased they ….. told me to give him a shot with the arquebus. I did so, without his perceiving anything, and with one shot caused him to escape all the torture he would have suffered ….. afterwards they cut off his head, arms and legs, which they scattered about: but they kept the scalp, which they had flayed. (Biggar, vol. 1. Pg. 101)

Champlain's written narrative records that at times torture would include cannibalism.

" They did another awful thing, which was to cut his heart into several pieces and to give it to a brother of the dead man to eat and to others who were prisoners. These took it and put it into their mouths, but would not swallow it." (ibid, pg. 101)

According to Champlain's writing, it was not only the warriors who inflicted torture on their captured enemies. After the Cap de la Victoire skirmish, Algonquin and Montagnais women participated in the torture of Iroquois prisoners.

" …… they were reserved to be put to death by the hands of the wives and daughters of these, who in this matter show themselves no less inhuman than the men; in fact, they greatly surpass the men in their cruelty; for by their cunning they invent more cruel torments and take delight in them. Thus they cause their prisoners to end their lives in the deepest sufferings." (ibid, pg. 137)

Champlain's Campaign to Defeat the Iroquois

Champlain began to plan an attack that he believed would be a crushing defeat for the Iroquois. He embarked upon a grueling campaign that would further shape French and Iroquois, and Iroquois and Wendat relations, for centuries to come.

Champlain travelled to meet with the Wendat (Huron) whom the French referred to as the *good Iroquois* because of their friendship with the Algonquin. The Huron in turn, called the French *Agnonha,* meaning *Iron Men* due to the metal cuirass they wore.

Accompanied by an interpreter, a French servant, a few Natives, and companion Etienne Brule, Champlain began his canoe paddle up the river the French called River of the Algonquin, present-day Ottawa River. On July 9, 1615, Champlain reached present-day Georgian Bay, Lake Huron. Champlain's canoe party turned south and followed the lakeshore until turning inland and finding the capital Huron village at Caragouha, in present-day Simcoe County, Ontario. Champlain was welcomed to Caragouha by Recollect missionary priest Father LeCaron who had established a mission there. After a wilderness journey of more than 600 miles, Champlain found a priest and six French traders already among the Huron.

Champlain moved forward with his campaign to crush the Iroquois once and for all. He sent his companion, Etienne Brule, with a Huron war party to the Andante (Susquehannock) tribe living on present-day Chemung River, New York State. The Huron called the Susquehannock people *Andastoerrhonon* meaning *people of the blackened ridge pole* which related to their building practices. The French adopted the Huron name and called the Susquehannock *Andaste.*

While Brule travelled southward toward the Andaste, Champlain was advancing from the north. Brule was faced with an arduous and dangerous detour route around the ancestral homeland of the Iroquois - present-day upper New York State - to avoid encountering the Iroquois,

Champlain, with his French companions and a war party of Huron, paddled across present-day Lake Huron, into Lake Erie, then down the Niagara River into Lake Ontario. The invading force landed on the south shore near their target, the Oneida castle located at present-day Nichols Pond, Madison County, New York State. Champlain arrived at the castle on October 10, 1615.

Waiting for the arrival of Brule and the Andaste reinforcements, Champlain had a difficult time controlling his Huron warriors. Discipline was non-existent and they insisted on frontal assaults against the Oneida palisade. Oneida arrows kept the attackers at bay while inflicting considerable casualties among the Huron. Champlain was twice wounded by arrows, in the knee and thigh.

The Huron attacks were repulsed. Champlain waited for Brule and the Andaste to arrive. With his Huron warriors growing increasingly impatient, Champlain abandoned the attack on October 16, 1615. Etienne Brule and his Andaste allies had endured hardships and travel delays in their circuitous route back to Champlain. Exhausted, Brule did not arrive until after Champlain had left. The Andaste melted into the forest and returned to their homeland. The Huron, now terrified of an assured Iroquois revenge, returned to their villages with great haste.

It was, by now, late in the season and winter was approaching. The Huron refused to escort Champlain back to Quebec. Champlain lived with the Huron until 1616 when he departed their company to make the journey back to Quebec. Upon his arrival, he was greeted as one returned from the dead.

While with the Huron, Champlain was not idle. He explored further west with Jesuit missionary Father le Carron. During the same period, Etienne Brule travelled with the Andaste and explored the Susquehannah River to the Atlantic coast. In later years, he also explored westward and visited Lake Superior.

In 1615, the Recollect missionaries arrived among the Wendat. In 1625, priests of the Society of Jesus (Jesuits) replaced the Recollect order of priests. The French, as did the Wendat Confederacy, recognized the need for strong bonding and alliance to ensure that the developing fur trade could be managed and sustained. In 1633, and again in 1635, Champlain, attempting to foster a strong alliance through intermarriage, asked the Wendat to consider intermarriage with the French. The initiative was fully supported by Jesuit Father Paul LeJeune. The Wendat, eager to please - but to a point - where not willing to surrender the time proven values of their clan system. Nor were they about to be coerced into conversion to Christianity as a condition of marriage. They rejected the French request. The Wendat view that marriage was a matter between two individuals, their family, and the acquiescence of respective clans, prevailed. In the Wendat view, marriage was too important to be used as an instrument of state policy.

The Wendat position on intermarriage did not prevent the French and Wendat from having families together. Of course not. After all, this matter involves human beings, and all the elements of humanity - loneliness, comfort, love. Tradition and policy could no more turn these things aside than could it change the seasons of the land. The Catholic missionaries could never accept the marriage of a Frenchman with an non-baptized `savage`. The clan system would not encourage unions between French and Wendat. However, relationships occurred without the blessing of the bride's clan, and certainly, without the blessing of the Church.

For the English, intermarriage was less about the restrictions of church, and more about perceptions of social impropriety. Indigenous partners were referred to as *summer wives*. When, a European wife arrived in the New World, or a European woman could be successfully courted, it was very likely that the Indigenous family would be abandoned. Hence the term *summer wife*, which spoke to the temporary nature of the arrangement.

By now the French had achieved success securing the fur trade of the region. They had established alliances with the Huron-Wendat, Montagnais, Algonquin, and the Susquehannock in the south. The longer term would prove this alliance to be a damaging strategic miscalculation for the French and their tribal allies.

Iroquois influence in the lower St. Lawrence River Region (Quebec) was gradually eroded and they were pushed south. The Montagnais and Algonquin had won control of the St. Lawrence River fur trade for the next two decades.

To summarize European relationships with the various Indigenous tribes and confederacies the Europeans encountered as the fur trade flourished we can say: the French embraced Indigenous people. The English disdained them. As for the Dutch, well, they were fair trading partners who saw the Iroquois as a proxy army against their fur trade competition - the French and the English. The Spanish in the far south of North America, and Central and South America were perhaps the most brutal of the European presence. Enslavement and total eradication of Indigenous populations was Spanish policy.

Old Enemies and New Alliances

The stage is now set in terms of old enemies and new alliances.

To provide the reader an appreciation for the complexity and scope of the Indigenous tribes, alliances, and confederacies with which the Haudenosaunee Confederacy interacted, the following descriptions will be useful.

The word *nation* is used throughout this book's narrative to identify Indigenous groups. The term *nation* began with the French reference to the tribes they encountered as *separate political and territorial entities, with similar cultures, a common origin in the distant past and who spoke similar but not identical languages.* In the view of the French explorers and fur traders, the Indigenous groups they allied with, and fought against, were *nations* by definition. The French managed their relations with Indigenous tribes accordingly. (Trigger, 1978)

Following is a description of the groups of Indigenous people who, over the next few centuries, dominated the struggles to build empires.

The table below shows tribal membership of each of the two dominant linguistic groups of the St. Lawrence River Region and Great Lakes Region. (Hessel, 1993. Pg. 39)

A tribe is defined as a group who speak one language. A particular tribe may be made up of a number of bands.

Algonkian Linguistic Group	**Iroquoian Linguistic Group**
Montagnais	Mohawk
Etchemins (Malecite)	Oneida
Abenaki	Onondaga
Micmac	Cayuga
Nipissing	Seneca
Ottawa	Wendat (Huron)
Ojibwa (Ojibwe)	Tobacco (Petun)
Cree	Neutral
Algonkin (Algonquin)	Erie

Before the arrival of the French in 1534, the tribes of eastern North America had either stood alone, or formed alliances for mutual benefit of trade and security. After the French began to develop the fur trade, and over the next two and a half centuries, tribal alliances were a critical aspect of both the building and ruination of empire – both Native and European. Considering this, it is important that some description be provided for the key alliances among eastern North America tribes.

During the time when the Iroquois Confederacy was building her empire, several Indigenous groups contributed significant roles in the ebb and flow of Iroquois Confederacy events.

The following Nations and alliances, influenced the fortune and misfortune of the Iroquois Confederacy and the imperial powers of Sweden, the Netherlands, France, and Britain.

Iroquois

Mohawk; Oneida; Onondaga; Cayuga; and Seneca.
The Five Nations of the Haudenosaunee Confederacy.

The Haudenosaunee Confederacy is a group of five distinct tribes of the Iroquoian linguistic group.

An analysis of archeological evidence, suggests the Confederacy was established in 1142 CE. The Confederacy is built on an armistice and constitution among the Mohawk; Oneida; Onondaga; Cayuga; and Seneca Nations. With the acceptance of the Great Binding Law brought by the Peacemaker, the five tribes had effectively agreed to an armistice among themselves and became a unified confederacy.

The followers of the Great Binding Law called themselves Haudenosaunee (Hotinonshonni in Mohawk) and referred to the five Confederacy members as nations.

The Five Nations of the Haudenosaunee Confederacy are:

Kanien'keha:ka **People of the Flint Place (Mohawk)**

After the Great Binding Law unified the Five Nations, the *Kanien'keha:ka* sometimes referred to themselves as *Ongwaano n sionni* meaning *'we are the extended lodge.'*

Although commonly referred to as Mohawk, there is no letter 'm' in the Kanien'keha:ka alphabet. Among the first Indigenous people the Dutch met on their arrival to the present-day Hudson River Region were a group calling themselves *Muh-heck Heeking Ing* (People of the Food Area Place). The Dutch transliterated the word to Mahican and Mohican. The Mahican called their *Kanien'keha:ka* neighbours *Maw Unk Lin* (Bear People). The Dutch heard and wrote *Maw Unk Lin* as Mohawk. The Dutch also referred to the Kanien'keha:ka as *Egil* and *Maqua*. The French, at first, called the *Kanien'keha:ka Aignier* and *Maqui*.

In Haudenosaunee Confederacy terms, the *Kanien'keha:ka*, because they are the most easterly of the five Confederacy Nations, are referred to as the *Keepers of the Eastern Door.*

Onyota'a:ka **People of the Upright Stone (Oneida)**

Within the Confederacy, the Oneida and Cayuga are referred to as the *younger brothers.*

Ononda'gega **People of the Hill Place (Onondaga)**

The Ononda'gega are the *'seat of the Confederacy.'* The Peacemaker gave the royaner (hereditary chief) Tadodaho the responsibility as Firekeeper for the Haudenosaunee Confederacy.

Gayogoho:no **People of the Canoe Carry Place (Cayuga)**

Onondowaga **People of the Great Hill Place (Seneca)**

Because the Onondowaga are the furthest west of the Five Nations, they are referred to as the *Keepers of the Western Door.*

Using fire to open forest cover for sunlight, the Haudenosaunee were a successful agricultural society. The Creator's gifts of the *three sisters* - corn, squash, and beans - were celebrated in ceremonies. Ceremonies acknowledged additional gifts such as tobacco, strawberry and maple syrup. Fishing was a significant food gathering endeavour. Hunting for game was a seasonal pursuit.

The Haudenosaunee lived in villages. The villages were built on high ground. A village would normally be surrounded by a palisade constructed of upright logs. Larger villages would have a palisade defensive wall that would be two or more rows in depth. Because of the villages location on high ground and the use of defensive walls, the Europeans began to refer to the Haudenosaunee villages as *castles*.

A family shelter was constructed of wooden frames covered with sheets of tree bark, normally birch and ash. Before the insatiable European logging devastated the forests, tree diameter was enormous. Sheets of bark peeled from mature trees were large in size. A single shelter would house several families. The shelter was long and narrow. The shape of the lodging is reflected by its name – *longhouse*. Many longhouses were sixty feet and more long. Villages would be moved when the soil would no longer support bountiful crops. A village could remain in one place for twenty years or more.

The Haudenosaunee are a matrilineal kinship society. Descent and inheritance is through the mother's line. Haudenosaunee society involves a clan system which serves as a socializing agent and also a political entity within society. Clans are led by Clan Mothers. Men and women cannot marry from within their own clan. The Clan Mothers nominate candidates from their clan to be considered for the leadership position of *royaner* [chief, lord]. Royaner are hereditary leadership positions, and, with exception, give lifetime service.

The Haudenosaunee have a strong animist spirituality that is supported by many stories of the Creator and his relations with the world and the beings that live on *Turtle Island* - our planet earth. The Haudenosaunee spirituality is celebrated with an annual cycle of celebrations that acknowledge and give thanks to the Creator for the many gifts He has bestowed upon Turtle Island and the people.

The people of the five tribes accepted the Great Binding Law brought by the Peacemaker. The people became known as Haudenosaunee - *followers of the longhouse teaching*. The Haudenosaunee Confederacy is a political and cultural alliance of five member nations.

In the beginning, the five tribes engaged in unrelenting and vengeful warfare between themselves. The wars were called *mourning-wars*. The raiding was intended to seize captives for adoption and, in extreme cases, revenge killing. The people were consumed by grief which fed a thirst for vengeance which fed continual atrocity between the tribes. Saddened by this, the Creator sent the Peacemaker to bring peace, justice, and harmony among the five tribes.

The Peacemaker was given a huge task - seek peace through diplomacy and spiritual means, not with the war club. The confederacy was established after the Peacemaker satisfied the royaner [lords] of the five tribes that they would be stronger politically and militarily if they ceased fighting among themselves, buried their weapons of war, and agreed to an armistice.

The Peacemaker succeeded in establishing the armistice among the five tribes, and the *Onkwehonwe* [the people] agreed to live by the teachings of the Great Binding Law. Upon consensual agreement among the lords of the Mohawk, Oneida, Onondaga, Cayuga, and Seneca tribes, a confederacy was established. The five united nations gave allegiance to the message of the *Great Binding Law* - the constitution of the five united nations. The Great Binding Law set out the process and rationale for governance, civil process, and social systems.

The followers of the Great Binding Law identified as *Haudenosaunee – followers of the longhouse teaching*. So, the armistice is referred to as the *Haudenosaunee Confederacy*. Upon their arrival, the French referred to the tribes they encountered as *nations*. They called the Haudenosaunee *Iroquois*. So, the unified Haudenosaunee tribes became known as the *Iroquois Confederacy*.

The English, accepting the French concept of *nation*, referred to the confederacy as the *Five Nation Confederacy*. The Tuscarora tribe was being systematically extinguished by the British in the present-day Chesapeake Bay region. The Tuscarora approached the Haudenosaunee Confederacy and asked to be adopted into the confederacy. In 1722, sponsored by the Oneida Nation, the Haudenosaunee agreed to adopt the remnants of the Tuscarora tribe. Later, with the adoption of the Tuscarora, the British began to call the confederacy the *Six Nations*.

All Haudenosaunee follow the teachings of the Great Binding Law. These are not Christian teachings. Over time, beginning with the arrival of the French

Jesuit priests, Iroquois citizens have been converted to Christianity. Converts to Christianity have, in varying degree, turned away from the traditional spirituality of the Haudenosaunee. All Haudenosaunee are Iroquois. Not all Iroquois are Haudenosaunee. Accepting that the constitution of the Haudenosaunee Confederacy is the Great Binding Law, and the followers of the Great Binding Law are Haudenosaunee, then perhaps the suitable name for the confederacy is the Haudenosaunee Confederacy.

The Great Binding Law is the Constitution of the Five Nations of the Haudenosaunee. The constitution is also spoken of as the *Great Immutable Law*; the *Great Law*; the *Great Law of Peace;* and the *Constitution of the Five Nations*. In the Mohawk language the Great Binding Law is the *Kaianerenko:wa*; in the Seneca language it is called *Gayanashagowa*.

The armistice and unity the Peacemaker achieved is a covenant for peace and unity only among the Five Nations. Nothing in the Great Binding Law prevented any one Nation, or all of the Five Nations together, from picking up the war club and engaging in warfare with tribes outside of the Haudenosaunee Confederacy.

Taken in the larger sense, the Great Binding Law never intended to abolish warfare. Terms were set out that banned warfare among the tribes which accepted the Creator's message brought by the Peacemaker. Tribes which capitulated to the Haudenosaunee Confederation and took shelter under the Great Tree of Peace, joined an alliance with the Haudenosaunee and received political representation and military protection of the Haudenosaunee Confederacy. With this in mind, the writer has refrained from referring to the Peacemaker's message as the Great Law of Peace, favoring instead, the term *Great Binding Law*.

The Peacemaker's vision of an enduring peace through the message of the Great Binding Law is a concept that held promise. The twists and turns of history crushed that promise. The Peacemaker's vision embraced the idea that the Creator's condolence ceremony - a gentler ritual and process for managing grief - would in time, replace the need for mourning-war. Tribes who sheltered under the Great Tree of Peace would also enjoy the peace and protection of the Haudenosaunee Confederacy. In this way, the peace would not be a limited to the Haudenosaunee. The Great Binding Law would indeed fan the promise of peace throughout the land and the rafters of the longhouse would be extended in peace.

Several events defeated the vision of a general peace among the Indigenous tribes and confederacies. First, the arrival of Europeans and the beginning of the fur trade brought new concepts to the Haudenosaunee. The new concepts of economic power and territorial expansion had been largely foreign to Haudenosaunee culture. However, in time both were inevitable choices for the Confederacy. The introduction of European trade goods changed the lives of Indigenous people. A dependence on the metal goods such as edged tools and metal containers made life easier. Competition for dominance over the fur trade introduced a thirst for economic power and the need for territorial expansion. With the introduction of European firearms, the war fighting strategy and tactics of the Haudenosaunee had to change. War casualties among friend and foe increased dramatically.

The arrival of European adventurers brought European diseases to the indigenous people of eastern North America. Depopulation and ensuing societal dysfunction brought about by disease epidemics disrupted the Peacemaker's vision of a broad peace. The devastating European diseases combined with greater casualities in the wars for trade dominance, ensured that grief was a constant within Haudenosaunee society. As long as grief overwhelmed the people and the tears of grief could not be dried by condolence ceremonies, there could be no hope that the Great Binding Law would provide the way to a wide and lasting peace.

The mourning-war raiding and skirmishing with the singular objective to seize captives to appease the grief for lost loved ones, began to change. The Haudenosaunee valued all life and certainly the lives of their warriors. Their war fighting tactics avoided casualties. Now, with the vicious competition for dominance in the fur trade and escalating use of firearms, casualties increased. An awful grief seized the people. More mourning-wars were needed to appease the grief of families; replace population; and maintain the physical and spiritual power of families, clans, and community.

The Peacemaker's vision that the Great Binding Law would bring peace to all the land was overwhelmed and defeated by unrelenting grief. There could be no peace until grief could be addressed in non-violent ways.

The unity of the Five Nations, their strong nationalist policies, and military power, allowed the Haudenosaunee Confederacy to become the dominant power in vast areas of the St. Lawrence River Region, the lower Great Lakes Region and the Hudson Valley Region.

The Haudenosaunee engaged a policy referred to as *extending the rafters of the longhouse*. The policy was actually a strategy for territorial expansion. The Great Binding Law allowed any tribe or confederacy that chose to accept the teaching of the Great Binding Law to shelter under the Great Tree of Peace. The Haudenosaunee would provide security through political leadership and military might. Those groups who chose not to accept the offer of alliance risked facing the military power of the Haudenosaunee Confederacy and forced cultural assimilation.

During the 1540s, the first records of the indigenous people of the Upper St. Lawrence River and lower Great Lakes Region were written by French explorer Jacques Cartier. About this time, it appears that the Haudenosaunee began to be called *Iroquois* by the French.

The northern and western Algonquin called the Iroquois *Nadowa* – meaning *real adders*. The eastern Algonquin who the French first encountered along the St. Lawrence River called their old enemies the *Iroqu*. The Algonquin word *Iroqu* [*irinakhoiw*] means *rattlesnake*. The French added the Gallic suffix *-ois* to the Algonquin insult and the word became *Iroquois*. The name *Iroquois* was soon adopted by the French to describe the five nations of the Haudenosaunee. The Haudenosaunee considered the French word for them to be less than flattering. (Day. 1970)

There are several other versions for the source of the word *Iroquois*. One source comes from the manner in which Mohawk orators ended a presentation, saying *Hiro Kone*. *Hiro* means I have spoken. *Kone* could mean *in joy; in sorrow; in truth*. Phonetically, for the French, the words *Hiro Kone* sounded like Iroquois. Another version for the source of the word *Iroquois* comes from the French translation of the Montagnais word *irnokue* translated as '*a terrifying and formidable being*.'

The Dutch and Abenaki called the Haudenosaunee *Maqua*.

Other names for the Haudenosaunee include: *Ehressaronon* (Wendat); *Massawomeck* (Powhatan); *Matchenawtowaig* (Ottawa word for 'bad snakes'); *Mengue* (French); *Mingwe* (Delaware); *Nautoaw* (Ojibwe word for 'bad adders'); *Mohowaanuck* (the Narragansett - a Rhode Island tribe - word for 'man eaters'); *Canton Indians*; and *Confederate Indians*. (Sultzman, 2014)

Regardless of the name source, it is safe to assume that the Iroquois did not enjoy a particularly kind and gentle reputation among their neighbours. The tendency to give the Iroquois unflattering and insulting names suggests that the Iroquois were both disliked and feared by their neighbours. Absolutely.

Never ones to feel inferior to any other tribe, the Mohawk had their own name for themselves. They recognized that they were the superior people and called themselves *Ongwi Honior,* meaning *the superior people.*

After the five-tribe armistice, the Haudenosaunee called themselves *ongwano n sionni* meaning *we are the extended lodge.*

The French put aside the word *Haudenosaunee,* preferring *Iroquois.* The Haudenosaunee Confederacy became known as the Iroquois Confederacy. The French, recognizing the distinct language, culture, and social and civic systems of government, began to call the tribes *nations.*

The English, realizing the *Iroquois Confederacy* was made up of five distinct tribes, adopted the term *nation* from the French and began to call the *Iroquois Confederacy* the *Five Nations.* Later, after the Confederacy adoption of the Tuscarora in 1722, the English began to call the Confederacy the *Six Nations.*

> *I recall listening to an Abenaki woman talking about her people's history.*
>
> *She dedicated some time in her discussion to Abenaki relations with the Iroquois.*
>
> *She said: "You know, a white mother will tell her children to be good, not go far from home, be home before dark. She will ensure her children listen by telling them that if they are disobedient the boogey man - a frightful creature who kidnaps children - will get them.*
>
> *Now, an Abenaki mother loves her children just as much. And she wants them to be safe. So, she tells them that if they are not good the Mohawk will get them. The Mohawk, that's our boogey man."*

When the Dutch built trading posts along the lower reaches of present-day Hudson River and Manhattan Island, a new alliance was established. The Dutch and Haudenosaunee Confederacy agreed to respect each other's cultures and coexist under the auspices of an agreement known as the *Covenant Chain*.

Later, the Haudenosaunee Confederacy would offer old enemies and, on occasion, defeated tribes, the opportunity to join the coalition of tribes and confederacies bound by the Covenant Chain. The Haudenosaunee assurance was that the Confederacy would represent the coalition in decision making for the benefit of the coalition. Also, the coalition would have the protection of the military power of the Haudenosaunee.

Over time, the Covenant Chain coalition members recognized the Confederacy served its own interests and agenda first. Still later, coalition members began to recognize that the military power of the Haudenosaunee Confederacy had diminished. It was becoming increasingly apparent that the ability of the Grand Council of the Haudenosaunee Confederacy to impose its will had weakened.

For a time, the Haudenosaunee Confederacy achieved political influence and military power that was equal to, and in many cases, superior to the Europeans in the New World.

Tuscarora Alliance Wampum

This wampum belt tells about the Tuscarora being adopted by the Haudenosaunee Confederacy, giving the Confederacy the name Six Nations. Five of the purple diagonal bars on a white wampum background represent the Five Nations Confederacy. The Nations are presented from left to right – the Mohawk Nation, the Oneida Nation, the Onondaga Nation, the Cayuga Nation; the Seneca Nation. The last diagonal bar represents the Tuscarora Nation adopted by the Confederacy in 1722. Source: pers. comm. Darren Bonaparte

Michael L. Hart

Women's Nomination Wampum

This belt tells the holder that women are equal. The belt reflects the Confederacy law that women hold the right of nominating the Confederacy Lords in their matrilineal clans. The women also have the right to depose the Confederacy Lord if he does wrong. Source: pers. comm. Darren Bonaparte

In a meeting of the Grand Council of the Haudenosaunee Confederacy, the tribal affiliation of the attending members is announced by the number and placement of feathers on their headdress. The headdress is called *kahstowa*. A Confederacy *royaner* [lord] can be identified by small deer antlers on his *kahstowa*. If a hereditary lord behaves in a manner unacceptable to his clan, the clan mother will remove him from his office. The process is called *dehorning* – the horns are taken from his *kahstowa*.

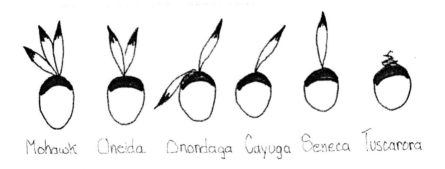

Five Nations Kahstowa

Algonquin Nation

The oral history of the Algonquin tells of their westerly migration from the Atlantic coast.

Their *'first stopping place'* was near present-day Montreal. Many of the Algonquin settled along the Kitcisipi, present-day Ottawa River. Other groups travelled further up the St. Lawrence River and arrived to settle at the *'third stopping place'*, near present-day Detroit City.

The Algonquin name is probably derived from the Maliseet word *elakomkwik - they are our relatives*. The Algonquin people call themselves *omamiwinini*. Culturally and linguistically, the Algonquin are closely related to the Ojibwe and Odawa.

The Algonquin lived in birch bark *wikiwams* or wooden *mikiwams*; sometimes surrounded by log palisades. The Algonquin animist spirituality was founded on the *Midewiwin* teaching. *Midewiwin* means *the right path*. The people accepted they were always surrounded by *manitok* [spirits] of the natural world.

In 1570, the Algonquin formed an alliance with the Montagnais. The ancestral land of the Montagnais flowed east along the St. Lawrence River to the area of present-day Quebec City, to the Atlantic Ocean. The term Montagnais comes from the French who referred to the tribe as *people of the mountains* because their ancestral land was mountainous.

In the early 17th century, seven distinct groups were recorded as part of the Algonquin family. Hessel (1993, pg. 17) identifies the groups, referred to as *Nations*, as:

- Kichesippirini (*people of the great river*), and *Island Algonkin*; the largest and most powerful group.

- Weskarini (*people of the deer clan*); also Petite Nation and Iroquet's Band. Their ancestral lands lay on the north side of the Ottawa River near present-day Lievere River and Rouge River, Quebec.

- Kinounchepirini (*people of the pickerel waters*), also Pickerel Band. Located on the Ottawa River below present-day Allumette Island. After 1650 they developed a strong association with the Ottawa people.

- Otaguottaouemin. Located along the upper Ottawa River above Allumette Island.

- Sagaiganininiwak (*people of the lake*).

- Saginitauigama Nation.

- Nibachis Nation. Located at present-day Muskrat Lake, Cobden, Ontario.

- Matawackariniwak (*people of the bulrushed shore*). Located near present-day Madawaska River in the Upper Ottawa Valley.

- Iroquet. Located along the South Nation River, Ontario.

The arrival of the French in the St. Lawrence River Region introduced competition for control of the fur trade. The *French and Indian Wars (1642-1698)* were not kind to the Algonquin. Algonquin survivors of Iroquois massacres sought refuge at the Jesuit missions at Trois Rivieres on the St. Lawrence River; and Sillery, a suburb of present-day Quebec City. At the missions, the Algonquin were almost extinguished as a people through disease epidemics and alcohol related conflicts. During this time the traditional values, lifestyles, spirituality, mythology, self-respect, and the skills of self-reliance were either tragically degraded or lost. It would be hard to argue such was not the case.

The Algonquin had also been pursued north on the River of the Algonquin, present-day Ottawa River. They arranged a temporary alliance with the Cree, their northern neighbours. The Algonquin established nine settlements in Quebec. Some historians take the position that if it had not been for 19th century protectorates at present-day Golden Lake, Ontario; and River Desert, present-day Maniwaki, Quebec; the Algonquin may have disappeared completely. (ibid, pg. 67)

Today, there are ten Algonquin communities. One in Ontario, and nine in Quebec. The Algonquin continue to speak their traditional language. Although most Algonquin converted to Christianity in the 17th and 18th centuries, many Algonquin continue to practice traditional *Midewiwin*.

Wendat Nation

Although members of the same linguistic group, and with very similar cultures, the Wendat and Five Nations of the Iroquois Confederacy clashed as enemies. Both were agrarian societies growing corn, beans, and squash. The Wendat also grew excellent tobacco. Their ancestral lands, located in present-day Simcoe County, Ontario, were fertile and productive.

In their ancestral territory, the Wendat occupied 18 to 25 villages. A few of the larger villages boasted populations exceeding 3,500 people. Prior to 1600, it is estimated that the Wendat population was 20,000 to 25,000 people. Between 1634 and 1642, the devastating European diseases of smallpox, influenza, tuberculosis, and measles had reduced the population to an estimated 9,000 persons. (Warrick, 2003, pgs. 258-275)

Both the Wendat and the Haudenosaunee were avid players of field lacrosse. Lacrosse was an excellent competition that provided all the physical stamina and skill that a warrior would require to survive the close quarter fighting of the day.

The Peacemaker may have been a Wendat. He had tried to bring peace and harmony to the Wendat without success. Frustrated, but refusing to give up on his vision of peace, he travelled in a stone canoe across Lake Ontario to the ancestral homeland of the Iroquois.

Both the Wendat and Iroquois lived in longhouses constructed of wood frames covered with sheets of bark. Archeological surveys tell us of longhouses in excess of ninety meters long. One longhouse would provide shelter for several family units. The Wendat are a matrilineal society with children born into the mother's clan. Young people could not marry within their mother's clan, but could marry a member of their father's clan. Both the Iroquois and Wendat followed the clan system. Clans were both a socializing agent and a political party with influence in civil governance.

The Wendat clans were tribes within a tribe. Like the Iroquois clan system, clans were political parties from which female clan mothers played a role in the nomination and selection of male clan members for leadership positions. The Wendat clans included: Bear; Deer; Turtle; Beaver; Wolf; Loon/Sturgeon;

Hawk and Fox. Some sources identify the Porcupine and Snake Clan as alternative to the Loon/Sturgeon Clan and the Fox Clan. Clan identity and allegiance was paramount regardless of tribe or village. (Soui, 1999. Tooker, 1991)

Village governance functioned under two councils. One council busied itself with civic affairs. The second council, when needed, was responsible for affairs of war. Consensual agreement in matters requiring decision was the intent. However, chiefs of the larger more powerful clans, and older, experienced men with practiced oratory powers, could influence council decisions. The Wendat system of governance differed significantly from the Haudenosaunee system. Wendat women had little influence in the work of council. Haudenosaunee women had great influence in almost all matters of importance, not only in the selection and removal of clan chiefs, but in matters such as determining whether a captive would be adopted or killed.

The Wendat, an Algonkian word meaning *people of the island*, were a confederacy consisting of five Iroquoian speaking nations located in present-day Simcoe County, Ontario, Canada.

The five members of the Wendat Confederacy were: Attinniaoenten (*people of the bear*); Hatingeenniahak (*makers of cords for nets*); Arendaenronnon (*people of the lying rock*); Atahontaenrat (two *white ears* - or `deer people`); and the Ataronchronon (*people of the bog*). (Tooker, 1991)

French contact with the Wendat occurred in the early 17th century. The French called the Wendat *Huron*. *Huron* is derived from the old French word *hure*, meaning *rough* or *ruffian*.

Throughout the narrative of this book the words Wendat and Huron are interchangeable. At times, the term Wendat-Huron is used. Preference, considering the origins and history of the people, is Wendat.

By 1609, Wendat trading alliances had been made with the Montagnais in the Stadacona area, present-day Quebec City; Hochelaga at present-day Montreal; and the Algonquin groups along the Ottawa River.

At first, the Wendat alliance with the Montagnais and Algonquin was formed around trading partnerships. However, as word of the availability of valued French trading goods in exchange for furs spread, a new player wanted to enter the fur trade. The new player was the Iroquois Confederacy. Competition for trade began in earnest and trading partnerships began to function as military alliances.

The French, attempting to capitalize on rich fur resources, understood they would only be successful if they built strong relations with trading partners and secured military alliances with various Native groups. In the summer of 1609, with the lure of lucrative trade promises, the French secured alliance agreements with the Wendat; Montagnais; Algonquin; and Etchemin (Maliseet). The same year, 1609, Samuel de Champlain founded the settlement of Habitation at the site of Stadacona. In the decades to come, the settlement of Habitation would be known as Quebec City.

The fires of old territorial conflicts and war fighting between the Iroquois Confederacy and the Wendat Confederacy were fanned by competition for the security and economic influence to be gained through control of the fur trade with the French.

For decades, the Wendat trading partnership with the French flourished. An estimated five hundred men from scattered Wendat villages managed the Wendat fur trade. They acted as middle men, collecting fur from trappers in the lower Great Lakes Region and along the Ottawa River. The fur was delivered to the French trading settlement at Hochelaga, renamed Ville-Marie by the French, and later, the present-day city of Montreal. By the mid-1630`s, the Wendat were the primary suppliers of fur to the French.

The *French and Indian Wars, 1642-1698*, would bring an end to the Wendat Confederacy and their political and military power in New France. After being devastated by war with the Iroquois Confederacy, and suffering the scourges of European diseases, the weakened Wendat became refugees in their ancestral lands. The *Great Pursuit* of the Wendat by the Iroquois Confederacy began in 1649. The vicious raiding by Iroquois war parties resulted in the dispersal of the Wendat population. The Wendat found refuge with other nations. First with the Petun; then the Neutral, then the Erie. In 1649-50, the Iroquois struck and dispersed the Petun. The Neutral had been dispersed by 1651; and the Erie by 1656. Many of the remnants of these nations were adopted by the Iroquois Confederacy.

Today, an estimated 3,000 Wendat live near Quebec City and Wendake near Loretteville, Quebec. Another group of about 350 Wendat - now called the Wyandot, or Wyandotte, an English corruption of the word Wendat - live in Oklahoma. Today, the Wendat language is extinct.

Petun Nation

The Petun, who called themselves Tionontati, are part of the Iroquoian linguistic group. The Petun were an agrarian society. Their ancestral homeland was in the southern part of present-day Grey and Simcoe Counties, Ontario. Their lands bordered Wendat territory.

The French visited the Tionontati in 1616 and gave them the name Tobacco because of their large fields of cultivated tobacco.

During the Great Pursuit of the Wendat by the Iroquois, Wendat refugees took sanctuary with the Tobacco. In 1649 the Iroquois attacked Tobacco villages. The Tobacco were destroyed as a Nation.

Some of the Tobacco and Wendat survivors were adopted by the Iroquois. Over time their culture and identity was lost. The relentless pursuit of the Iroquois forced other Tobacco survivors to join groups of wandering Wendat as refugees.

Over time, the remnants of the pursued Tobacco Nation were assimilated into the Wendat society. In 1670, after a time of hardship and wandering, the people settled in Mackinac, Michigan. The two groups intermarried and became known as the Wyandot. The Tionontati are extinct as distinct people and culture.

Neutral Nation

The Neutral, an agrarian society, were part of the Iroquoian linguistic group. Their ancestral homeland was in southeastern Ontario, between the present-day Grande River and Niagara River. The majority of their forty villages were located near western Lake Ontario.

The largest population group was called Chonnonton, *Keepers of the Deer*. Another group, the Onguiaahra, *Near the Big Waters*, populated the southern Niagara peninsula area. This group provides the origin of the word *Niagara*.

The Neutral allied with the Iroquoian language-speaking Wenrohronon to provide strength of arms for protection against the Iroquois. The confederacy broke up in 1639, leaving the Neutral vulnerable to Iroquois attack. At the same time the Wenrohronon were overwhelmed by the Seneca, their eastern neighbour, during the early 17th Century before the Iroquois began their Great Pursuit of the Wendat. Wenrohronon survivors were adopted and assimilated by the Seneca. Some escaped north and were assimilated into the Wendat (Huron) culture. Today the Wenrohronon are extinct as a distinct people and culture. Their language is extinct.

The name Neutral was given by the French. Their tribal name reflects their determination to avoid being involved in the wars between the Wendat and the Iroquois.

The Seneca embarked on a campaign of westward expansion and attacked and destroyed a Neutral village in 1647. The Neutral remained docile, hoping to avoid becoming engaged in the Iroquois invasion. After the Wendat and Tobacco had been devastated, the Iroquois turned to the Neutral as their next conquest. Although attempting to remain neutral, they had given sanctuary to Wendat and Tobacco refugees, and refused to surrender sheltered people to the Iroquois. Using this as an excuse for war, the Iroquois attacked the Neutral throughout 1650 and 1651. The last mention of the Neutral in French records was 1671.

The Neutrals are extinct as a distinct people and culture. Their language is extinct.

Mahican Nation

The Mahican (*Muh-he-ka-neew*, translated as *people of the continually flowing waters*) lived on ancestral lands in the Hudson River Valley around present-day Albany, New York State, and western New England. The first Mahican contact with Europeans was with Henry Hudson and the Dutch, in September, 1609.

The Dutch called this nation the *River Indians*. Other common names were *Mahigan, Mahikander, Mahinganak, Maikan,* and *Mawhickon.* Later, the English corrupted *Mawhickon* to *Mohican* or *Mahican.* The French called the Mahican *Loups* - wolves in English.

Mahican villages were large fortified affairs made up of from 20 to 30 longhouses. The Mahican were agriculturalists and enjoyed particular success with corn. Fish, and to a lesser extent, wild game, added to their food supply. Mahican governance consisted of hereditary chiefs advised by a council of clan elders.

The Mahican Confederacy included five nations occupying an estimated 40 villages. The confederacy nations included:

- Mahican proper; the *Fireplace of the Mahican Nation,* in the vicinity of present-day Albany, New York State. The primary village was Shodak, east of present-day Albany.

- Mechkentowoon Nation along the west shore of the Hudson River above present-day Catskill Creek.

- Wawyachtonoc Nation; *eddy people* or *people of the curving channel.* This nation was situated in present-day Duchess County and Columbia County eastward to the Housatonic River in Litchfield County, Connecticut State.

- Westenhuck Nation; *on the other side of the mountains.* Sometimes called the Housatonic people, the people lived in the Housatonic Valley in Connecticut and Massachusetts.

- Wiekagjoc Nation; *upper reaches of the river.* This nation was situated east of the Hudson river near present-day Hudson City, Columbia County, New York State.

After the arrival of the Dutch and during the next century, the fur trade was the root cause of conflict between the Mahican Confederacy and the Iroquois Confederacy. The tensions with English and Dutch settlers forced many of the Mahican to migrate east across the Hudson River into western Massachusetts. Many Mahican settled near the town of Stockbridge, Massachusetts, and over time, they became known as the *Stockbridge Indians*. In 1710, the Mahican chief *Etow Oh Koam,* accompanied by three Mohawk chiefs, sailed to England on a state visit with Queen Anne. In England, the four chiefs were referred to as the *Four Mohawk Kings*.

In the *American Revolutionary War, 1765-1783*, the Mahican allied with the Colonists and participated at the siege of Boston, and the battles of Saratoga and Monmouth. In 1778, the Mahican were ambushed by British soldiers at the Bronx, New York, and lost 15 warriors killed. General George Washington acknowledged the bravery of his Mahican ally by issuing a written commendation. (Brasser, 1978)

Things would not go so well for the Mahican after the Revolutionary War. In the 1820s and 1830s, many Mahican moved to Shawano County, Wisconsin, where the new United States government had promised them land under the federal policy set out in the *Indian Removal Act, 1830*. In Wisconsin, the Mahican settled on reservation land with the Munsee Delaware. The two nations formed one nation that became known as the *Stockbridge-Munsee Band of Mohican Indians*. The 22,000-acre reservation is situated near the present-day town of Bowler, Wisconsin. The Mahican language, like the Mahican Confederacy, is now extinct. (Starna, 2013)

Susquehannock Nation

The Susquehannock Nation was a notable political and military power before, and for a short time, after the 1609 Dutch arrival in their ancestral homeland. The introduction of European disease epidemics; the social destruction wrought by the fur trade; the ravages of war with the Iroquois Confederacy; and the violence and murder inflicted by English settlers encroaching on Susquehannock land in the James River region of present-day State of Virginia; contributed to the extinction of this strong and independent nation.

The agriculturally rich ancestral lands of the Susquehannock were vast. They included land adjacent to the present-day Susquehanna River and its tributaries in the southern part of present-day New York State; through east central and central Pennsylvania; with lands extending into Maryland along the west bank of the Potomac River at the north end of Chesapeake Bay. (Hahn et al, 1977, pgs. 12-13)

The Susquehannock called themselves the *Andaste*. But the names given to them by others are numerous and serve to tell a story in themselves.

- The Wendat called the Susquehannock '*Andastoerrhonon*', meaning *people of the blackened ridge pole.*

- The French shortened the Wendat name and called the Susquehannock *Andaste.*

- The Lenape (Delaware) offended the Susquehannock with the name they gave a traditional enemy, *Mengwe*, meaning *'without penis'*. In a better mood, the Lenape might call the Susquehannock *Miqui*, meaning *'foreign, different, far off.'* From *Miqui*, the Dutch and Swedes derived the name *Minquas*. On a good day, the Lenape would call the Susquehannock *Sisawehak Hanna Len*, meaning *'Oyster River People'*. (Brinton et al, 1888, pg. 132)

- The Powhatan called the Susquehannock the *Sasquehannock.*

- The English settlers in Maryland and Virginia used the Powhatan *Susquehannock.*

- The Pennsylvania English called the Susquehannock *Conestoga,* after their principal Pennsylvania village called Conestoga Town, from the Mohawk word *Kanastaoge* meaning *place of the upright pole.* (Mithun, 1981, pgs. 1-26. Hewitt, 1907, pgs. 335-337)

In the year 1600, the Susquehannock population may have been 5,000 to 7,000 people. Pre-European – and indeed post-European – Indigenous population estimates should be considered as informed guesses. In 1608, Captain John Smith of Jamestown, wrote that the Susquehannock had a fortified village at present-day Lancaster, Pennsylvania, and that the population included an estimated 600 warriors. In 1615, French explorer Samuel de Champlain wrote of the Susquehannock in his *Voyages of Samuel de Champlain*. In his writing, he mentioned seeing 20 villages. A village named Carantouan was located near the upper Susquehannah River. Carantouan, with two additional villages, could raise 800 warriors. Modern estimates for the year 1600, put the Susquehannock population at around 7,000 persons. At the time, the Susquehannock were a regional power with the population and military capacity to defend against Iroquois Confederacy attacks. (Tyler, 1907)

The English colony of Maryland was coveting more land for settlement. The Susquehannock pushed back. In 1642, Maryland declared war on the Susquehannock. The Swedish colony, New Sweden, established in 1638 by the Swedes along the lower reaches of the present-day Delaware River, allied with the Susquehannock against the English. English colonial government ceased hostilities in 1644. However, the Susquehannock and English continued to engage in intermittent raiding against each other until 1652.

A peace treaty with Maryland was in place by 1652. The treaty ceded large sections of land on both shores of Chesapeake Bay. During this time the *Beaver Wars, 1640 -1701*, were being fought over dominance of the fur trade. The Susquehannock had allied themselves with the Wendat, and had traded with the Erie and the Neutrals. The Iroquois Confederacy, seeing itself surrounded by enemies on all sides, raided Susquehannock territory with a vengeance. Throughout the period 1658 to 1662, the Susquehannock and Iroquois Confederacy were engaged in sporadic warfare.

By 1661, Maryland and the Susquehannock agreed to ally themselves against the Iroquois Confederacy. In 1663, the Susquehannock, responding to an attack on their village on the upper Ohio River, defeated a large and determined Iroquois raiding party of Seneca, Cayuga, and Onondaga. The Susquehannock defeated a second large Iroquois raiding party in 1672. By 1675, the table had turned in favour of the Iroquois. To establish a buffer between the Iroquois and Maryland settlements, the colony of Maryland invited the Susquehannock to relocate to the region of Maryland adjacent to Pennsylvania.

The Dutch, in the *Second Northern War, 1655*, had defeated the Swedes and incorporated New Sweden into New Amsterdam. During the period 1659-63, the Esopus tribe; the Lenape tribe; and the Dutch had been engaged in the *Esopus Wars* being fought for regional control of the fur trade. The Susquehannock used their influence to bring an end to the *Esopus Wars in* 1663.

Sometime around 1666, the Susquehannock defeated the Seneca and Cayuga Nations of the Iroquois Confederacy. The Susquehannock power and political influence peaked in the mid 1660s. However, their decline was rapid. The decline is probably due to the epidemics of European diseases that ravaged villages. In this weakened state, the Iroquois Confederacy, also weakened by disease, but with a larger population to draw warriors from, overwhelmed the Susquehannock. By 1667, many of the surviving Susquehannock had been adopted by the Haudenosaunee. By 1700, the Susquehannock population may have been a mere 300 persons. Small surviving populations of Susquehannock and Delaware were further decimated when General George Washington sent troops into Pennsylvania's Wyoming Valley in 1778. (Josephy, 1961, pgs. 188-89)

In 1676, the Iroquois Confederacy made a peace with Maryland and Virginia, and the Lenape (Delaware). The Susquehannock were offered an opportunity to shelter with the Iroquois and most moved north to Upper New York State, and were adopted and assimilated by the Seneca and Onondaga. The adoption was not solely about Iroquois Confederacy generosity. Through the adoption, the Confederacy acquired territory rights to Susquehannock territory along the Susquehanna River.

Warfare and the devastation wrought by European disease epidemics had battered the once politically influential and militarily powerful Susquehannock. Around 1697, a few hundred surviving Susquehannock settled in a village in Lancaster County, Pennsylvania, called Conestoga Town. In 1763, a census counted 22 Susquehannock people in Conestoga Town. About this time, *Pontiac's Rebellion* had started on the western frontier, and a vigilante group known as the *Paxton Boys* attacked the Susquehannock and killed six people. The victims were scalped and mutilated in other ways and their shelters were burnt. The colonial government held an official inquest and found that the killings were murder. A reward for the Paxton Boys was posted without success.

The Pennsylvania government moved the remaining sixteen Susquehannock to shelter in a Lancaster workhouse. Undeterred, the *Paxton Boys* attacked the sheltered Susquehannock in December, 1763. At the workhouse, fourteen Susquehannock were killed, including women and children. The murdered victims were scalped. Six adults and eight children were dismembered. None of the attackers were arrested and called to account for their heinous actions. (Eshleman, 1909)

Benjamin Franklin, sickened and furious with news of the *Paxton Boy's* atrocity, personally organized a Quaker Militia to control the white population and strengthen the government.

Franklin used the Paxton Boy massacres to reinforce his point that no race had a monopoly on virtue. He called the Paxton vigilantes 'Christian White Savages'. In his grief, Franklin called out to a just God to punish those who carried a Bible in one hand and a hatchet in the other. In the most part, Franklin praised the Native American way of life, their customs and hospitality, and the effectiveness of their councils which were able to reach agreement through discussion and consensus.

Lazarus Stewart, once a leader of the Paxton Boys, was killed by Iroquois warriors in the *1778 Wyoming Massacre*.

In the early 1700s. some groups of surviving Susquehannock had migrated to Ohio. In Ohio, they merged with the Seneca and Cayuga who had migrated west to the Ohio Valley. The people intermarried and became known as the *Mingo*. The Susquehannock were now extinct as a distinct people and culture. Some 100 words of the Susquehannock language have been preserved in the *Vocabula Mahakuassica* written by Swedish missionary Johannes Campanius in the 1640s. The Susquehannock language is no longer spoken. (Mithun, 1981, pgs. 1-26)

Anishinaabe and Mississaugas

The Anishinaabe include three principal member groups: Ojibwa, Odawa, and Potawatomi. The groups are members of the Algonquian language family.

The word *Anishinaabe* has several meanings. Elders speak of the meaning as *people from whence lowered*. Another meaning is *the good humans*. This phrase means the people are good people who are on the proper path laid out for them by the Creator known as *Gichi-Manidoo*, the Great Spirit.

The Ojibwa scholar Basil Johnston identifies the name Anishinaabe with the literal translation *beings made out of nothing*, or *spontaneous beings*. This translation is based on the belief that the people were created by divine breath, made of flesh and blood and gifted with a soul and spirit. The people are special creations of the Great Spirit and separate from the animistic spirits of rock, fire, water and wind.

The Ojibwa, Odawa, and Potawatomi people [always presented in that order] of the Anishinaabe are part of the *Council of Three Fires*. The Nipissing, Algonquin and Mississaugas identify as Anishinaabe but are not part of the *Council of Three Fires*. The Mississaugas are close relatives of the Ojibwa.

In the Beginning:

Oral tradition and the translation of markings on birch bark scrolls called *wiigwaasabak*, tell a story of the migration of the people from the east coast of North America. The homeland was called *Turtle Island*. Anishinaabe oral history tells us that the people are descendants of the Abenaki people who are referred to as *Fathers*. Another version tells us that the Abenaki are descendants of the Lenape Delaware, whose ancestral lands lay in present-day New Jersey and Pennsylvania. The Anishinaabe defer to the Lenape as *Grandfathers*. Another twist comes from Cree oral traditions. The Cree, who live well to the north of the Anishinaabe, believe the Anishinaabe to be descendants of the Cree, not the Abenaki.

The Anishinaabe oral history speaks of seven great *miigis*. The *miigis* are radiant beings who present themselves in human form. The *miigis* showed themselves to the Anishinaabe in the *Waabanakiing* (Land of Dawn) and taught the people about the *Midewiwin* way to live a good and honourable life.

One of the *miigis* was not of the same mind as his fellows and threatened to kill any people who he found in his presence. This awesome and spiritually powerful *miigis* returned to the ocean depths leaving the remaining six *miigis* to share the *Midewiwin* teaching with the people.

The six *miigis* each created a *doodem* (clan) for the people. After creating the clans, the *miigis* returned to the depths of the ocean. The work of the *miigis* resulted in the founding of six clan systems. The clans are:

Awaazisii (Bullhead)

Baswenaazhi (Echo-Maker, or Crane)

Aan'aawenh (Pintail Duck)

Nooke (Tender, or Bear)

Moozoonii (Little Moose)

Waabizheshi (Marten)

Oral histories talk of the creation of another doodem, the *Animiki* Thunderbird Clan. This doodem would have been founded as well had the seventh *miigis* not become angry and returned to the ocean.

After a time, the *miigis* returned to the people in a vision and told the Anishinaabe of the pending arrival of a new people who would build numerous settlements. The Anishinaabe were told they needed to travel west to keep their traditional ways alive. The people were told that their journey would involve visits at a number of small Turtle Islands. The Turtle Island layovers are symbolized by the cowry shells presented to the people by the *miigis*. The people spoke to their *Fathers* the Abenaki, and their *allied brothers* the Mi'kmaq, and gained their promise of a safe passage across their respective tribal territories.

Moving inland, the people reached the St. Lawrence River and travelled upstream to the Ottawa River. They moved up the Ottawa River to the Mattawa River and then entered Lake Nipissing. From Lake Nipissing, they travelled down the French River into Georgian Bay, Lake Huron.

The people had reached the first of the smaller Turtle Islands at *Mooniyaa*, present-day Mooniyaang. Now the people divided into two groups. One group turned eastward, returning the way they had come, and settled along present-day Ottawa River. The second group moved south along Lake Huron, into Lake Erie and arrived at the *second stopping place* at present-day Niagara Falls.

The people continued to move through the land. They arrived at the *third stopping place* at present-day Detroit, Michigan State. By now the Anishinaabe had divided into six distinct Nations: Algonquin, Nipissing, Mississauga, Ojibwa, Odawa, and Potawatomi.

After a time, the people began their migration from the *third stopping place* to the *fourth stopping place* on present-day Manitoulin Island, Lake Huron, Ontario.

The principal Odawa settlement is on Manitoulin Island. The Ojibwa settled in the Sault Ste. Marie region of Ontario, Canada. In the years ahead, as the French and English fur trade competition and expansion grew in intensity, groups of the Ojibwa, Odawa, and Potawatomi, migrated south to the Ohio River Region, southwest along the Illinois River, and west along Lake Superior, the Lake of the Woods Region, and the northern Great Plains. The western Ojibwa divided and formed the Saulteaux tribe. The Saulteaux became the seventh group of the Anishinaabe.

The Council of Three Fires:

The ethnic identities of the Ojibwa [also known as Ojibwe and Chippewa], Odawa [also known as Ottawa, Outaouais], and Potawatomi emerged after the Anishinaabe arrived at Michilimackinac during their journey west from the Atlantic coast. Michilimackinac is the Odawa name for present-day Mackinac Island in the Straits of Mackinac between Lake Huron and Lake Michigan.

Sometime around 796 CE, after reaching Michilimackinac, the Anishinaabe established the *Council of Three Fires.*

Potawatomi Elder Shup-Shewana shares the following. At the *Council of Three Fires,* the Ojibwa were addressed as *Older Brother,* the Odawa were referred to as the *Middle Brother,* and the Potawatomi were known as the *Younger Brother.* Each of the three groups are assigned functions. The Ojibwa are the *keepers of the faith,* the Odawa are the *keepers of trade,* and the Potawatomi are *boodawa-adam,* the *keepers of the fire.*

The *Council of Three Fires* met for military and political business and decision making. The favored meeting place, due to its central location, was Michilimackinac. The Council maintained relations with other nations. Fellow Anishinaabeg included Sac, Meskwaki, and Menominee. The non-Anishinaabeg relations included the Wiinibiigoo (Ho-Chunk), Naadawe (Iroquois Confederacy), Nii'inaa-Naadawe (Wyandot), and Naadawensiw (Sioux).

Europeans were included as well: Wemitigoozhi (France), Zhaaganaashi (England), and Gichi-Mookomaan (the United States).

In the 18th century, the French constructed Fort Michilimackinac at the council meeting site. At the end of the *Seven Years War, 1756-63*, the victorious British claimed the fort and used it as a trading post.

HISTORICAL ALLIANCES AND RELATIONS:

Through the strategies of both alliance and conquest, the Anishinaabe brought other tribes into the Anishinaabe Nation. The *Noquet*, originally part of the Menomini Tribe, and the *Mandwe*, originally part of the Fox Tribe, were absorbed. Membership of the *Migizi-doodem* (Bald Eagle Clan) and *Ma'iingan-doodem* (Wolf Clan) of the Santee Sioux represented ancestors from present-day United States.

To the north of their territory, the Anishinaabe enjoyed a strong alliance with Cree people which included the distinct groups of Swampy Cree, Moose Cree, Plains Cree, Atikamekw, and Montagnais. Alliances were maintained with the *Noos (Abenaki), Miijimaag, Nii'inaa-naadawe (Wendat), Oanoominiig, Wiinibigoog* and *Zhaawanoog*. Further alliances were established with the *Zhiishiigwan* and *Amikwaa*.

The *Council of Three Fires* enjoyed a largely peaceful co-existence with neighbours. From time to time, unresolved disputes turned into conflicts. The most notable adversaries were the Iroquois Confederacy and the western Sioux. The ferocity and persistence of the Sioux had won them the reputation as the Iroquois of the West.

The Anishinaabe Alliance presented a diverse and powerful military and political force to both the expansionist Haudenosaunee Confederacy (Iroquois) and the European powers of France and England who were seeking their own alliances to win dominance in the fur trade. Indeed, the Anishinaabe alliance is a reason why Iroquois expansionism did not move north and northwest. Picking a fight with the powerful Anishinaabe would not have had a happy ending for the Iroquois.

The Ojibwa, Odawa, and Potawatomi, were the first of the Anishinaabe to come into contact with the European arrivals. In a few decades, contacts between Anishinaabe people and Europeans spread over time and geography to include contacts in present-day states of Illinois, Michigan; Indiana; Ohio, Pennsylvania and present-day provinces of Ontario and Quebec, Canada.

During the *Seven Years War, 1756-63*, the *Three Fires Council* fought as an ally of France against England. This choice of ally was due in a large part to a long and fruitful trading partnership with France,

In the years ahead, the *Three Fires Council* would be a founding partner in the alliance known as the *Three Fires Confederacy*. This alliance was formed to address the escalating conflict arising from settler encroachment in the Ohio Region and growing tensions between the British government in Upper and Lower Canada and the government of the new United Sates of America.

Letters of record written by British Army Officers Colonel Henry Bouquet and Jeffrey Amherst tell of a 1763 plan to disable and kill Anishinaabe people using the intentional distribution of smallpox infected materials at Fort Pitt. Similar efforts to implement germ warfare were initiated by employees of the American Fur Company trading at Mackinac in 1770. A keg of liquor was wrapped in an American flag and gifted to the Anishinaabe. Instructions provided with the keg directed that the keg should not be opened until the people arrived back at their home community. The keg was opened at the village of Fon Du Lac. People became sick. A person who had seen the sickness before, in Montreal, recognized the symptoms as smallpox. (Harstead, 1959)

After the *American Revolutionary War*, the *Three Fires Confederacy* entered into conflict with the United States. The cause of tension was the flood of settlers into their territory in the Ohio Region. The *Three Fires Confederacy* allied themselves with the *Western Lakes Confederacy* (also known as the *Great Lakes Confederacy*) consisting of the Wyandot, Algonquin, Nipissing, Sac, and Meskwaki.

The *Northwest Indian War, 1785-95*, and the *War of 1812* saw the *Three Fires Confederacy* fight against the United States. As refugees of these wars, many Anishinaabe, the largest part of which were Odawa and Potawatomi, migrated to British Upper Canada, present-day Province of Ontario.

The *Three Fire Confederacy* people who chose to remain in the Mississippi River Region suffered the draconian policies of the *Indian Removal Act, 1830*. The Potawatomi were most affected by the policies. The Odawa had already been removed from settler paths and few Odawa remained to be removed. The Ojibwa removals culminated with the *1850 Sandy Lake Tragedy*.

The *Sandy Lake Tragedy* occurred after the Ojibwa had been relocated to Sandy Lake, Minnesota. Before attempting to move the Ojibwa from Sandy Lake west to the Mississippi River Region, the United States government decided to keep the Ojibwa at Sandy Lake over winter to reduce their resistance to a forced spring relocation. Promised supplies never arrived at Sandy Lake. The failure of food and warm clothing reaching the people resulted in the deaths of some 400 Ojibwa from starvation, disease, and freezing. The Ojibwa used the tragedy to pressure the government to secure permanent reservations for them in their ancestral territories.

Mississaugas:

The Mississaugas, closely related to the Ojibwa, are a part of the Anishinaabe people. The name *Mississauga* is derived from the Anishinaabe word *misi-zaagiing* meaning *those at the great river mouth.*

After leaving the *Second Stopping Place* near Niagara Falls, the Mississaugas became lost, in both a physical and spiritual sense. They called upon the Anishinaabe to be allowed to take up the teachings of Midewiwin, the *return to the path of the good life.*

The Mississaugas migrated along the Credit River northwards to Georgian Bay. The ancestral lands of the Mississauga are believed to be the shores of northern Lake Huron around the Mississagi River and the shores of lower Lake Superior.

When French explorers arrived in the area in 1534, they identified a distinct tribe of the Anishinaabe people living along the Mississagi River and on Manitoulin Island. The French explorers called this group Mississaugas. By 1675, the Mississaugas had migrated southward into the Kawartha Lakes region of Ontario. From there, a group moved further south to settle along the Credit River, a little west of present-day Toronto, Ontario.

As the *American Revolutionary War* came to a conclusion, the British Crown began to purchase land from the Mississaugas through a number of transactions that covered much of present-day southern Ontario. The objective of the British was to obtain land to enable them to award grants to Loyalists who were forced to abandon property in the Thirteen Colonies. Land grants were a reward to both Native allies and British loyalists for loyalty to the Crown. The British also wanted to secure the lands along the north shore of Lake Ontario through increased settlement of farms and villages. The pending threat of invasion from the new United States was not lost on the British government in both Upper Canada (Ontario) and Lower Canada (Quebec). A populated border was a strategic necessity.

The land sales to Britain by the Mississaugas, particularly the islands in that part of the St. Lawrence River between Kingston and Brockville, Ontario, infuriated the Mohawk, Oneida, and Onondaga. The islands are recognized as ancestral lands by the Iroquois.

> *The author recalls talking about Mississaugas land claims with Salli Kawennotakie Benedict, (1954-2011) a land claim researcher in Akwesasne.*
>
> "Mike, I have a bridge I want to sell you. Those lands were never Mississaugas territory. They accepted money in exchange for fraudulent land surrenders. They are worse than pirates."

Although Queen Victoria never visited Canada, during her 64-year reign (1837-1901) she did engage First Nation leaders from a distance. At times the relationship was more personal. At Windsor Castle, in 1838, Queen Victoria met with Chief Kahkewaquonaby of the Mississaugas First Nation. The chief presented a petition to Queen Victoria pleading for title deeds to land along the Credit River, Upper Canada (Ontario).

In recent times, the Canadian government awarded the Mississaugas of the New Credit First Nation, nearly $145 million dollars in settlement of a land claim due to the Crown's underpayment in the 1700s.

Today, there are six Mississaugas Nations, all are located in Ontario. The First Nations are:

- Mississaugas of the New Credit First Nation. The largest community with a population of 1,375.
- Alderville First Nation
- Curve Lake First Nation
- Hiawatha First Nation
- Mississaugas of Scugog Island First Nation
- Mississaugas First Nation – Mississagi River #8 Reserve

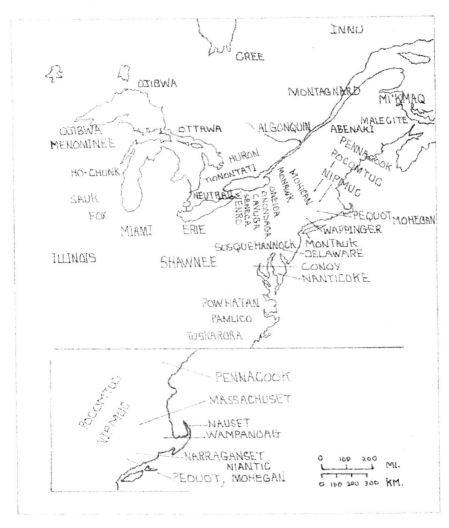

Indigenous People of eastern North America, 1600

Summary

Adventurers arriving in the European new found land of Northeastern America needed a rationale to claim the resources and territory for their sovereign. They needed a justification to take what they wanted. After all, the Europeans were a civilized people with laws about such things. So, the Papal Doctrine of Terra Nullius was taken down from the shelf and interpreted as justification.

Terra Nullius is Latin for *nobody's land*. Terra Nullius decreed that *nobody's land* was land that has never been subject to sovereignty of any state. The doctrine of Terra Nullius told the European adventurers and missionaries that the newly European discovered world was fair for the taking. This was a good start, but could not stand alone.

A second consideration is a religious interpretation. After all, in those times of discovery of new lands, the first ashore were soldiers with their swords and flag to claim land for their sovereign. The soldiers were followed ashore by priests with their cross and holy word to claim souls for God.

The Holy See *[Sancta Sedes]*, at that time and place, provided a supporting rationale particular to Terra Nullius. The Vatican's interpretation was that until converted to Christianity, the Indigenous people were soulless heathens. Without souls, they were savages, not people. Certainly, not people capable of governance, civil process, and spirituality. If the Indigenous people had no souls, then the land was unoccupied. The doctrine of Terra Nullius stood, it could not be disputed.

> *My friend, Ernest Kaientaronkwen Benedict (1918-2011), Haudenosaunee, Mohawk Elder, supporter of the Methodist Church, and the last of the Akwesasne Rotinonkwisere [Long Hair Chiefs], was granted a private moment with Pope John Paul II during his September 15, 1984, visit to the Martyrs Shrine, Huronia, Ontario.*
>
> *Pope John Paul II was no doubt intrigued to meet and speak with a Mohawk ancestor of the warriors who had tortured and killed the Church's Jesuit missionaries.*

Kaientaronkwen presented the Pope with an eagle feather and spoke briefly with the Pope. Whatever Kaientaronkwen shared, it is said the Pope apologized and confirmed that even non-converted Indigenous people have souls and are welcomed by God.

After looking briefly at the complex cultures of the amazing confederacies and alliances of the Indigenous people populating Northeastern America at the time of European arrival, it seems the European position that the territory was *nobody's land*, that it was unoccupied by people, is a difficult rationale to justify.

Friendship Wampum

This wampum belt, purple lines on a white background, represents the relationship between the Haudenosaunee and the first European arrivals. The broad diagonal bands on either side of the narrow central band represent the Haudenosaunee. The narrow band between the broad bands represent the Europeans. The wampum tells how the onkwehon:we [the people] supported the first Europeans by showing them how to survive on the land. Source: pers. comm. Darren Bonaparte

Chapter 3

The Fur Trade

Foundations for a Wilderness Empire

It would be negligent to proceed further without providing the reader with an overview of the fur trade that began to emerge soon after the first visits of the Swedes, Dutch, French and English to eastern North America.

The fur trade would become the crucible that founded empires, both Native and European. Over time, the fur trade would also undo empires, both Native and European.

The era of the fur trade lasted from 1600 to 1830. Competition between Native and European political and military powers for territory and control of the fur trade, provided fertile ground to cultivate all the horror humankind is capable of.

Genocide and the extinction of cultures; an arms race; biological warfare; scorched earth policies of reprisal; human diasporas; and the despair and hopelessness of proud peoples reduced to refugees in their ancestral lands, all of this was integral to the fur trade package.

The immense scale of treachery and betrayal of Indigenous people by European powers during, and after, the wars spawned by the fur trade, was fed by unquenchable greed and quest for power. The fur trade sowed the seeds of ruination for cultures and society.

The fur trade did introduce things of value to the Indigenous people. Iron implements such as axes, hatchets and knives, cooking pots and utensils made life much easier for the people. Animal traps multiplied the effectiveness of trapping effort a hundred-fold. Of course, the trade of firearms, powder and ball changed the balance of power among many tribes and tribal alliances. The Indigenous people became dependant on European trade goods.

As the fur bearing animals were depleted through unrestricted harvest over vast areas, the Indigenous hunters and trappers were forced to move further and further from their villages. This brought about unwanted and uninvited incursions onto lands of neighbouring tribes. The competition for fur resulted in skirmishing and loss of life which fed vengeance reprisals. Disputes turned into conflict which escalated into open warfare.

The men began to be absent from home for longer periods, either seeking furbearers or engaging in raids against their competition. The absence of the men forced changes in duties and responsibilities among the families and within their villages. These were difficult adjustments that had never been experienced. The social stability provided by clans, family, and villages was sorely tested, and in some cases, began to unravel.

From the earliest days of the fur trade, the dysfunctional cultural and societal shift within established Indigenous societies and alliances became obvious to the Jesuit missionaries. The Jesuit missionaries, witnessing the extinction of cultures and fragmenting of societies brought about by the competition for control of the fur trade, began to petition the French Monarchy to impose economic restriction that would slow the growth and impact of the fur trade. The Jesuits, a tough and pragmatic Catholic order of educators and missionaries, knew that a total prohibition against the fur trade was not going to happen. Perhaps the Jesuits could somehow find a way to influence a reversal to the cultural genocide they watched unfolding around them.

When revenue could be assured, any change that would reduce the flow of money into the king's coffers was not going to happen. Too much money was being made by too many prominent and politically influential people. The beaver was already out of the bag, so to speak. The Jesuits would bide their time. The Society of Jesus would strike when economic conditions supported their appeal. In the meantime, winning control of the fur trade would determine the survival and sustainability of European and Indigenous empire in eastern North America.

In the beginning, the French disregarded the beaver as the prime pelt of value in favor of furs used to trim European garments. Fox, fisher, and marten were preferred. For a time, the most valued furbearer was the weasel, known in the fashion industry as ermine. Brown in summer, turning a brilliant white with black tipped tail in winter, this pelt was a favorite fashion icon of European royalty.

Soon, the beaver became the preferred furbearer of the fur trade. In addition to the skin and valued oils given up by beaver castor, the beaver pelt offered two qualities. Pelt quality consisted of a soft glossy long hair that skilled craftsman could make into beautiful and warm coats. Under this guard hair, lay a dense mat of short soft hair called beaver plew. The plew was made into beaver felt which was used to make fashionable, warm, and weather resistant hats of all shapes and fashions. Furbearers became known as 'soft gold.'

The fur trade in eastern North America was dependant on water transportation routes. Using two principal paddling routes, furs were moved from the Great Lakes Region to Ville Marie, present-day Montreal. The first route was by way of Lake Huron into Georgian Bay, upstream on the French River into Lake Nipissing, along the La Vase River to Trout Lake, the Mattawa River, and into the Ottawa River at present-day Mattawa, Ontario. From there the route followed a downstream paddle to Ville Marie. Of course, fur cargoes would need to be paddled from Ville Marie, present-day Montreal, down the St. Lawrence River to Habitation, present-day Quebec City, where they were loaded on ships bound for Europe.

Another principal fur trade route was from Lake Michigan into Lake Huron, entry to present-day Lake St. Clair and then Lake Erie. Canoes and fur bundles would be portaged around Niagara Falls; move down the Niagara River into

Lake Ontario. The long paddle across Lake Ontario brought the fur laden canoes to the mouth of the St. Lawrence River and the French settlement of Cataraqui, present-day Kingston, Ontario. The arduous paddle down the St. Lawrence River was encumbered with numerous and difficult portages before the paddlers arrived at Ville Marie.

A third principal trade route was in the southeast. This trade route was dominated first by Sweden, and then by the Dutch. At Manhattan, present-day New York City, the Dutch traders established a fur collection and debarkation point for furs going to Europe. The Dutch established their primary fur trading post at Fort Orange, present-day Albany New York, on the Hudson River. Fort Orange was on the southern boundary of the Mohawk ancestral lands. Furs could be paddled to Fort Orange from the St. Lawrence River Region by a route south through Lake Champlain. The Dutch also established important trading posts on the Delaware River.

In the beginning, there were three major tribal players involved in competing for control of the trade routes. The Wendat (Huron) acted as middle-men for fur coming from the Great Lakes Region. The Algonquin controlled the movement of people and goods on the Ottawa River and the St. Lawrence River. The Susquehannock controlled the fur trade with the Dutch. The five united tribes of the Haudenosaunee Confederacy, realizing their growing dependence on European trade goods, entered the fur trade with great ambition. The Haudenosaunee, called Iroquois by the French, had a goal of controlling the fur trade and being the sole dominant power in trade with the French and the Dutch. Competition would either be neutralized through diplomacy or squashed with military force.

Henry Hudson, sailing under Dutch charter aboard his ship the De Halve Maen [The Half Moon], arrived in present-day Hudson River region in 1609. Similar to Jacque Cartier's charter in 1534, the principal purpose of Hudson's Dutch charter was to find a short route to Asia.

During the years 1610-1614, the Dutch established seasonal trading posts on the Hudson and Delaware Rivers. The Netherlands granted a charter to the *Dutch West India Company* to trade for furs in New Netherland, often referred to as New Amsterdam. The first Dutch settlement was Fort Nassau, on the Hudson River. The Dutch fort was built in 1614, on the foundation of an abandoned

French trading fort built in 1540. The first permanent Dutch settlement was built at present-day Albany, New York. Named Fort Orange, the trading post replaced near-by Fort Nassau in 1624. Fort Orange was later named Fort Albany.

Fort Albany had the monopoly on regional fur trading. The Dutch required all fur trading to occur at Fort Albany and all fur would be shipped to Europe from their settlement at present-day Manhattan, New York. The Dutch paid twice the price for fur that the French paid. Also, Dutch trade goods, particularly their firearms, were a superior quality to French trade goods.

Samuel de Champlain founded New France in 1608. Soon after his arrival, trading with the Indigenous tribes for the pelts of furbearers began. In 1613, *The Company of One Hundred Associates* was given a royal charter granting a fur trade monopoly. The royal charter required the company to pay a portion of profits to France, cover military expenditures, and continue to aggressively encourage settlement of New France.

In 1627, the *Company of New France* was founded when the French king issued the company a licence as the sole fur trader of New France. The condition was that the company would bring settlers to New France and help them become established. For the French monarchy, the fur trade provided the incentive to begin a process of occupation of New France.

The French built trading forts at strategic locations. The forts provided the French with a military presence to assert control over the fur trade. The trading posts also defined the boundaries of a growing French empire. In addition to the trading post at Ville Marie, present-day Montreal; French posts extended south across present-day Lake Champlain and down the Hudson River to Fort Albany. Pushing along the St, Lawrence River, the most westerly French trading forts were established at Fort Niagara and Fort Oswego on Lake Ontario. Eventually, the chain of French trading forts extended into present day Lake Huron, Lake Michigan, the Ohio Valley Region, and south along the Mississippi River.

The French entered into an alliance with the Wendat. The French traders and missionaries referred to the Wendat as Huron. The French-Huron alliance angered the Five Nations of the Haudenosaunee, called Iroquois by the French. The Iroquois wanted control of the fur trade and over the next century and a half, warfare was constant and engaged numerous tribes, tribal confederacies, tribal alliances, and the European powers of France, England and the Netherlands.

The English began their colonization in 1607 with a settlement at Jamestown, present-day State of Virginia. The English, in the beginning, were not interested in the fur trade. Their interest was primarily in colonialization and extraction of reginal resources, particularly the vast stands of magnificent and valuable old growth White Pine forest.

Swedish traders played a minor European role in the fur trade in eastern North America. Beginning in 1610, Swedish fur traders, competing with the Dutch, began to establish trading posts on both sides of the Delaware River in present-day states of Delaware, New Jersey, and Pennsylvania.

In 1628, the Mohawk defeated the Mahican, a Dutch ally, and established a fur trade monopoly with the Dutch at Fort Orange. This conflict was the beginning of the *Beaver Wars (1628-1701)*.

Sweden, at the time an important northern European military power, had ambitions of colonization in eastern North America. In 1638, Sweden planted her flag with the building of her first fort at the present-day Wilmington, Delaware. The fort was named Fort Christina, in honor of Queen Christina of Sweden.

Sweden's fur-trading and colonial ambitions were short lived. In 1655, during the *Second Northern War, 1655-60*, New Sweden was defeated by the Dutch. Swedish settlements and trading posts were incorporated into the Dutch colonies of New Netherlands.

During 1660 through 1763, the French and English won and lost tribal alliances, fought wilderness wars, and struggled mightily to expand their empires and win control of the fur trade. At the same time, various Native tribes, alliances, and confederacies, strategized about which European power would serve their purposes best.

During this time the Iroquois Confederacy was the political and military equal of France and Britain. The Iroquois Confederacy was fighting as hard as the French and British to win control of territory, dominant the fur trade, and build their empire.

In time, the British defeated the French and won control of Canada. During the *American Revolutionary War, 1775-1783,* destructive social and cultural shifts occurred across the vast landscape of eastern North America. Great Native confederacies and alliances were shattered beyond any hope of recovery. Tribes became extinct. Many of the Native tribes who had been allies of the British or Americans during the turbulent years of the *American Revolution* and the following *War of 1812, 1812-15,* had become refugees in their own ancestral lands.

The American Revolution had forced the British to abandon their fur trading posts south of the Great Lakes Region. The new United States of American attempted to put life back into the fur trade but their emphasis was on settlement and the challenges of settler expansion into the Ohio Valley Region.

By the 1830s, the fur trade was in disarray. Markets had weakened as well as world demand for fur bearer pelts. The fur trade no longer played a key part in the strategies of empire building.

Chapter 4

The Covenant Chain

A Coalition of Tribes

The *Covenant Chain* agreement with the early Dutch explorers and traders of New Netherlands, in the Hudson River Valley of present-day New York State, provides an example of Iroquois statesmanship and diplomatic skill in nation to nation relations. The term *Covenant Chain* was suggested by the Dutch at the time of a treaty signing with the Mohawk in 1618.

As the Haudenosaunee Confederacy expanded in pace with military success and diplomacy, the cultural practice of adoption of conquered tribes began to change. Adoption of entire populations of defeated non-Iroquoian speaking tribes and nations was no longer an option. The alternative was to offer membership in the Covenant Chain.

Friendship Treaty Wampum

This wampum, purple figures connected by a purple line on a white background, represents a covenant of friendship between the Onkwehon:we [the people] and the Europeans. The belt speaks of friendship, peace, and good minds. Source: pers. comm. Darren Bonaparte

The Covenant Chain defined a relationship between nations. The cultural identity of members would not be threatened, allowing a trust to build between parties.

Today, the Covenant Chain arrangement would be called a 'coalition' of nations. Being invited to join the Covenant Chain tribes was an opportunity to become a member of an assembly of tribes united towards a particular goal that, when achieved, would benefit all the members. In the case of the Covenant Chain, the Haudenosaunee would protect the members of the Covenant Chain. They would act on any coalition member's behalf for their benefit and the benefit of all the Covenant Chain members.

Jennings (1985, pg. 117) writes: *" There was a long series of treaty relationships that had begun with a rope between the Mohawks and the Dutch at Fort Orange. The rope apparently signified a nonaggressive pact for purposes of trade. It was converted into an iron chain connecting the Mohawks with all the Dutch of New Netherlands in a bilateral mutual assistance alliance at about 1643. The iron chain was renewed by the English of New York in 1664, at which time it also included the Seneca. In 1677 the chain became silver as a multilateral, bicultural confederation of the Iroquois League and certain English colonies and thus began the Covenant Chain proper."*

In a 1993 research paper written by Paul Williams, a researcher with the North American Indian Travelling College, Akwesasne, Ontario; several historical references to the Covenant Chain are provided. A few of the references shared by Williams follow.

An address particular to the Covenant Chain was spoken by Sir William Johnson, Imperial Superintendent General, at Onondaga, Keepers of the Iroquois Confederacy Fire, April 25, 1748.

The account reads: *"Brethern of the Five Nations, I will begin upon a thing of long standing, our first Brothership. I found out some of the old writings of our Forefathers which was thought to have been lost, and in this old valuable Record I find that our first Friendship commenced at the arrival of the first great Canoe or Vessel at Albany, at which time you were much surprised but finding what it contained pleased you so much, being Things for your Purpose .... you all resolved to take the greatest care of that Vessel that nothing should hurt her Whereupon it was agreed to tye her fast with a great Rope to one of the largest nut trees on the Bank of the River. But on further Consideration in a further Meeting it was thought safest, Fearing the Wind should blow down that Tree, to make a long Rope and tye her fast at Onondaga which was accordingly done and the Rope put under your feet That if anything hurt or touched said Vessel by shaking of the Rope you might know it, and then agreed to rise all as one and see what the Matter was and whoever hurt the Vessel was to suffer. After this was agreed upon and done you made an offer to the Governor to enter into a Bond of Friendship with him and his People which he was so pleased at that he told you he would find a strong Silver Chain which would never break, slip or Rust to bind you and him in Brothership together, and that your Warriors and ours should be as one Heart, one Head, one Blood."* (Jennings. 1984, pg. 145)

In 1755, Sir William Johnson, meeting with representatives of the Iroquois Confederacy, provided a reply to the Confederacy's request for written copies of their past transactions with the Crown. From records in the National Archives of Canada, Record Group 10, Indian Affairs Papers, Vol. 1822, pp. 35, 22, we have the following:

Johnson addressed the Council: " *Behold Brethern these great books, four folio volumes of the records of Indian Affairs which lay upon the table before the Colonel. They are records of the many solemn Treaties and the various Transactions which have passed between your Forefathers and your Brethern the English, also between many of you here I present us your Brethern now living. You well know and these books testify that it is now almost a hundred years since your Forefathers & ours became known to each other. That upon our first acquaintance we shook hands & finding we should be useful to one another entered into a Covenant of Brotherly Love & mutual Friend-ship. And tho we were at first only tied together by a Rope, yet less this Rope should grow rotten & break we tied ourselves together by an Iron Chain. Lest time or accidents might rust & destroy this Chain of Iron, we afterwards made one of Silver, the strength and brightness of which would subject it to no decay.*

The ends of this Silver Chain we fix'd to the Immovable Mountains, and this in so firm a Manner that no Mortal enemy might be able to remove it. You know also that this Covenant Chain of Love & Friendship was the Dread and Envy of all your Enemies & Ours, that by keeping it bright and unbroken we have never spilt in anger one drop of each other's blood to this day. You well know also that from the beginning to this time, we have almost every year strengthened & brightened this Covenant Chain in the most solemn and public manner. "

At the commencement of a 1774 Treaty Council meeting in what is now Pennsylvania, Governor Clinton of New York spoke on behalf of the British Colonies:

" Brethren

This interview gives me the greatest pleasure as I am persuaded we meet with equal sincerity in order to renew, strengthen, brighten the Covenant Chain which has so long tied you and the subjects of His Majesty the Great King of Great Britain your Father and my Master in mutual ties of friendship and benevolence which I hope will forever be invilably preserved and continue as long as the sun and the moon endureth. "

In reply, and on behalf of the Iroquois Confederacy, Haudenosaunee representative Canesatago, spoke on the history of the Covenant Chain:

" Brother.

You came out of the Ground in a Country that lies beyond the Seas, there you may have a just Claim, but here you must allow us to be your elder Brethren, and the Lands to belong to us long before you knew anything of them. It is true, that above one hundred years ago the Dutch came here in a ship, and brought with them several Goods, such as Awls, Knives, Hatchets, Guns and many other Particulars, which they gave us; and when they had taught us how to use their Things, and we saw what sort of People they were, we were so well pleased with them, that we tied their Ship to the Bushes on the Shore; and afterwards, liking them still better the longer they staid with us, and thinking the Bushes too slender, we removed the Rope, and tied it to the Trees; and as the Trees were liable to be blown down by high Winds, or to decay of themselves, we from the Affection we bore them, again removed the Rope, and tied it to a strong and big Rock [the interpreter says this means the Onondaga country] *and there we tied it very fast, and rowll'ed Wampum around it ; and to make it still* more secure, we stood upon the Wampum, and sat down upon it, to defend it, and to prevent any hurt coming to it, and did our best endeavours that it might remain uninjured forever. During all this time, the new-comers, the Dutch, acknowledged our Right to the Lands, and solicited us, from Time to Time, to grant them parts of our Country, and to enter into League and Covenant with us, and to become one People with us.

After this the English came into the Country, and as we were told, became one people with the Dutch. About two years after the arrival of the English, an English Governor came to Albany, and finding what great Friendship subsisted between us and the Dutch, he approved it mightily, and desired to make as strong a League, and to be upon as good terms with us as the Dutch were, with whom he was united, and to become one People with us. And by his further care into looking into what had passed between us, he found that the Rope which tied the Ship to the great Mountain was only fastened with Wampum, which was liable to break and rot, and to perish in a Course of Years; he therefore told us he would give us a Silver Chain, which would be much stronger, and would last forever, this we accepted, and fastened the Ship with it, and it has lasted ever since. " (Treaty Minutes, Pa. Council Minutes, June 16, 1774, 4:706-09)

The Covenant Chain, in addition to serving as a memory of treaties between the Haudenosaunee, the Dutch and English, includes many elements of the Great Binding Law of the Iroquois Confederacy. The agreement is consistent with the Two Row Wampum which confirms that the two Nations will travel in different canoes side by side [each Nation with its own culture and spirituality without interfering with the other]. The two parties recognized and accepted that they must, from time to time, meet and reaffirm the commitment created by the Covenant Chain. The Chain must be grasped firmly to remain binding, and so to must the Lords of the Confederacy grasp one another's arms firmly to maintain the Great Binding Law so firmly that a falling tree could not break the strength of the circle. The *winds* that are recorded in the accounts of Johnston and Canesatego refer to war which could threaten the Tree of Peace which stands at the symbolic centre of the Iroquois Confederacy.

The descriptions of the intent and history of the Covenant Chain by the Haudenosaunee leaders and English officials provide a record for the development of relations between the Iroquois, Dutch, and English.

Michael L. Hart

Two Row Wampum

This wampum belt, purple lines on a white background, signifies the relationship between the Dutch and the Haudenosaunee. The two separate purple bands signify the canoe of the Europeans and the canoe of the Haudenosaunee. The canoes may travel together on the same water, but neither canoe will interfere with the culture, custom, or laws of the other. Source: pers. com. Darren Bonaparte

The French Period, 1615-1763

Chapter 5

The French Period 1615-1763

In 1615, the French and their allies raided Onondaga Iroquois territory. Furious about French raiding in Onondaga territory on the south shore of Lake Ontario, the Iroquois struck back.

The Iroquois began to campaign against the French and their allies. They successfully disrupted travel routes of the Lake Ontario fur trade. This forced the French to use the Ottawa River Valley route to gain access to the western Great Lakes Region. This travel route was long and arduous. From Ville Marie, trade goods laden canoes travelled upstream on the Ottawa River to the Mattawa River; paddled across Lake Nipissing; then down the French River to Lake Huron.

By 1610, Dutch traders had established a presence on the Hudson River, in present-day New York State. The Dutch began to supply the Iroquois with steel knives, hatchets and good quality firearms, powder and ball. With good quality weapons the previously disadvantaged Mohawk now had parity with the French and their allies.

In 1613, a truce between the Mahican and Mohawk was negotiated by the Dutch. The truce lasted four years. The years 1617 through 1624 were not peaceful. The Mohawk and Mahican continued to skirmish.

In 1615, the Montagnais, Algonquin, and Huron-Wendat continued to attack the Mohawk in the north. The Mohawk were now fighting a war on two fronts. In the south, the Mohawk were waging war on their old enemies, the Susquehannock. (Sultzman, 2014)

The Dutch allied themselves with the Mohawk against the Susquehannock. This new alliance with the Dutch did not come easily for the Mohawk. To reach their Dutch trading partners, the Mohawk had to travel through Mahican territory. The Mahican, seeing an opportunity for advantage, demanded payment from the Mohawk in return for their safe passage across Mahican territory. The Mohawk were not happy with this arrangement. They began skirmishing with the Mahican.

The Dutch had succeeded in preventing total war between the Mohawk and Mahican, but they were frustrated by what they saw as stalled trading opportunities. The Dutch initiated a venture to open trade with the French on the St. Lawrence River. Their strategy was to have the Mahican approach the Algonquin, a strong ally of the French, and have the Algonquin make trade overtures to the French on behalf of the Dutch. The initiative was a strategic blunder on the part of the Dutch.

The Mohawk learned what was happening and were furious. In 1624, they attacked the Mahican with a vengeance. The Dutch found themselves on the sidelines. The Mahican called upon the Pocumtuc and western Abenaki to help them fight the Mohawk. The Dutch stepped back into the fray and allied themselves with the Mahican. Dutch soldiers were killed and the Dutch became fearful of the loses being inflicted on them by the Mohawk. The Dutch could see Mohawk military superiority and decided that the wise move for them would be to pull out of the conflict and declare neutrality.

By 1628, the Mohawk had defeated the Mahican and driven them east across the Hudson River. The Mahican sued for peace and the Mohawk were happy to oblige. The Mohawk peace terms offered the Mahican forced them to pay tribute in wampum, or, pay a share of their profits acquired through trade with the wampum suppliers, the Delaware of Long Island.

During the *Pequot War (1634-1638)*, the Pequot and allied Algonquin tribes of coastal New England were being displaced by the English settlers and their tribal allies of the region. The Pequot petitioned the Mohawk for assistance. Weakened by smallpox epidemics, the Mohawk refused the Pequot request of alliance. In a tragic turn of events, the Mohawk killed the Pequot chief Sassacus who had come to the Mohawk for refuge.

The *Pequot War* was a brutal affair that extinguished the Pequot Confederacy—consisting of the Western Niantic and Mattabesis tribes—as a viable polity in present-day southern New England. Many of the Pequot captured by the British during the war, along with those who surrendered after the war, were sent to the Bermudas and the West Indies to be sold into slavery.

Hunt (1940, pg. 72) writes that during the years 1630 through 1640, the Huron raided Iroquois territory with impunity. However, the Iroquois began to obtain good quality firearms from the Dutch traders. They quickly learned to be efficient with these new weapons and were soon the equal of the French soldiers in terms of accuracy and speed of reloading. The Iroquois began reprisal raiding. War parties, dominated by Mohawk warriors, attacked the Huron-Wendat and their Algonquin allies " *armed with good Dutch harquebuses which they can use as well as our Europeans.* " (JR vol. 22, pg. 269)

Samuel De Champlain, the *Father of New France*, died in 1635. Since his first skirmish with the Iroquois in 1609, warfare had changed significantly. Wooden armor and cornstalk shields had been cast aside as useless against lead balls. When trade allowed, firearms began to replace warrior's powerful long bows. The Iroquois, well armed with good quality Dutch weapons, were now the hunters and not the hunted.

Between 1630 and 1640, hundreds of Kichesippirini and Weskarinin Algonquin abandoned their ancestral lands in the Ottawa River Region. Seeking safety from Iroquois war parties, they resettled at the St. Lawrence River Jesuit mission at Trois Rivieres.

In 1642, A Mohawk war party was seen in the vicinity of Trois Rivieres. Some of the Trois Rivieres Algonquin fled upriver to shelter with the Kichesippirini band living at Morrison Island on the Ottawa River, adjacent to present-day Pembroke, Ontario. The island population included a strong force of warriors.

Unlike most Algonquin villages, Morrison Island functioned as a permanent fortified village. Unusual for Algonquin villages, some agriculture for beans, corn and peas was conducted on the island and lands adjacent to the island. Morrison Island was a unique Native settlement in another way. The Kichesippirini were managing a flourishing and lucrative seasonal business. Every fur laden canoe paddling downstream was charged a transportation tax. Every trade goods laden canoe paddling upstream was charged the same tax. (Hessel, 1993, pg. 27)

In the winter of 1642, Mohawk scouts learned that many of the Morrison Island warriors were away hunting. The Mohawk war party, travelling across difficult terrain in adverse winter weather conditions, used surprise to full advantage and captured the settlement. Many Algonquin were killed in the attack, others were taken prisoner.

" About thirty young women were tortured and received terrible wounds, but their lives were spared, and they were kept as 'wretched slaves' by the Iroquois." (JR vol. 22, pgs. 251-267)

In the spring of 1642, the Mohawk attacked the Weskarini. Some were killed and entire families were taken away as captives. (ibid, pg. 269)

At about the same time, Mohawk raiding parties attacked a group of Huron-Wendat traders at the Chaudière Falls, Ottawa River, in the vicinity of the present-day city of Ottawa. Another raid attacked Fort Richelieu, north of the French settlement of Ville Marie, on present-day Montreal island (ibid, pg. 273)

The Mohawk raiding strategy intended to disrupt the fur trade was not as effective as the Mohawk had hoped. Beginning in the summer of 1643, the Mohawk changed tactics. They separated into small war parties and located themselves at strategic points along the Ottawa River and the St. Lawrence River. When one party had served a tour of duty, another arrived to provide relief. By 1644, there were ten river based war parties ready to attack canoe flotillas. A war party was stationed on the upper Ottawa River to be closest to the Huron-Wendat canoe routes coming east out of the French River and Lake Nipissing. Two parties were located in the vicinity of Chaudière Falls on the Ottawa River at the present-day city of Ottawa; one party waited at Long Sault Rapids on the Ottawa River near present-day Carillon, Quebec. One party waited near the settlement of Ville Marie, another war party bivouacked somewhere along Rivieres de Prairies, present-day Montreal island. Four additional Mohawk war parties were situated between Ville Marie and Trois Rivieres.

This was an amazing war effort on the part of the Mohawk. The river blockading strategy demonstrated the military sophistication that enabled such a wide dispersal of Mohawk warriors. Military planning included rotating warriors to provide relief.

The Mohawk strategy began to have results. The constant harassment of Huron-Wendat and Algonquin fur canoes along the water routes leading to Ville Marie and Habitation (present-day Quebec City) degraded the paddler's ability to get furs to the French. Something had to be done to break the Iroquois blockade.

Kiotsaeton's Treachery

Charles Huault de Montmagny replaced Samuel de Champlain as Governor of New France. The Natives gave Montmagny the name *Onontio* [*Big Mountain*]. The new Governor sent 22 newly arrived French soldiers up the Ottawa River to protect the Algonquin traders. The soldiers wintered at the Jesuit mission of Sainte-Marie in Huronia, the Huron-Wendat homeland known today as Simcoe County, Ontario. At the same time, Montmagny was making overtures to the Iroquois to open negotiations for a peace treaty. His overture began by sending Mohawk prisoners home with the message *'Onontio wishes to discuss a truce.'*

In 1645, Kiotsaeton, a Mohawk statesman and orator of reputation, arrived with his delegation at Trois Rivieres. Montmagny was accompanied by Father Vimont, the superior of the Jesuit Mission at Trois Rivieres, and Father Le Jeune. Representatives from tribal allies also attended to participate in the negotiations. A problem emerged when it was discovered that the Algonquin were not represented by their chief, Tessouat. This meant that the Algonquin could not speak with the authority needed for a treaty negotiation. Kiotsaeton gave seventeen wampum belts to the French and the Huron delegates. This was a good will gesture. However, the Algonquin did not receive a belt. The Mohawk had grown suspicious of the few Algonquin attending the meeting because they failed to show any enthusiasm for peace.

Kiotsaeton asked for a private meeting between him, the two Jesuits, and Montmagny, the Governor of New France. A peace treaty with secret articles known only to those present was proposed by Kiotsaeton. The proposal involved a peace which excluded the Algonquin. Kiotsaeton's proposal set forth a plan that would have the French and their allies abandon the Algonquin. The solution was certainly dishonorable in the least, and outright treacherous at most. Montmagny could not agree. However, the attending Jesuits offered a solution. They suggested to the Governor that he could promise, in secret, that if the Mohawk would agree not to attack Christian Algonquin, then the French could accept that all non-Christian Algonquin were excluded from a peace treaty. (JR vol. 28, pgs. 149-151)

Kiotsaeton's treacherous plan was accepted by Montmagny, Father Superior Vincent, and Father Le Jeune. The agreement was written into the Jesuit Relations in Latin. Other Jesuits learned of the political treachery a year later. The Algonquin never did learn about the covert agreement. (ibid, pg. 315)

So it was that the Algonquin, loyal and faithful French allies since Champlain gave them French military assistance in 1603, were betrayed with *'thorough going duplicity'* a mere decade after Champlain had died. (Hunt, 1940, pg. 78; Trigger,1976, Vol II, pgs. 648-49)

The political reality of 1645 had made the non-Christian Algonquin an expendable ally. Governor Montmagny and the Jesuits knew that there was no doubt at all that if the Algonquin were no longer seen by the French as a necessary ally in the fur trade, the Iroquois would begin to campaign against the Algonquin. The awesome military might of the Iroquois against the abandoned Algonquin would be a terrible thing.

The fate of the Algonquin was sealed. The formal and public treaty negotiation began in September, 1645. The French, Mohawk, Wendat, Montagnais, and the Algonquin were in attendance. The unsuspecting Algonquin were now represented by their Chief Tessouat of the Kichesippirini. The Kichesippirini were the strongest of the Algonquin bands in terms of military strength and political influence. The Jesuit priest, Father Lalemant, unaware of the treachery, watched the proceedings *'with eyes full of joy.'* A second meeting was held in Mohawk territory. A third meeting was held at Trois Rivieres in February, 1646. At this meeting the Algonquin Chief Tessouat presented gifts to the Mohawk as a gesture of trust and to satisfy all the parties that the Algonquin wanted peace.

Hessel writes: *"Tessouat prayed to the sun to be a spectator and to serve as a witness. Tessouat promised the Mohawk that he would never break the peace and 'in token* of the truth', he presented them with a number of beautifully painted and trimmed robes of moose skin. He said he wanted the gifts to dispel his suspicion of the Mohawk. Other Skins were for the 'ambassadors to repose on, in order to be refreshed from the toil of their journey.' " (1993, pgs. 52-53)

Hessel also writes: *"Tessouat presented other gifts to the Mohawk, to assure freedom of the hunt everywhere, to assure the Mohawk that ' they could freely come to warm themselves at the fire which Onontio had kindled for them at Trois Rivieres '* " (ibid, pg. 53)

Chief Tessouat reminded Montmagny *"that his happiness should also be common to the Algonkin and Huron."* The Jesuit Priest Lalemant criticized Tessouat for being *"so utterly distrustful and suspicious"* and *"afraid that the French might make their peace in private, without troubling themselves about the Savages, their allies."* (JR vol. 28, pg. 299)

Chief Tessouat, although still without any evidence to the contrary, must have sensed that things were happening behind the scenes that could bring no good for his people.

When the Jesuits learned of the secret articles, Father Lalemant wrote: *" What was surprising therein was that our Fathers sent us no word of that at all."* (JR vol. 27, pgs. 147-155)

Mohawk truce with the French, Algonquin and Huron

The peace treaty of 1646 was completed. The Jesuits sent Father Jogues and a companion to begin a mission among the Mohawk. Their task, in addition to converting the Mohawk to Christianity, was to persuade the Mohawk to deny other Iroquois Nations a passage through Mohawk territory to reach Dutch trading posts. Matters did not work out well for the missionaries who had arrived in the Mohawk territory during a time of famine. The Mohawk blamed Father Jogues and his companion for the famine. They were killed after being accused of sorcery. (Trigger,1976, vol. II, pg. 657; Hunt, 1940, pg. 83)

By the summer of 1646, the fur trade was again back in business. Record numbers of furbearer pelts were being transported down the Ottawa River to Ville Marie by Huron-Wendat and Algonkin paddlers. The Mohawk were keeping the peace. However, Oneida warriors attacked Chief Tessouat and a party of Kichesippirini on the Ottawa River above the Long Sault Rapids. This same Oneida war party was later attacked and defeated by the Weskarini.

The Mohawk had kept to the truce with the French and the Huron, while, at the same time the 'secret articles' allowed them to attack the Algonquin in both their winter hunting grounds and along the fur trade canoe route.

But the peace would not last. On Ash Wednesday, March 6, 1647, a Mohawk war party attacked. The Mohawk warriors wiped out the entire Kichesippirini Band who had been living and trapping in the vicinity of Trois Rivieres, where they believed their close proximity to the French would guarantee a measure of security from Iroquois raiding. Many of the dead Algonquin were baptized Christians. It was obvious that the Mohawk did not differentiate between Christian Algonquin and a non-Christian Algonquin. (JR vol. 30, pgs. 231-253).

Things were about to get a lot nastier. After the Mohawk attack, a group of Weskarini travelled to Trois Rivieres and discovered that their fellow Algonquin had been massacred. A Weskarini party travelled upriver to Morrison Island, near present-day Pembroke, Ontario, with the intention of warning the people of the pending Mohawk danger. On the way, Weskarini scouts spotted a large group of Mohawk with an estimated forty Algonquin captives. Warned of the approaching Mohawk paddlers, the main party of Weskarini set up an ambush. The ensuing battle resulted in a bloody defeat for the Mohawk. The Algonquin captives were freed, although some were killed in the fighting. The freed Algonquin captives told their rescuers that they had been captured during a Mohawk raid on their island stronghold at Morrison Island. (JR vol. 30, pgs. 283-84)

The Iroquois Destruction of the Huron Begins.

In the winter of 1647-48, a Huron peace delegation travelling to Onondaga was attacked by a Mohawk war party. This may have been an attempt by the Mohawk to prevent contact by the Huron with the four other Iroquois Nations – Oneida, Onondaga, Cayuga and Seneca. In the meantime, another Huron group was attacked and wiped out by a war party of Seneca. The two attacks were the beginning of full scale war in Huronia. The Iroquois Confederacy was about to begin their destruction of the Huron Confederacy.

In the winter of 1648, an Iroquois force of over 1,000 warriors, mostly Mohawk and Seneca, spent the winter camped north of Lake Ontario. The Iroquois strategy was to be in a position to attack the Huron before the winter snows had melted. The sudden, and totally unexpected attack, destroyed the villages around the heart of the Huron homeland at Sainte-Marie.

The Huron were reduced to refugees. Many of the Huron survivors died of starvation. More were hunted down and killed by Iroquois war parties scouring the land for bands of fleeing stragglers. The raiding, captive taking, killing, and burning of villages and crops was relentless.

The Iroquois needed prisoners to satisfy their mourning-war culture, and the conflict with the Wendat provided ample opportunity to raid and seize prisoners. For almost a decade after the defeat and collapse of the Wendat, the Great Pursuit of the Wendat and their allies by the Iroquois Confederacy raged across the land. The time was known as the Wendat Dispersal.

Some Huron refugees sought sanctuary with the Tobacco. This safe zone did not last. Angry about the Tobacco involvement, the Iroquois raided Tobacco villages and the destruction was completed by the end of 1649. An estimated 300 Wendat survivors of the Iroquois raids, along with surviving Jesuit priests, fled to the French settlement at Habitation, present-day Quebec City. (Hessel, 1993, pgs. 54-55)

The Iroquois were unyielding in the pursuit of the Wendat refugees. The few Wendat refugees finding sanctuary at present-day Quebec City were aggressively petitioned by the Iroquois to join their Confederacy. By 1657, many of the exhausted Wendat, with a French policy of non-interference, walked away from their Quebec City sanctuary. The Arendaronon Wendat were adopted by the Onondaga. The Attignawantan Wendat were adopted by the Mohawk.

In time, many of the surviving Huron and Tobacco were adopted by the Iroquois and absorbed into their communities. The Iroquois were adept at using adoption to replace their own populations depleted after years of disease epidemics and war causalities. The adopted peoples would be totally assimilated in

Iroquois society. With time, the cultural identity of the adopted people would fade and be erased.

The astute Dutch, with their lucrative trading settlements on the Hudson River, watched the flow of events. The Dutch approached the victorious Mohawk and suggested that the Mohawk become the principle trading partners with the Dutch. The Mohawk realized the advantage of such an arrangement. Dutch firearms and steel weapons were superior quality. The Mohawk, from recent experience, had learned that a few skilled and motivated warriors with quality firearms could defeat a larger force with insufficient and poor quality firearms. The Dutch had superior quality firearms, powder and ball, and were willing to trade these weapons on generous terms with the Mohawk. Besides, the Mohawk liked the Dutch. With the exception of a few strategic blunders by the Dutch, their relationship had been largely favorable for both parties.

So now, with a renewed alliance with the Dutch, good weapons, and with the taste of recent victory still fresh, the Iroquois began planning to expand their empire. They would go to war against the French and fight for control of the St. Lawrence River Region. The prize would be control of the fur trade. The *Beaver Wars* had begun.

Chapter 6

The Beaver Wars, 1640-1701

Beginning in the mid 17th Century, the sixty-year long *Beaver Wars* were brutal, even by today's standards. Large numbers of refugees from defeated tribes struggled for survival. The Iroquois destroyed several powerful and regionally influential tribal alliances including the Algonquin, Wendat, Neutral, Erie, and Susquehannock.

The Beaver Wars are also referred to by historians as the *French and Indian Wars; Iroquois Wars*, and the *French and Iroquois Wars*.

The Iroquois victories and their aftermath realigned the tribal geography of North America. The Iroquois forced some eastern tribes to relocate west of the Mississippi River, and pushed other tribes southward into the Carolinas. From 1670 onward, the Ohio Valley lands had become the hunting grounds for the Iroquois. Various tribes had been pushed from the Ohio Country and the Lower Peninsula of Michigan. As refugees fled westward to escape marauding Iroquois, the land was emptied of people.

This is an appropriate place to provide background information for the Ohio Valley Region. In the decades to come, we learn more about the Ohio Country, sometimes called the Ohio Territory and Ohio Valley. The territory was the first frontier region of post *Revolutionary War* United States. The Ohio Valley Region consisted of all present-day Ohio; northwestern West Virginia; western Pennsylvania; and eastern Indiana.

Struggles over this region were pivotal to a number of major historical events of North America. The British; the Natives whose ancestral lands included territory within the Ohio Valley Region; the Iroquois Confederacy who claimed the territory by right of conquest; and the New England colonies all claimed the Ohio Valley Region as theirs. Indeed, historians believe the political and social pressures associated with Anglo-American settlement in the Ohio Valley Region were a primary cause of the *French and Indian War, 1754 -1760;* and a contributing factor to the *American Revolutionary War, 1775-1783*. Certainly, the Ohio Valley Region conflict served to erase any influence that an already shattered and dysfunctional Iroquois Confederacy had managed to cobble together after the *American Revolutionary War*.

The pressures from land speculators and the illegal 'invasions' and 'occupations' by frontier settlers and timber harvesting interests forced the new United States government to act on the expansion of territorial boundaries. Indeed, the Colony of Virginia had claimed the Ohio Valley Region as their territory, and had upheld this claim into the *American Revolutionary War* years. The fact that the British Crown had tried to stop emigration and settlement west of the Appalachian Mountains was a flashpoint for the American Revolution against British rule.

In 1774, the Colony of Virginia had formally issued a declaration of war against the Shawnee Nation. The declaration of war brought about the conflict known as *Lord Dunmore's War*. This conflict led to a treaty ceding rights to settle the eastern lands of the Ohio River Valley. The war and its result was totally inconsistent with official British policy on settlement.

The *Northwest Ordinance of 1787* established the boundaries of the Ohio Valley Region, now called the Northwest Territory. This new territory description was far larger than the original description for the Ohio Valley Region. The *Northwest Ordinance of 1787* boundaries included: all the land of the United States west of Pennsylvania and northwest of the Ohio River. This description included all of the present-day states of Ohio; Indiana; Illinois; Michigan; Wisconsin; and the northeastern part of Minnesota. The area was vast. It covered more than 260,000 square miles (670,000 square kilometers).

But these events and consequences were yet to come. We need to go back to the year 1629 and the *Beaver Wars*.

The year is 1629. The Mahican are defeated. Now the Mohawk look towards the Mahican allies - the Abenaki [Sokoki] and Pennacook. The Mohawk understand the concept of total war. Enemies must either capitulate totally and agree to terms of surrender which reduced the people to vassals and penury, or be adopted and assimilated into the Iroquois Empire.

By now there were three major European players in the fur trade: Dutch; French; and English. Although Sweden had established a colony on the lower Delaware River in 1638, she was never more than a lesser player in the fur trade.

The intention of the Iroquois Confederacy (Mohawk; Oneida; Onondaga; Cayuga; Seneca) was to monopolize the fur trade. If they could monopolize the fur trade, then the Iroquois would also dominate all trade between the European markets and the tribes of the Great Lakes Region. If the Iroquois Confederacy could accomplish their objectives, they would achieve their expansionist goals of Empire. They would establish the economic, political, and territorial strength and security needed for an Iroquois Empire.

The Iroquois war against the Abenaki and Pennacook would have continued for years had it not been for the intervention of Great Britain. The British had begun colonizing New England in 1620. The *Thirty Years War* in Europe between Britain and France also had campaigns in the New World. During 1628 and 1629, English privateers under Charter from King Charles I and commanded by David Kirke, successfully executed a blockade of the French settlement at Quebec. Samuel de Champlain, whose position had been weakened when his resupply convoys were captured, was forced to surrender to the English on July 19, 1629. This was the first surrender by France of Quebec to the English.

At the time of surrender, the *Thirty Years War* in Europe had ended with the *Treaty of Susa*. Champlain argued that the seizure of St. Lawrence River lands by the English was illegal. Years after, in 1632, Charles I agreed to return the lands to France if, among other things, Louis XIII would pay Charles wife's dowry.

The French monarch agreed and the 1632 *Treaty of St. Germaine en Laye* was signed and Quebec was restored to France.

In the meantime, French influence was diminished and they could no longer support their old allies the Algonquin and Montagnais. The Algonquin and Montagnais were now in a weakened state as well. The Mohawk were quick to take advantage of the situation. They negotiated a truce with the Abenaki. After the truce, the Mohawk destroyed the Algonquin and Montagnais village at Trois Rivieres. For three years after the village was destroyed the Algonquin and Montagnais suffered raiding loses to the Mohawk. Relief from Mohawk incursions came after the English returned the St. Lawrence River settlements to France in 1632.

By 1632, the Iroquois had nearly won control of all the ancestral territories of the Algonquin, Abenaki, and Montagnais in the upper St. Lawrence River Region and the Huron-Wendat ancestral territory in southern Ontario.

Furbearers were becoming more difficult to find. Furbearer populations had begun to show the results of years of intense trapping pressure. The Iroquois ancestral lands in upper New York State had never been a rich fur area and now the fur bearer population had been depleted through overharvest.

If the Iroquois were going to be able to continue to dominate the French, English, and Dutch fur trade, they needed to seize territory in which to take fur. Another strategy was the use of military force to win a capitulated agreement with a defeated tribe that a portion of their fur harvest would be allocated to the Iroquois. The Iroquois began to expand their empire. Empire building began with raids into fur rich southern Ontario and the Ottawa Valley.

The Iroquois did not have an easy time of it. Their ambitions were stalled by push back from the Wendat [Huron]. The Huron had persisted as a regional military power in their own right. The historical Huron alliance with the French give the Huron added weight in terms of military support, a supply of firearms and ammunition, and a security blanket for negotiation and diplomacy as advantage inevitably shifted from side to side.

The Iroquois changed strategies. They were dependant on the metal tools, good quality firearms and ammunition they traded for with the Dutch. Without a supply of furs to trade, the Iroquois knew the supply of European trade goods would dry up. So, they decided that perhaps they could get the furs they needed by trading with the Huron instead of fighting with them. Seeking a trade alliance with the Huron was not a precedent. Before the arrival of the Europeans and the competition for furs and trade alliances, the Iroquois and Huron had been successful trading partners. Actually, they had been on rather good terms with one another.

The Iroquois would first try diplomacy. They sent a delegation to negotiate with the Huron. However, the Huron, sensing they had a position of influence with the French, did not want to risk having that influence reduced. They refused to negotiate with the Iroquois delegation. A strategic blunder that would have tragic consequences for the Huron.

Sometime after their refusal to negotiate, a party of Huron killed a group of Iroquois hunting in disputed territory. The Iroquois took up the war club. Iroquois war parties began raiding in southern Ontario. Their objective was to obstruct the Huron trade route to the French at Ville Marie (Montreal) and Habitation (Quebec). Although the Iroquois were outnumbered, their skill at arms and superior strategy enabled them to defeat the Huron.

While the fighting ebbed and flowed, Iroquois diplomats worked to keep the French neutral. The Algonquin had not been forgotten by the Iroquois. The peace made with the Algonquin in 1634 came to end when the Algonquin initiated efforts to open trade with the Dutch in the Hudson River Valley. When they learned of the Algonquin plan, the Iroquois raided throughout 1636 and 1637 and drove the Algonquin north into the upper Ottawa Valley. While this was happening, on a second front, the Iroquois were also busy fighting the Montagnais and succeeded in driving them towards present-day Quebec City.

About this time, the non-discriminating scourge of European smallpox struck. The Iroquois may have been the first to be affected. The ravishes of this European disease forced an end to the Mohawk ambition to gain dominance over the fur trade in the east. However, in the west, the Seneca, as yet untouched by smallpox, began attacking the Huron and their allies in western Ontario.

Smallpox, a terrible relentless plague upon the land, certainly influenced the destinies of both the Iroquois and Huron, the two dominant military powers in the region. During the period 1637 through 1641, smallpox epidemics struck Huron populations. When the epidemics had run their course, it is estimated the Huron had lost half their population. The disease claimed many of their most experienced warriors and statesmen.

Human mortality associated with disease and causalities of war was not selective of tribes and confederacies. All the people suffered great losses. The leaders of the weakened populations understood that if they were going to be able to hold a position of strength sufficient to keep their military and political advantage, they needed to secure good quality firearms and ammunition in sufficient quantities to arm warriors. So now we have the makings of an arms race.

The arms race heated up when the French began to trade firearms to the Huron and Algonquin. As an incentive to accept Christianity, the French had been trading firearms to Christian converts only. This condition was now waived by the French. The French knew that a critically important strategic element in the struggle was to have a large force of allies equipped with an abundance of firearms.

The Iroquois found solid allies in their Dutch friends. In response to the French arms initiative, the Dutch unconditionally supplied good quality firearms with unlimited powder and ball to the Iroquois.

The arms race was gathering momentum. By 1638, Sweden had entered the lucrative fur trade and had established a small settlement on the lower Delaware River. The Swedes traded firearms to the Susquehannock, whose territory in southern Pennsylvania bumped against the ancestral lands of the Iroquois. The Swedish initiative caused great concern for the Iroquois. With the arming of the Susquehannock, the Iroquois began to be concerned about their old enemies.

The Iroquois demanded more firearms and ammunition from their Dutch trading partners. The Dutch, angered over Swedish encroachment on the fur trade, did not hesitate to supply quality firearms and ammunition to the Iroquois. Through the arms race, the Dutch established an alliance with the Iroquois that served to counter the influence of Swedish fur traders.

For the Iroquois, the availability of quality weapons to arm their warriors created a military advantage over the Huron. However, the Iroquois strategy was not to immediately began a campaign against the Huron to the north. Rather, the first campaign was directed against the Wenro tribe of western New York state. The anticipated alliance with old friends of the Wenro, the Erie and Neutral, did not come about. By 1639, the Wenro had been defeated and assimilated by the Seneca. The Wenro offered scattered resistance to the Iroquois occupation, but by 1643, the Wenro had been decimated in number, demoralized, and thoroughly defeated. Wenro refugees sought shelter with the Huron and the Neutral.

The arms race continued. In 1640, New England traders from Boston sought a piece of the lucrative fur trade. The traders organized and attempted to break the Dutch trade monopoly by offering the Mohawk a restricted quantity of firearms and ammunition at cheaper prices. This dickering in the arms market by Boston traders violated British law.

The Dutch, responding to the Boston initiative, stepped up the arms race and traded all the firearms, ball and powder the Mohawk asked for. For the small number of Mohawk warriors, this was a significant force-multiplier. The market free flow of weapons associated with the *Beaver Wars*, this proliferation of small arms, resulted in an escalation of the inter-tribal violence. The Iroquois knew they had secured a firepower advantage over the French and their allies.

The winds of war are always fickle. Military might can be sabotaged by poor planning and bad timing. In 1640, and again in 1641, the Huron won two significant victories against the Iroquois. However, the superior strategy and tactics of the Iroquois allowed the Mohawk and Oneida to regroup and force the last of the Algonquin and Montagnais from the lower St. Lawrence River.

This was neither a lucrative nor peaceful time for the French. In 1642, the Montagnais interfered with Abenaki [Sokoki] trading with the French at Quebec. Skirmishing between parties occurred and war broke out. The Abenaki, seeking an advantage to their favor, sought out their old Mohawk enemies in hopes of an alliance. The Mohawk, already fighting the Montagnais, agreed to the alliance. The Mahican, allied with the Mohawk since 1628, joined the Mohawk and Abenaki alliance. In 1645, alliance warriors raided the Montagnais village near Sillery, Quebec.

Learning of the Mohawk, Mahican, and Abenaki alliance, the Dutch grew uneasy. They could see an intrigue in the making and were eager to seek an advantage. In 1640, the Dutch had started to trade firearms and ammunition to the Mahican. By 1642, the Mohawk and Mahican were well armed with quality weapons, powder and ball. The Mohawk and Mahican initiated tribute demands on the Munsee and Wappinger Delaware (Wiechquaeskeck) of the lower Hudson River, present-day New York State.

In the winter of 1642-43, growing increasingly fearful of the powerful Mahican and Mohawk, the Wappinger Delaware moved south to Manhattan Island and also settled among the Tappan and Hackensack villages at Pavonia, present-day Jersey City. Hope persisted that the Dutch presence in that area would be a deterrent to Mohawk and Mahican aggression. The Wappinger Delaware were now war refugees.

The Dutch saw the arrival of the Wappinger Delaware refugees as a threat to regional stability. The Dutch, in an unusually aggressive move on their part, attacked and killed an estimated one hundred Wappinger Delaware. This incident became known as the *Pavonia Massacre*. The *Pavonia Massacre* was the catalyst for a new war. This war was called the *Wappinger War*, also known as *Governor Kieft's War of 1643-45*.

The fighting in this new war grew in intensity and territory. The Munsee (New Jersey); the Unami (Delaware); the Meloac (Western Long Island) were pulled into the fighting. The Dutch began to grow uncertain as to the war's outcome and petitioned the Mohawk and Mahican for assistance. In 1643, a treaty of alliance was arranged and the Mohawk and Mahican entered the fray on the side of the Dutch. In 1645, after years of brutal skirmishing, a peace was arranged at Fort Orange, a fortified Dutch settlement, present-day Albany, New York.

By the time peace was declared, more than 1,600 Wappinger, Munsee, and Meloac had been killed. Settlements had been destroyed and refugees roamed the land. The Mohawk and Mahican had secured control of the desirable and valuable wampum trade of western Long Island.

During the final twenty years of Dutch influence, Munsee hatred for the Mohawk festered. The Munsee hatred was held in check by the knowledge that an uprising on their part would be met with a brutal response by the Mohawk who were ready, able, and willing to crush resistance. After a time, five Munsee tribes allied with the intent to fight against the new Dutch settlements in the Esopus Valley. The Mohawk struck back, attacking Munsee villages and killing hundreds. At the end of the *Esopus War, 1660-64,* the Munsee had been defeated. The surviving Munsee were now subject to Iroquois rule.

While the Dutch were having an anxious and disruptive time, the French to the north were not faring much better. 1644 was particularly nasty. The Iroquois had forced the Algonquin (Atontrataronnon) from their Ottawa River territory. The Algonquin sought refuge with the Huron. Iroquois war parties had successfully fought and captured three large canoe flotillas attempting to bring furs to Ville Marie. The fur trade along the St. Lawrence River had been brought to a standstill. The Iroquois proposed a truce. The French were ready and eager to listen to terms.

In 1645, a treaty was agreed to. The Iroquois would allow the French to resume their fur trade. The treaty advantage for the Iroquois was time. Time to heal and rebuild communities and military power after years of warfare and devastating disease epidemics. However, the treaty did not address the main source of conflict between the French and their allies, nor the Iroquois and their allies. The issue that needed to be addressed for a lasting period of trade stability and reduced inter-group conflict was the trade competition and struggle for dominance between the Huron and the Iroquois. This festering conflict fed the vicious cycle of treachery and war that created a land of devastated settlements and war weary refugees.

To the credit of the Iroquois, they believed that their treaty with the French could establish a resumption of the historic and mutually beneficial pre-European trade between the Huron and the Iroquois. Sadly, and certainly most tragically, the Huron turned away from Iroquois approaches to resume trade as partners.

Events of unimaginable human and social consequence were about to be set into motion. The horrors of war in the New World would include monumental battles and an Iroquois strategy of genocide through a devastatingly cruel and unrelenting *Great Pursuit of the Huron* and her allies to the edges of cultural oblivion. The outcomes of events would be monumental in terms of power shifts and a changed social, political, and military landscape for both the Indigenous people and Europeans.

The Pine Tree Chiefs, a temporary appointment as war chief by the Grand Council of the Iroquois Confederacy, had work to do. Their task was to gather, excite, motivate, and lead warriors to war.

The time had arrived for the Pine Tree Chiefs of the Iroquois Confederacy to begin to do what they did best. Preparations for war began.

Chapter 7

Seizing an Empire

The Great Pursuit and Dispersal of the Huron

This was a time when the coming storms of violence began to gather strength.

By the early 1640s, disease epidemics had finished their devastating work among the Great Lakes Region Native peoples. None were left unscathed. While both the Iroquoian and Algonquian settlements lost an estimated half of their populations, it was the less populous Algonquians who suffered the greatest decline. For the sick and weakened Algonquian group, starvation compounded the impacts of disease.

The surviving Algonquian leadership were conflicted on how to move forward. The Huron were also divided. Do they allow the missionaries to continue to live among them, thereby keeping their alliance with the French, or should they cease their alliance? The majority Huron position favored keeping the French alliance. Maintaining the alliance was essential for French military support in their battles with the Iroquois. Hardly a reliable assessment given the record of French duplicity.

To sustain dominance as a political and military power, the Iroquois understood they needed to rebuild their devastated population. The women's councils, always influential in times of crisis, saw the adoption of people from defeated groups who had cultures similar to their own as the means to rebuild the Iroquois population. From a military perspective, the leadership saw an opportunity to *extend the rafters of the longhouse* through territorial expansion and adoption of defeated groups into one nation. Politically, it was believed that this strategy would ultimately establish a lasting peace. Ancient foes would be absorbed and assimilated into one universal community of extended families.

In 1645, the Huron sent sixty fur laden canoes to Ville Marie. These were soon followed by other fur flotillas in 1646.

The Iroquois, particularly the Mohawk, persisted in their diplomatic initiatives with the Huron. The Mohawk objective was to satisfy the Huron that a trade partnership between Iroquois and Huron was in everyone's best interests. The Iroquois statesmen sent to talk to the Huron insisted that all parties would benefit from the peace and community well-being that a mutually agreeable trade partnership would bring. Sadly, and once again, the Huron made the strategically tragic mistake of presenting a hard-nosed approach to Iroquois petitions. The Huron rejected the Iroquois efforts for reconciliation and trade partnership.

Never a confederacy to let disappointment stagnate initiative, the Iroquois began to move from diplomacy to a war footing. But first, there was more diplomacy to be initiated by the Iroquois statesmen. The French were uneasy about developing events. They harboured doubts about the capacity and tenacity of their Huron allies to come out of a protracted war with the Iroquois Confederacy as the victorious party. Iroquois diplomacy satisfied the French that they need have no fear of Iroquoian reprisal provided that they remain neutral in the coming war with the Huron. The Iroquois plea was successful. The French would sit this one out and let the dice fall where they may with their Huron allies.

In 1647, the Iroquois struck. They raided and destroyed the Arendaronon Huron villages. This was an early strategic move on the part of the Iroquois to interrupt the Huron trade route to Ville Marie. The noose was set and began to tighten. But not without bold and courageous Huron resistance. Pushback came in 1648 when a 250 paddler Huron canoe flotilla battled its way through an Iroquois blockade on the Ottawa River. The Flotilla managed to reach Ville Marie.

The Iroquois knew that the number of warriors needed for such a large canoe fleet had drained considerable warrior power away from Huron settlements. The Pine Tree Chiefs seized the opportunity presented by absent Huron warriors. They raided and destroyed the Huron Mission village at St. Joseph and tortured and killed the resident Jesuit priest. The Attigneenongnahac Huron were scattered.

The Dutch continued to be players in the fur trade. They also continued to be power brokers, but to a lesser degree than previous years. The Dutch could see a total Iroquois victory on the horizon. On credit, they supplied the Iroquois with 400 superior quality flintlocks and unlimited powder and ball.

In March, 1649, a devastating blow was delivered the Huron by Mohawk and Seneca warriors. The war party struck the Huron homeland mission villages of St. Ignace and St. Louis. Hundreds of Huron were killed or captured. Two French Jesuit priests were tortured to death. Huron resistance collapsed. Survivors of the raids scattered and fled to be hunted down and captured or killed.

Many of the captured Huron were adopted by the Iroquois. The cost of victory for the Iroquois in terms of depopulation due to war causalities and the devastating horror of disease epidemics, was catastrophic. It is estimated that the Iroquois had been reduced to 1,000 healthy and skilled warriors. For centuries, the Iroquois Confederacy had applied a cultural policy of selective adoption to replenish and sustain their population. The Iroquois strategy to destroy the Huron was, in part, fuelled by the critical need to replace population through selective adoption and acculturation.

The affairs of March, 1649, brought forth a horrifying chain of events. The Iroquois, flushed with victory, knew they had the Huron panicked and disorientated. Resistance was expected to be minimal and scattered. After twenty years of war and disease epidemics, fear and hatred had festered among the Iroquois. The Iroquois leadership were not satisfied with this one victorious engagement.

They sought to inflict maximum damage on the Huron. They wanted the Huron gone from the land. A strategy of cultural genocide was moving forward.

The Great Pursuit

The relentless Iroquois Confederacy pursuit of the Huron is known as the *Great Pursuit*. By present-day definition, the Iroquois campaign against the Huron was an act of genocide. The Iroquois campaign was intended to deliberately inflict on the Huron *conditions of life calculated to bring about its physical destruction in whole or in part.* (genocide definition source: Convention on the Prevention and Punishment of Genocide, United Nations, 1948.)

The *Great Pursuit* was a strategy to eliminate Huron military and political competition in the fur trade. In a large part, the *Great Pursuit* was also driven by Iroquois vengeance. The persistent search for the Huron and her allies also flowed from the culturally sanctioned adoption of captives to replenish depleted populations. So, in this sense, the *Great Pursuit* can be explained as a very long and intense mourning-war.

The *Great Pursuit* began after several major Iroquois and Huron engagements had left the Huron a defeated confederacy. The Iroquois victories over the Huron resulted in the dispersal of the Huron from their ancestral homelands. The once powerful military ally of the French had been reduced to a refugee population. The remnants of the Huron empire found themselves being aggressively and relentlessly pursued by the Iroquois. The military objective of the Iroquois Confederacy was the total destruction of the Huron Confederacy.

While a Mohawk captive in 1643, French Jesuit Father Joques wrote in his diaries:

"the Iroquois plan is to take all the Huron if possible, put to death the most important ones along with a large part of the others, and with the rest to make one country. The rallying cry to those they were about to attack was 'come join us that we be one people in one land'".

During the period 1642 through 1646, the Iroquois managed a two-front offensive. In the east, they pushed the Algonquians from the Ottawa Valley. In the west, they attacked the Huron villages. The 1648-49 Huron campaigns resulted in the Dutch armed Iroquois bringing an end to Huron resistance. The surviving Huron were now refugees in their ancestral land.

The Iroquois planned to inflict a terrible vengeance on the Huron, their old fur trade partners and competitors. The Iroquois military strategic goal was the defeat and unconditional subjugation of the Huron and any ally who rendered aid or abetted Huron resistance. The military might of the Iroquois was about to be unleashed on the Huron. The Huron would be fought and decimated, remnants of villages who refused to capitulate would be pursued without rest or mercy.

In December, 1650, the Iroquois were ready to begin the *Great Pursuit*.

The Wendat population included a traditional anti-Iroquois faction. No doubt this group of Wendat were of special interest for the Iroquois. They represented a threat to social stability and had the potential to instigate a future uprising. The Iroquois pursuit would not slow down until the complete annihilation or a fully neutralizing dispersal of this radical Wendat group had been accomplished.

The Iroquois campaign began with raids against the Attignawantan Huron (Wendat) who had taken refuge with the Tionontali (Petun). The main Tionontali village was overrun and it is estimated that less than 1,000 Tionontali and Huron refugees managed to escape the slaughter and find temporary refuge on Michilimackinac Island (Upper Michigan) near present-day Sault Ste. Marie, Ontario.

The Jesuit Relations tell us that Michilimackinac Island was *" a favorite resort for all the Algonkin tribes, many are returning to it since the peace with the Iroquois, on this account, the Jesuits have begun a new mission, opposite Mackinac, called St. Ignaces. Thither have fled the Huron, driven from Chequamegan Bay by fear of the Sioux, 'the Iroquois of the West.' (1671, pg. 12)*

By 1651, the Tionontali and Huron refugees were forced further west to Green Bay, Wisconsin. In the years to come, the Tionontali and Huron refugees would become known as Wyandot.

In the spring of 1652, the Nipissing, who had been allies of the Huron and had sheltered Huron refugees, were raided by the Iroquois. The defeated Nipissing became refugees themselves and fled north to seek protection of the Ojibwe. The last groups of Algonquin were forced to flee the upper Ottawa River Valley. As war refugees, the Algonquin fled north and joined an alliance with the Cree. The Algonquin and Cree alliance would last another twenty years.

During the skirmishes of the Great Pursuit, the Tahonaenrat Huron fled southwest to seek refuge among the villages of the Neutrals. The Neutrals had been constant in their refusal to side with either the Huron or Iroquois in their many wars. War parties from the military powers of both the Huron and the Iroquois regularly passed through Neutral territory to raid one-another. The Neutrals had remained rigidly neutral. But that was soon to change.

Resistance fighters of the Tahonaenrat Huron found shelter among the Neutrals. They used Neutral territory as a base for raids against the occupying Iroquois. The Iroquois asked the Neutrals to surrender their guests. The Neutrals, in a difficult bind, made the humane but tragic choice to ignore the Iroquois request.

The Neutrals and their troublesome guests did not have long to wait for the Iroquois response. The Iroquois attacked.

In the first year of the war the Neutrals had the support of the Susquehannock. The Susquehannock had been Huron allies before 1648. They were known as fierce and stubborn warriors. In 1651, the Mohawk and Oneida had attacked the Susquehannock. In the same year, Kimika, the principal Neutral settlement, was overwhelmed by the Seneca. Surviving Neutrals had a choice of surrendering or fleeing. The resident Tahonaenrat Huron surrendered as a group and were adopted by the Seneca. The adoption was a generous allowance from the Iroquois, especially the Seneca whose reputation for fierceness in war is matched only by the Mohawk.

The consequences of this war continued unabated. The land was full of terrorized survivors and fleeing refugees. Groups of Huron and Neutral fled south in hopes of finding refuge with the Erie. The Erie, with real cause for concern, were reluctant to accept the refugees.

The Iroquois were merciless in prosecuting their *Great Pursuit*. They demanded that the Erie surrender the refugees to them. The Erie, in a surprise bit of resistance, refused the Iroquois demand. They had been emboldened by the influx of hundreds of refugee warriors who were eager to have another go at the Iroquois. This Erie refusal would not be forgotten by the Iroquois. The fleeing Huron and Neutral had not found sanctuary without a cost being extracted by the Erie. The relationship between the Erie and their unwanted refugee guests was akin to semi-slavery.

In 1653, the Erie raided the Iroquois homeland. A Seneca chief was killed in the skirmishing. The Iroquois, reluctant to begin a new conflict, arranged a peace conference with the Erie. The environment was tense. An Erie warrior, obviously not the brightest warrior in the deck, killed an Onondaga. The Iroquois were furious. They struck back, killing 30 of the Erie representatives to the peace conference.

The same year, on the western front, the Seneca attacked the Huron and Potawatomi fortified settlement near Green Bay, Wisconsin. The Huron and Potawatomi fought back and the attack turned into a siege campaign. Over time, the Iroquois were forced to withdraw due to a shortage of food. The Huron retreated to the Mississippi River Region, and then, after a time, moved again to Michigan and the south shore of Lake Superior.

The Iroquois recognized that peace was not going to occur in the immediate future. The Erie were respected as a strong military force. Once again, a part of the Iroquois strategy included securing French neutrality in the coming conflict. The Iroquois knew if the French allied with the Erie, this would be a force multiplier for the Erie that would prove disastrous to Iroquois campaign objectives.

Having pushed the French into a position of neutrality in the face of superior Iroquois military capability, the way was clear for the Mohawk and Oneida to move against the only Erie ally left, the Susquehannock. The combined military force of Mohawk and Oneida kept the Susquehannock bottled up in the south. In the northwest, the Seneca, Cayuga, and Onondaga attacked the Erie.

This war would prove to be a long fight. The Erie had insufficient firearms to meet the Iroquois skirmishers, and there was no opportunity to acquire what they needed. The Erie fought hard, and although outgunned, their reputation as disciplined and skilled warriors enabled them to resist the Iroquois for three years. In 1656, the Erie ceased hostilities and the survivors were adopted by the Iroquois.

Iroquois hostilities continued bringing both victory and defeat. In 1657, the Iroquois destroyed a Fox village. In 1662 a combined force of Ojibwe, Ottawa, and Nipissing surprised a large war party of Mohawk and Oneida at Iroquois Point on the east end of Lake Superior. The Iroquois war party was annihilated.

The French position of neutrality meant they had no hope of negotiating with the Iroquois Confederacy to salvage something of their fur trade empire.

The Huron-Wendat Dispersal, 1653-1667
A Diaspora of Epic Proportion

During the Iroquois campaigns against the Wendat, an estimated 3,000 Wendat had been adopted by the Iroquois. The Wendat adoptions included all of the Deer Clan, and a good part of the Rock Clan. Both clan populations settled among the Seneca. In 1649, another 1,000 Wendat of the Christian faction, knowing that the likelihood of adoption by the Iroquois was slim to nil, fled with their Jesuit mentors to Christian Island in Georgian Bay, Lake Huron.

Christian Island could not have been a worse place for safe refuge. The island was soon stripped of any source of food. Wood supplies for heat and cooking were depleted. The people starved, froze to death, and died of disease. At this point in time and place of the Great Pursuit, cannibalism among the Wendat may have occurred out of sheer desperation to cling to life, as brutal and hopeless as life was for the refugees.

When the snows began to melt in the spring of 1650, an estimated 300 Huron-Wendat were left alive. These sick and dying people began a journey of despair that took them to Ile d'Orleans, a small island about five kilometers east of present-day Quebec City. The time it took for a sick and demoralized refugee band to move this impressive distance through wilderness, and the loss of life during the journey, is not recorded. A conservative estimate is the journey probably exceeded two months. On Ile d' Orleans, the Christian Island refugees were joined by another group of 300 Huron-Wendat refugees. This group of Wendat was made up of Bear Clan, remnants of the Rock Clan, and the Cord Maker Clan.

In 1653, the French had managed to persuade the Iroquois to negotiate for peace terms. The Iroquois demand was that the Wendat under French protection, accept adoption into the Iroquois Confederacy. The French were anxious to secure a peace and were aggressive in their insistence that the Wendat accept the Iroquois demand. The Rock Clan was adopted by the Onondaga; a part of the Bear Clan went with the Mohawk.

Another part of the Bear Clan and all of the Cord Maker Clan refused to go with the Mohawk. These Wendat moved from the strategically weak Ile d'Orleans to the French settlements at Sillery and Lorette. At the time, Sillery and Lorette were small enclaves pushing against the French town of Habitation, present-day Quebec City. Today, Sillery and Lorette are the homes of the descendants of the Wendat refugees.

In 1665, Nicolas Perot and Jesuit Priest Father Claude-Jean Allouez, with four other Frenchmen and 400 Huron, Ottawa, and Ojibwe paddlers, fought their way through Iroquois skirmishers to Green Bay, Wisconsin. The conditions they found upon their arrival were appalling even to the hardened travelers. According to their estimate, more than 30,000 refugees had overwhelmed the resident Winnebago and Menominee population. The refugees were a consequence of the Iroquois raiding campaigns and *Great Pursuit* of the Huron-Wendat. Refugees also included Fox, Sauk, Ottawa, Macouten, Miami, Kickapoo, Ojibwe, and Potawatomi tribe members. The area's natural resources had been exhausted. The land was not suitable for growing the traditional crops of corn, beans, and squash. The refugees were starving. Fighting among the refugees for subsistence food was common place.

The scarcity of food forced the Green Bay population to begin to hunt and forage further afield. A new war started when the traditional hunting territory of the Dakota Sioux was invaded by the Green Bay inhabitants. The Dakota Sioux were ferocious warriors the French referred to as the *Iroquois of the west*. To make matters worse, the refugees continued to suffer from sporadic raiding by Iroquois war parties searching for Huron survivors of the *Great Pursuit*.

The *Great Pursuit* of the Huron-Wendat by the Iroquois ended in 1667. That year, a treaty to end hostilities was signed between the French and the Iroquois Confederacy. The treaty also included a cessation of hostilities between the

Iroquois and Native groups allied with the French in the western Great Lake Region fur trade.

By 1704, the Wyandot and Odawa had moved near the village of Detroit, present-day Michigan State, which had begun to be settled in 1701. In 1738, the Wyandot were entangled in disputes with the French and Odawa, and the Wyandot split into two groups. One group moved to Sandusky, present-day Ohio State, and later, they moved further into the Ohio Valley. The second group moved across the river to present-day Windsor, Ontario.

In the *Seven Year's War, 1756-83*, the Detroit Wyandot fought as allies of their old friends the French. After the war, the Detroit Wyandot joined Pontiac against the English. The descendants of this group of Detroit Wyandot now live in the area adjacent to Windsor, Ontario.

The Ohio Wyandot were forced to surrender their lands to the newly formed United States after the *American Revolutionary War, 1775-83*. In 1830, the passage of the *Indian Removal Act, 1830*, passed by the United States Congress and signed by President Andrew Jackson, forced the removal of the Ohio Wyandot to Kansas. In 1867, the *Kansas - Nebraska Act of 1854* was applied to the detriment of the estimated 200 Wyandot residing in Kansas. The Wyandot were forcibly transported to reserve lands in Oklahoma, where they began a residence with relocated Seneca, their former enemies.

Today, the Wendat population is estimated to be about 3,000 persons. The eastern population live on land near Quebec City and also at Wendake, near Loretteville, Quebec. The majority of the surviving Wendat are Catholic and their first language is French. Today, the western descendants of the Wendat, the Wyandot, numbering some 350 souls, continue to live in Oklahoma and their first language is English.

> *I recall a sunny afternoon, sitting on Mohawk Haudenosaunee Elder Ernie Benedict's porch, looking out over his extensive garden, and talking about things.*
>
> *We were discussing something about the many Christian churches that resided in Akwesasne and how that was working with the revival of the Haudenosaunee teachings in the community.*

Somehow, the conversation moved to history and the work of Jesuits at St. Regis, Akwesasne Territory.

I asked Ernie what the Mohawk name for the Jesuit priests is. He thought for some time, and pronounced two Mohawk words. I waited a while, and asked what the words meant. After a short time, Ernie smiled and said 'black and crispy'. He laughed.

Thinking I was on a roll, I asked Ernie something about the Huron. Ernie grew still, and after a moment he said " there are no more Huron. Even their shadow has gone from the earth."

And so, truly, that is how it is.

Chapter 8

The Battle of Long Sault

The Battle of Long Sault was fought in the vicinity of the Long Sault Rapids, Ottawa River, at present-day Carillon. Opposing forces were French militia supported by Huron and Algonquin allies, against the Iroquois and adopted Huron warriors. The battle was fought over a five-day period in early May, 1660.

In April, 1660, Adam Dollard des Ormeaux, the commander of Ville Marie's (present-day Montreal) garrison, was given permission by Governor Paul Chomedey de Maisonneuve, to take a military expedition up the Ottawa River to attack an Iroquois war party that was reported to be camped in the vicinity. Information received by the French suggested that the Iroquois had gathered to prepare for an attack against Ville Marie. After finishing with Ville Marie, the French believed the Iroquois plan was to raid Trois Rivieres and Habitation, present-day Quebec City. Dollard's mission was to find the Iroquois raiders, attack first and inflict sufficient damage to discourage their plans to raid French settlements.

Dollard's expedition consisted of himself, sixteen volunteer soldiers, and four Algonquin warriors including a Chief named Mituvemeg. In late April, the canoes set off. The small flotilla paddled up the St. Lawrence river from Ville

Marie, then turned northwest into the Ottawa River and the Lake of Two Mountains. The trip would have been arduous. Swift currents from recently melted snow and lake ice made the upstream paddling a slow and exhausting labour.

On or about May 1st, the paddlers found a site they believed would be an excellent place for an ambush. The Ottawa river shore site was an abandoned Algonquin village. The village included a deteriorating log palisade. Not long after the French and Algonquin had settled in to await the Iroquois arrival, a party of some forty Huron under the leadership of Chief Etienne Annahotaha, arrived at the old fort. The meeting was mutually pleasing and the Huron joined with the French to await the Iroquois. Dollard directed his men to reinforce the old log walls with a new palisade. However, before the work could be completed the Iroquois arrived.

The Iroquois had been camped a few miles from Long Sault. The canoe flotilla was made up of 200 Iroquois warriors and a small, unknown number of adopted Huron. Dollard, expecting an advance scouting party of Iroquois would land at a particular place along the shore, set up his ambush. Eventually, two Iroquois canoes landed at the expected location. Dollard's men opened fire. Four of the five Iroquois were killed or wounded. Shortly after the first skirmish, the main party of Iroquois canoes arrived.

Soon after beaching their canoes, the Iroquois attacked the fort. The attack was repulsed. Preparing to lay siege, the Iroquois began building their own fortification. While the work was progressing the Iroquois leader asked for a parley. Dollard suspected the request for a parley was a ruse for a surprise attack and he refused the offer. The Iroquois were quick to take action after Dollard's snub. They found and broke up two undefended French canoes. In the second Iroquois attack, the broken parts of the two canoes were set against a section of fort wall and set afire. The French soldiers and their Algonquin and Huron allies beat back the second Iroquois attack. The Iroquois received heavy casualties from the defenders. The Seneca chief leading the war party was killed.

Seeing the Seneca chief fall, several French soldiers fought their way out of the fort to the chief's body and cut off his head. Returning to the fort they spiked it on the palisade for all to see. An ugly business. The Iroquois, infuriated, attacked a third time. This attack was pushed back again by the defenders. The Iroquois sent a canoe to find another Iroquois war party of some 500 warriors who were preparing to raid Ville Marie. The warriors abandoned their Ville Marie plans and paddled to the siege site. When the Iroquois arrived, it was the fifth day of fighting. (Karr, 1970. Pgs. 41-46)

Prior to the second war party arriving, the Huron fighting with the Iroquois called to the Huron allied with the French, promising they would be treated well if they abandoned the French. The Huron fighting at the siege site with the Iroquois were captives who had been adopted by the Iroquois. With a promise of fair treatment, all the Huron with the French, except Chief Etienne Annahotaha, left the fort. This was not a wise choice on the part of the deserters. The Iroquois, still smarting from the killing and beheading of their Seneca chief, killed all except five of the original forty Huron who had joined Dollard. The surviving five Huron were released to return to Ville Marie to tell the French of an Iroquois victory.

Planning to end the siege as soon as possible, the Iroquois built mantelets. The mantelets were large shields consisting of three logs bound together to protect the warriors from musket fire. The Iroquois attacked the fort a fourth time. Advancing with their mantelets in the front, the attackers were well protected from the barrage of French musket balls sent to greet them.

The French defenders, with their four Algonquin and one Huron warrior, were in bad shape. They were exhausted. Their nourishment over the last several days had consisted of corn dust mush and muddy water. The Iroquois were now pushing against the palisade. Protected from musket fire by their wood shields, they began to chop a breach in the fort's wall. The breach was completed and the Iroquois flooded into the fort. Standing along the top of the breached wall, Dollard lit the fuse attached to a keg of gunpowder and, lifting it above his head, he made his move to heave the keg into the mass of Iroquois below him. The keg hit the palisade and bounced back into the fort where it exploded. Many of the defenders, who had gathered to defend the fort at the breached wall, were either wounded or killed. Dollard was dead. The Iroquois, recovering from the blast, quickly resumed their attack and overpowered the survivors. Four French soldiers were captured alive. Three of the soldiers were seriously wounded and the Iroquois burnt them alive within the fort. The fourth French prisoner was tortured and killed some time after the fort was captured. (ibid, pg. 41-45)

There is another version of Dollard's initiative to take the fight to the Iroquois. Did Dollard and his men paddle up the Ottawa River not knowing that a war party of Iroquois were approaching Ville Marie? In this version, Dollard's intention may have been to intercept and capture any fur laden Iroquois canoes returning from a season of upriver raiding.

Whatever Dollard's motive for the expedition, he is a hero of New France. Dollard's seven-day fight with the Iroquois is a matter of record in official Catholic Church history. Dollard is considered a martyr for the Church and for the French colony. Adam Dollard des Ormeaux is one of the heroic figures of New France.

After the battle, the Iroquois did not continue on to raid Ville Marie. Historian Peter Moogk (2007), believes that the Iroquois did not continue on to Ville Marie because, after their hard-won victory, the booty of battle would have satisfied the Iroquois.

The French conflict with the Iroquois over control of the fur trade had significantly diminished the influence of the French Jesuits among the Huron. French trading partners and allies had been destroyed or scattered as refugees across the land. The Iroquois now controlled the Ottawa River and St. Lawrence River fur routes. The movement of people and fur to Ville Marie and Habitation, present-day Quebec City, had become a hazardous journey fraught with unexpected raiding and vicious skirmishing.

Chapter 9

Victors and Vanquished

Aftermath of War

Competition for control of the lucrative fur trade had begun with the arrival of the Dutch and French to the New World. This new-found fur treasure and the ensuing competition for control had brought about escalations of ancient animosities between Indigenous groups of the region. New alliances were struck between tribes and the Europeans. Tribal tactics involved distant raiding and decades long campaigns with the strategic objective to assimilate, subjugate, or destroy neighboring and distant tribes. The proliferation of small arms changed warfare from melee skirmishing to deadly encounters with high casualty rates.

The conflicts for fur trade dominance had provided an opportunity for the Iroquois to expand their empire in many directions. By now, the Iroquois had laid claim to the north shore of the St. Lawrence River from Lachine, a present-day Montreal suburb, west to the mouth of the Gananoque River, present-day Gananoque, Ontario.

By 1667, the *Beaver Wars* had brought great change to the social, political, and military landscape of the embattled region. Refugees moved across the land seeking safe haven with old friends and past enemies. Defeated tribes relocated, were adopted and assimilated into other cultures. Pandemics of European diseases such as smallpox; measles; and tuberculosis had reduced tribal populations by halves, and more.

Iroquois du Nord

The territorial expansion of the Iroquois Confederacy was moving forward. The *Great Pursuit* of the Huron from their ancestral lands had been completed by 1667.

During the years 1665 and 1670, the Iroquois had established seven settlements along the north shore of present-day Lake Ontario. The French referred to the Iroquois settlements as the *Iroquois du Nord*. The villages were settled by the Seneca, Cayuga, and Oneida.

The Oneida settled *Ganneious* on the eastern edge of Lake Ontario - present-day town of Napanee. The Cayuga settled three villages: *Kente* - on the Bay of Quinte; Kentsio - on Rice Lake; and *Ganaraske* – on the site of present-day Port Hope. The Seneca also established three settlements: the westernmost village of *Ganatsekwyagon* - at the mouth of the Rouge River; *Teiaignon* – at the mouth of the Humber River; and *Quinaouatoua* – near present-day Hamilton. (Jordan, 2013)

Each of the seven settlements shared common attributes. All were located at strategic points along Lake Ontario. Each village represented a major staging point for fur trading and north bound Iroquois hunting and raiding parties. All were in proximity to seasonally abundant fish and wildlife resources. Six of the seven villages were located on the richest agricultural land along the north shore of Lake Ontario. (Adams, 1986)

The motivation for the north shore Iroquois villages was mostly economic. By the 1640s the beaver population had been extirpated throughout much of the ancestral homeland of the Iroquois in present-day upper New York State. Competition among the Iroquois, Huron, Algonquin, and Ottawa for control of the fur trade was fierce. Settlement of the north shore of Lake Ontario strengthened the Iroquois control of fur movement from the north and west to the

Dutch and French fur receiving points at Albany, present-day Albany, New York State; and Ville Marie, present-day Montreal City.

During the mid 17th century, the Iroquois expanded their territory into present-day Ohio, Pennsylvania, and Lower Canada, present-day Province of Quebec. Historians, reflecting upon the expansionist strategies of the Iroquois Confederacy, refer to the territorial expansion as *Iroquois colonies*. Interpretation of archeological evidence recovered from the Bead Hill site of a Lake Ontario north shore Seneca village, tells of multinational and multilingual Iroquois communities, far from their ancestral homeland. (Jordan, 2013)

By 1668, French missionaries focused their attention on the seven villages. Their work was to convert the people to Christianity. In 1668, Bishop Francois de Laval sent missionaries Claude Trouve, Sulpician priest and missionary, and Francois de Salignac de la Mothe-Fenelon to the village of Kente. The mission failed and was abandoned in 1680.

Fenelon, an Abbe of the Church, visited other north shore villages and spent the winter of 1669 at Ganatsekwyagon. For a brief time, the early French explorer and Jesuit priest Jacques Marquette visited Ganatsekwyagon on his way to Lake Superior. Father Marquette was the first European to see and map the northern portion of the Mississippi river. (Marcel, 2014)

Although the Iroquois villages were settled during a time of minimal conflict, the *Beaver Wars* ensured a constant tension existed between the Iroquois and the French. In 1673, the French established their first Lake Ontario settlement at Cataraqui, present-day Kingston, Ontario. Here the French built Fort Frontenac. For ease of trade, many of the inhabitants of the nearby Oneida village of Ganneious moved closer to Cataraqui and Fort Frontenac. (Adams, 1986)

With the new settlement at Fort Frontenac, the original importance of Ganatsekwyagon shifted to Teiaiagon. Until Fort Frontenac, Ganatsekwyagon had been the more important settlement because of its strategic position on the Rouge River known as the *Toronto Carrying-Place Trail*. Now the Seneca village Teiaiagon became the dominant village. The French found that Teiaiagon provided a much better anchorage for their trade barques than Ganatsekwyagon. (Konrad, 1981)

In 1687, the French attacked the Iroquois Confederacy. Villages were destroyed in both the Iroquois ancestral homeland in present-day New York State and along the north shore of Lake Ontario.

Anishinaabe oral tradition tells that decisive battles won by the Anishinaabe during the *Beaver Wars* caused the Iroquois to abandon their north shore settlements. In the *Great Peace of Montreal, 1701,* the Iroquois Confederacy agreed to stay on the south shore of Lake Ontario. In 1701, the settlement void was filled by the Anishinaabe Mississaugas when they settled into the area between Lake Erie and the Seneca village Ganatsekwyagon, at Rouge River.

Researchers believe the eastern villages of Kente and Ganneious were attacked and destroyed by Jacques Rene de Brisay de Denonville. Two hundred residents of both villages were taken prisoner. After fighting began in 1687, there is no record of the fate of Ganatsekwyagon or Teiaiagon. The possible outcome is that, no longer believing themselves secure, the residents abandoned their settlements and fled to the south shore of Lake Ontario. (Myrvold, 1997)

Chapter 10

Campaigns of the Eastern Iroquois

The French Offensive

The western Iroquois - the Onondaga, Cayuga, and Seneca - had been busy conquering the Ohio Valley Region. At the same time, on another front, the eastern Iroquois - Mohawk and Oneida - had been busy with their own military campaigns.

By 1647, the ongoing Iroquois war with the Algonquin and Montagnais had involved the Abenaki (northern region of the State of Maine) who had allied themselves with the Montagnais. By this time the Mohawk alliance with the Sokoki against the Montagnais had fallen apart over hunting area disputes east of Lake Champlain.

By 1649, the Huron had been seriously mauled by the Iroquois. The Mohawks stepped up their pressure on the French and began raiding small French settlements along the St. Lawrence River. They brazenly raided groups of Christian Huron living outside the gates of the fortified French settlement of Quebec. The French, uneasy with the collapse of their old Huron allies, knew they needed new alliances if they were to survive.

The French put together a plan to secure new alliances. In 1650, they dispatched a Jesuit priest and a Montagnais chief to New England to search out an eastern alliance with the Sokoki; Pennacook; Pocumtuc; and Mahican. The British in the New England colonies were also approached but declined the invitation to join an alliance against the Iroquois.

The French succeeded in bringing the new eastern alliance together. Firearms and ammunition began to flow to the alliance tribes. The Mohawk tested the new French alliance with the occasional raid against the Sokoki in the Vermont region. The raids were intended as intelligence gathering probes. The Iroquois were overextended and they knew it. Their war with the obstinate and strategically astute Susquehannock in Pennsylvania was proving difficult. Now was not the time to open a second front with the French alliance.

The Susquehannock had a history as formidable warriors. They had been well armed through trade with Swedish fur traders on the lower Delaware River. During their years of skirmishing, both the Iroquois and the Susquehannock had been sorely hurt. The Mohawk and Oneida had succeeded in capturing only a small piece of Susquehannock territory.

The war was stalemated. Then the Dutch gained control of the Swedish settlements in 1655. The tide of war changed in favor of the Iroquois. Without the supply of Swedish firearms and ammunition, the Susquehannock knew that their losses from continued conflict with the Iroquois were not sustainable. They sued for peace. The Mohawk accepted.

By now the French found themselves isolated to the areas adjacent to present-day Montreal and Quebec. The Mohawk and Oneida had initiated an effective blockade on French trade. The Ottawa, after the Huron collapse, began to fill the void in fur trading left by the Huron. This infuriated the Mohawk. They attacked the Ottawa who had settled on the fur route among the islands of Lake Huron. The Ottawa were pushed west to Wisconsin and the upper Michigan peninsula.

Among the few Frenchmen who were successful in west bound journeys were Pierre-Esprit Radisson and Medard des Groseilliers. The two fur traders reached the west end of Lake Superior in 1658. When they returned to the settlement of Quebec the following year, rather than being celebrated, they were arrested by French officials for the offence of fur trading without a licence.

During this time, the Susquehannock had been sidelined. The Mohawk and Oneida could now open their new front in New England. The outbreak of fighting between the Mohawk and Mahican caused concern for the Dutch. In 1658, the Dutch persuaded the Mahican to leave the French alliance and cease hostilities with the Mohawk. But the Mahican chose to remain in the game. The Mohawk learned that the Mahican had been arranging opportunities for trade between the Dutch and the Montagnais and Sokoki. The Dutch attempted to defuse the Mahican subterfuge but the Mohawk prepared for war. In 1662, the Mohawk attacked the Mahican. After two years of war the Mahican left their primary settlement at Shadoc, near present-day Albany, New York State. Soon, they had abandoned most of the Hudson River Valley.

The remaining alliance of Sokoki, Pennacook, Pocumtuc, and Montagnais, supplied with French and English firearms and ammunition, continued to fight the Mohawk.

The uneasy French and Iroquois truce ended in 1658, when a Jesuit ambassador was murdered and the Iroquois were suspect.

Tensions between the Iroquois Confederacy and the Susquehannock Confederacy simmered. The Iroquois grew apprehensive when Susquehannock warriors began to gather in large numbers. The matter boiled over when the Susquehannock made a fatal mistake of massing their military might in one impregnable fortified village.

The Iroquois strategy left the Susquehannock bottled up by their own choice. The Iroquois went after the Susquehannock allies. They attacked and damaged the Munsee Delaware along the Delaware River and then scattered the Shawnee. Pursuing the fleeing Shawnee, as the Iroquois are wont to do, they skirmished with the Cherokee and Catawba. It must have been a shock to have an Iroquois war party, so far from home, arrive on your village doorstep with war clubs in hand.

Iroquois war-fighting strategy once again proved superior. Perhaps the Susquehannock leadership believed the Iroquois would throw themselves at the walls of their fortified stronghold and be ground down through attrition.

The final blow for the fortified Susquehannock village was not from an Iroquois war club. The devastating blow was a smallpox epidemic that struck the crowded fortified village in 1661. Over time, the ranks of Susquehannock warriors had been decimated by disease and war. The point had been reached where warrior strength was insufficient to sustain warfare.

The Iroquois never favored static siege warfare. They certainly valued their warriors and were always reluctant to sacrifice lives in frontal assaults against fortified enemies and superior numbers. Indeed, the refusal to fight in straight lines facing withering musket fire in the European fashion had earned the Iroquois a reputation from the British as cowards. They would not stand in orderly rows and fight like men. Instead, warriors skulked about, blending into the forest in a manner that provided very difficult targets for the muskets of British infantry. The Iroquois excelled at guerilla warfare - hidden ambush, fast hit and run raiding. The French were quick to adopt such tactics as their own. In the early days, the British ranted and raved and called upon the Iroquois to come out in the open and fight like men.

In the decades ahead, the Catawba who had allied with the Susquehannock would not be forgotten by the Iroquois. To satisfy the social and repopulation needs of the Iroquois, the Catawba would suffer the consequences of Iroquois mourning-war raids.

The French Offensive

By 1658, the influence of the Dutch in North America was in decline. The French saw this as an advantage for them and a disadvantage for the Iroquois.

However, British and Iroquois relations had begun to improve, and this greatly alarmed the French.

Recognizing an advantage to securing stability in the region, the Governor of New York agreed to ally with the Mohawk if they arranged a peace with the Mahican and Sokoki.

The alliance between the English and the Iroquois, at this time, was beneficial to both parties in a number of strategic ways. The benefits for parties included:

- The English and Iroquois alliance would protect both from the French.

- The alliance would enhance Iroquois power and influence by ensuring British neutrality toward Iroquois campaigns to extend Confederacy authority over other tribes by gathering them into the Covenant Chain coalition.

- The English position on the territorial expansion and Covenant Chain alliance building by the Iroquois was one of non-interference. Expanding Iroquois influence was, at the time, an asset for the British and their own alliance with the Iroquois Confederacy. The Covenant Chain tribes were kept from establishing alliances with the French.

- Negotiations and treaty making with the numerous Indigenous tribes of the region were simplified for the British. With the Covenant Chain alliances, the British need only approach the Iroquois Confederacy.

- In the matter of possible conflict with a tribe, the Iroquois could be used as enforcers of British will. When the Wampanoag tribe tried to use the Mahican village at Schaghlicoke as a refuge during *King Philips War (1675-76)*, the governor of New York called upon the Mohawk to force the Wampanoag back to Massachusetts. The Mohawk later helped New England force King Philip's Sokoki and Pennacook allies to retreat into northern Maine and Canada. Of course, the down side to the expulsion of the Sokoki and Pennacook was that they became French allies.

Matters would not be easily resolved for any of the parties. The Mahican, exhausted and battered, were ready for quieter times. The Sokoki refused to talk about a cessation of hostilities. That summer the Mohawk raided the Pennacook. In retaliation, the Sokoki and Kennebec struck Mohawk settlements.

In 1663, Pocumtuc warriors brazenly attacked a Mohawk village. The attack resulted in a high number of causalities for the raiders. Alarmed at the hornets nest they had kicked, and running out of warriors, the Pocumtuc asked the Dutch to arrange a truce. The Dutch were silent. In December of that year, a Mohawk and Seneca war party attacked the primary Pocumtuc village at Fort Hill, present-day Deerfield, Massachusetts.

The attack was beaten back by the defenders. But not without a grievous butcher's bill. The Pocumtuc suffered a catastrophic loss of some three hundred warriors. The badly bruised defenders managed to abandon their capital settlement. After catching their breath, the Pocumtuc sought peace terms. The Mohawk agreed to meet to discuss terms. Then things went from bad to worse for the Pocumtuc. Someone, not believed to be a Pocumtuc, attacked and killed the Iroquois ambassadors travelling to the peace conference. Enraged, the Mohawk resumed their campaign and forced the Pocumtuc from their Connecticut River territory.

The French had grown tired of Iroquois threats to their lucrative fur trade. Worried about the possibility that with an Iroquois alliance, the English could gain advantage in the fur trade, the French Crown declared formal possession of the vast wilderness of the St. Lawrence River and Great Lakes Region.

In 1665, to secure the French territorial claim, the 1,200 soldier Carigan-Salieres Regiment was sent to New France. During the winter of 1665-66, the regiment set about planning a robust campaign to begin the subjugation of the Iroquois to French rule. The Mohawk villages of Tionnontoquen and Kanagaro were attacked and burnt. The following spring the Mohawk asked the English for support.

In 1667, the French made several successful raids on Mohawk villages. The Mohawk, feeling the losses, arranged a truce with the French. Now, the western Iroquois - the Seneca, Cayuga, and Onondaga - could turn their campaign towards their old enemy the Susquehannock.

The year 1667 proved to be a momentous year in the wilderness of the Great Lakes Region and the St. Lawrence River. Early in the year the French had raided Mohawk villages. Then the Mohawk arranged a truce with the French. A while later that same year, a peace treaty between the French and the Iroquois was signed. The treaty had secured the consent of each of the five nations of the Iroquois Confederacy; the Mohawk, Oneida, Onondaga, Cayuga, and Seneca. The peace also included the French fur trading partners in the western Great Lakes.

In 1667, the Mahican became the first member of the Covenant Chain coalition arrangement originated by the Dutch and Iroquois Confederacy.

In 1668, the Mohawk drove the Pennacook across New Hampshire to the protection of the Abenaki in Maine. By 1670, many of the Sokoki had been defeated and were living under French protection along the St. Lawrence River.

The relentless and merciless pursuit of the Wendat by the Iroquois ended. The French could now attempt to rebuild their fur trade.

French missionaries began to travel west. Soon after their arrival, order began to be shaped from the *Great Pursuit* refugee chaos at present-day Green Bay, Wisconsin.

By 1669, the French were able to explore the Ohio Valley for the first time. This opportunity resulted in the French claiming this fertile and resource rich territory for France. The Iroquois, having already claimed this region by right of conquest, were riled by the French claim and tensions simmered.

In 1672, the English brokered a peace between the Mahican alliance and the Iroquois. By design, the peace overture was actually an unconditional surrender by the Mahican alliance. After the treaty, the Iroquois managed all Mahican relations with the Europeans.

The French were on a roll. In 1673 explorers Louis Jolliet and the Jesuit priest Jacques Marquette arrived on the shore of the Mississippi River. In 1677, the French and the Iroquois Confederacy agreed to a peace accord – again. In 1682, Rene-Robert Cavelier, Sieur de LaSalle, claimed the territory of Louisiana for the French Crown.

Once again, fur began to reach the French trading posts at present-day Montreal and Quebec. The French gradually assumed the role of mediator of intertribal disputes. This role increased French influence among the Indigenous peoples of the region. A rejuvenation of French confidence was occurring. With this renewed French strength and confidence, the risk of eventual belligerence was also inevitable. The makings were now in place for the beginning of an organized Algonquin resistance against the Iroquois.

With a renewal of the fur trade came a revitalization of French military power in the region. Waking from their slumber of inattentiveness, the British began to grow uneasy with the French rebuilding of military power and their expanding influence.

The British responded with their own increase in military power. Matters had begun to escalate and the ground was set for the beginning of a period of conflict between the French and British. Their respective tribal allies would also be pulled, willingly and unwillingly, into the approaching conflict.

This new period of conflict would last a century. It would become known as the *Hundred Years War*.

Chapter 11

The Iroquois Confederacy and Aftermath of the Beaver Wars

The 1677 Iroquois peace accord with the French brought subtle change to how the Iroquois would function in future.

The 1677 peace with the French was a peace agreed to by each of Five Nations of the Iroquois Confederacy. This was the first 'Five Nation' agreement made by the Confederacy.

From their past experience with other Confederacies and the Europeans, the Iroquois had learned that they must resolve their own internal differences independent of outside interference. Crucial to keeping their empire and maintaining their position as a political and military power, the Iroquois knew that they must always present a unified position in face of opportunity or threat. The fierce Iroquois culture of nationalism was the foundation for their unity. The unity of the Five Nations was their core strength. This strong unity was something that enemies and allies did not have or cherish with the same degree of Iroquois zealousness.

In future decades, members of the Confederacy would sometimes step away from the unity of the Great Binding Law. They would choose to negotiate separate agreements and would, from time to time, conduct their own wars. Such choices would inevitably do great harm to the cohesiveness and strength of the Iroquois Confederacy.

The 1677 peace with the French presented advantage and opportunity for the Iroquois. The Iroquois began to repopulate the Huron and Mississauga homeland along the north shore of Lake Ontario. The shore lands had been largely uninhabited since 1650. In the absence of hunting and trapping during the war years, the furbearer population was able to rejuvenate itself. The area was once again a prime fur producing region.

But this was not always a time of peaceful opportunity and advantage. The Iroquois were not ready to bury old grievances. The western Iroquois picked up the war club and began to plan a renewed campaign against their old enemies the Susquehannock. The Susquehannock's long war with the Mohawk and Oneida had ended in 1655. Now, they faced a new war with the Onondaga, Cayuga, and Seneca.

In 1655, the Susquehannock had lost their firearm suppliers, the Swedish traders, as an ally. New alliances with the English colonists in Maryland were formed in 1661 and 1666. The new partners would guarantee firearm and ammunition supplies for the Susquehannock and their allies. The new alliance against the Iroquois was a rich blend of tribes. The Algonquin, Shawnee, Delaware, Nanticoke, Conoy, Saponi, and Tutelo all seemed eager to renew the fight against the Iroquois.

While war preparations were brewing among the western Iroquois, the Mohawk were engaged in their own skirmishing in the New England region.

The Mohawk had allied themselves with their old friends the Dutch. The Mohawk were attempting to avoid returning to conflict with the Susquehannock, a Dutch ally.

The Mohawk fought alongside the Dutch to crush the Munsee Delaware during the *Esopus War, 1664*. This engagement resulted in the loss of the Munsee

Delaware as an ally of the Susquehannock. This was certainly a dangerous time of complex relationships.

Regardless of their tragic setbacks in previous decades, the Susquehannock continued to fight. In 1668, the Onondaga, Cayuga, and Seneca conducted raids in Susquehannock territory. The Susquehannock were hard pressed. With barely three hundred fit warriors available to defend villages and territory, the stubborn and courageous Susquehannock continued to fight for another seven years.

Over the next decade, the Iroquois campaigned against the allies of the Susquehannock. They subdued the Nanticoke and Conoy and brought them into the Covenant Chain as allies. Iroquois raids continued against the Saponi and Tutelo in Virginia and the Catawba in South Carolina.

Victors and Vanquished

The Iroquois Confederacy had destroyed tribal confederacies powerful in their own right, such as the Huron, Neutral, Erie, Susquehannock, and Shawnee. The Iroquois were now the dominant political and military power in the region. Many eastern tribes were pushed west of the Mississippi River. Other tribes were forced southwards into the Carolinas. From 1670 onward the Iroquois controlled the Ohio Valley Region. As refugees fled westward to escape the Iroquois war parties, the Ohio country and the lower peninsula of Michigan were emptied of people.

To provide a sense of substance and scope to this tumultuous era of Iroquois Confederacy conquest, consider the following:

- The Huron Confederacy, and the Susquehannock Confederacy had been destroyed.
- The Wenrohronon (Wenro), were an Iroquoian language speaking people, whose ancestral lands lay adjacent to the western boundary with the Seneca. After the Wenrohronon lost their alliance with the Neutral, they were overwhelmed by the Seneca. Survivors were adopted and assimilated by the Seneca.

- Iroquois raiding in 1630 through 1640 had forced many Algonquin, mostly of the Kichesippirini and Weskarina bands, to flee their traditional Ottawa Valley lands and seek refuge with the French at Trois Rivieres on the lower St. Lawrence River.

- The Algonquin, a once independent and flourishing confederacy of tribes, suffering defeats from raiding Iroquois, had been forced from their lands along the Ottawa river and St. Lawrence River and fled inland to the wilderness area of Ontario we know today as Algonquin Park. Other groups moved inland away from the Ottawa River into northern Quebec, others sought the protection of French missionary settlements along the St. Lawrence River. Similar to other confederacies before them, the Algonquin were now a scattered collection of demoralized refugees on what was once their own ancestral land.

- The Potawatomi, Fox, Sauk, and Mascouten had fled lower Michigan and were living as refugees in villages scattered through Wisconsin.

- The Shawnee, Kickapoo, and part of the Miami had been forced from Ohio and Indiana. The Kickapoo and Miami found refuge in Wisconsin. The Shawnee scattered and spread across Tennessee, Illinois, Pennsylvania, and South Carolina.

- In retribution for giving refuge to the Wendat and Neutrals, the Seneca attacked the Illinois in 1655, and forced them west of the Mississippi River.

- The Dhegiha Sioux (Osage, Kansa, Ponca, Omaha, and Quapaw tribes) abandoned the lower Wabush Valley and moved to the Missouri River Region. The Quapaw separated from the other tribes and settled near the mouth of the Arkansas River.

- The defeated Wendat, Tionontati, Wenro, Neutrals, and Erie were killed or captured by the Iroquois. Many were adopted into the Iroquois Confederacy. An estimated one thousand Wendat and Tionontati escaped capture and fled first to Wisconsin, then further inland to Minnesota, and finally back to the south shore of Lake Superior.

- The Ottawa had fled from their ancestral lands among the islands of Lake Huron and moved west to the upper Michigan area.

- The Nipissing and southern bands of the Ojibwe had been forced north to the Sault Ste Marie area.

- Some tribes in the Ohio Valley Region disappeared altogether and are remembered today only by their name: A few of these extinct tribes include: Casa; Cisca; Iskousogom; Moneton; Mospelea; Ouabano; Teochanontian; Tomahitan; and Tramontane. Who they were, their culture, and their history, has been lost for all time.

Having won their campaigns, the Iroquois now pondered how they would proceed as the dominant military and political confederacy of the St. Lawrence River and Great Lakes Regions. Their decision was strategic. They would not bring a military campaign against the Europeans. The Iroquois Confederacy would treat the Europeans on a nation to nation basis. Iroquois Confederacy political influence and military power ensured the Iroquois could accept the Europeans as their equals.

Iroquois Empire, 1667

Chapter 12

Second Phase of the Beaver War Begins

After 1667, a short-lived and certainly less than perfect peace hovered over the region.

In 1671, the Seneca attacked the settlement of Mackinac, an island sanctuary located in the eastern end of Lake Huron near the entrance to lake Michigan. The Dakota were skirmishing with the Ojibwa and Fox along the shores of Lake Superior. But, throughout the region, matters were much less chaotic than what the French had found in 1665.

In 1675, the Mohawk and the Mahican were pressured by English officials in Albany to make a peace between them. The ensuing peace brought to an end a decade of fighting that had cost both parties dearly. 1675 also saw the Susquehannock withdraw from Pennsylvania to Maryland, bringing an end to the long, vicious war with the Oneida, Onondaga, Cayuga and Seneca.

The Iroquois peace with the Mahican and Susquehannock was an opportunity for the Iroquois Confederacy to look westward for captives and furs. During the later part of the 1670s and early 1680s, the Iroquois raided the Illinois, Miami, and other western tribes. At the same time, Iroquois relations with remnants of the Huron - now called Wyandot - and the Ottawa, fluctuated between raiding each other and attempts among themselves to form alliances against common enemies.

The importance of the Iroquois policy of territorial expansion with the intent to acquire furs is expressed by the Onondaga orator *Otreoti* whom the French called *La Grande Gueule,* or *Big Mouth.*

Otreoti speaks about why the Iroquois attacked other tribes in the beaver hunting grounds.

The Iroquois *"fell upon the Illinese and the Oumamies because they cut down the trees of peace that ser'd for limits or boundaries to our Frontiers. They came to hunt Beavers upon our Lands; and contrary to the custom of all the Savages, have carried off whole Stocks, both Male and Female."* (Lahontan, 1703)

Until the later part of the 1670s, the French were the only European imperial power the Iroquois Confederacy had to compete with. The Iroquois relationship with the Dutch of New Netherland and the English in their eastern seaboard colonies had, up until now, been based on trade. Imperialist policies and intrigue with the British did not become a factor until 1674. By now the British had pushed the Dutch aside. The British governor, Sir Edmund Andros, viewed the Iroquois Confederacy as a critically important part of his strategy to pacify and settle the new colonies along the eastern seaboard.

Governor Andros intended to include the political influence and military power of the Iroquois Confederacy in his plans to seize land from present-day Connecticut State to add to New York territory. To do this, Governor Andros encouraged the Iroquois Confederacy to fight as allies of the British against Pauquunaukit Wampanoag Confederacy (anglicized as Pokanoket) leader Metacomet. Metacomet led a confederacy that included the Wampanoag, Nipmuck, Podunk, Narragansett, and Nashaway tribes. Metacomet adopted the name King Philip in recognition and honor of his father's friendly relations with the Mayflower Pilgrims.

The ensuing war, known as *King Philips War, 1675-1678,* is also referred to as the *First Indian War;* and *Metacomet's War.* The war ended with the *Treaty of Casco*

Bay, 1678. At the cessation of hostilities, the Wampanoag and Narragansett tribes had been destroyed.

In 1675, during *King Philip's War,* Metacomet, unannounced and uninvited, brazenly set up a winter camp near present-day Albany, New York State. This was in the heart of the Iroquois ancestral homeland. Enraged, the Mohawk attacked and killed 360 of the 400 Wampanoag.

In the years after Sir Edmund Andros, the British colonial and Iroquois Confederacy relations would change. Governor Andros successors continued to attempt to engage the Iroquois Confederacy as a tool for English imperial policy of seizing territory and pacifying Indigenous resistance to settler encroachment on ancestral tribal lands.

In 1683, Governor Thomas Donga attempted to entice the Iroquois Confederacy to come under his jurisdiction. He distributing the Duke of York's coat of arms to Iroquois villages for display. Such a shallow symbolic gesture meant nothing to the Lords of the Iroquois Confederacy. The efforts of Governor Andros and his successors to enlist the Iroquois Confederacy as a proxy military force was not something the Iroquois Confederacy was about to accede to.

The Iroquois Confederacy had its own plans for building an Iroquois empire. Their strategy involved territorial expansion and seizing economic power through dominance of the fur trade. The Iroquois Confederacy considered themselves the political and military equal of the European powers of France and Britain.

By 1680, the power and territory of the Iroquois Confederacy had reached its zenith. The Iroquois Confederacy had won a vast empire by virtue of the power of unity, wise use of statesmanship, diplomacy, and the measured application of military power supported with intelligent strategy.

Although Iroquois warriors had skirmished and fought battles in every state east of the Mississippi River, they had not raided west of the Mississippi.

In 1680, on the upper Illinois River, Robert LaSalle established Fort Crevecoeur to trade with the Illinois Confederacy. The fort was built on the east bank of the Illinois River, near present-day Peoria, Illinois.

The Illinois Confederacy is also referred to as the Illiniwick or Illini. What we know today about the Illiniwick is from the writings of the French Jesuits recorded in Jesuit Relations.

At the time of first European contact in the 17th Century, the confederacy included the following tribes of the upper Mississippi Valley region: Kaskaskia; Cahokia; Peoria; Tamaroa; Mongivena; Michigamea; Chepoussa; Chinkoa; Coiracoentanon; Espeminkia; Maroa; and Tapoura. The confederacy population was estimated to be more than ten thousand persons. Their ancestral lands included an area in the shape of a triangle that spread from modern-day Iowa to the proximity of modern-day Chicago, and then south to Arkansas.

The fortified French settlement at Fort Crevecoeur, present-day Creve Coeur, a suburb of Preoria, Illinois, attracted large numbers of Algonquin seeking safety from Iroquois raiders and the hope of trade opportunities. The large number of potential enemies gathered in the vicinity of Fort Crevecoeur concerned the Iroquois. Their concern was compounded by the growing number of Illiniwick hunters and trappers moving into the Ohio, Indiana, and lower Michigan trapping territory claimed by the Iroquois by right of conquest. The important beaver population in this rich furbearer territory was being overharvested. The Iroquois knew that the fur resource could not support such a heavy pressure and remain self-sustaining.

The Iroquois made their concerns known to the Illiniwick. During this rapprochement, a Seneca chief was killed by a member of one of the Illiniwick Confederacy tribes. The year was 1680. The second phase of the *Beaver Wars* would now fall into play.

In their ancestral homeland in western present-day New York State, the Seneca gathered a large war party and set out to punish the Illiniwick Confederacy. While making their way to the Illiniwick villages near Fort Crevecoeur, the Seneca recruited warriors from the Miami tribe. The Miami where old enemies of the Illiniwick.

The French received a warning of the approaching Iroquois and Miami war party and they abandoned Fort Crevecoeur, and began a retreat toward present-day Wisconsin. Many of the Illiniwick retreated west of the Mississippi River. However, the Tamaroa, Espeminkia, and Maroa remained in the area in hopes of reconciliation. A fatal mistake. The combined war party of Iroquois and Miami were apparently in no mood for reconciliation. The raid ended with huge numbers killed and villages burnt. The Tamaroa and Maroa were massacred. The Espeminkia were annihilated.

The Iroquois, having returned to the territory, discovered that in 1682, Henri Tonti had built Fort St. Louis on the upper Illinois River, present-day Utica, Illinois. The protection offered by this new French stronghold, also known as Starved Rock, enticed the Illiniwick to return from their refuge west of the Mississippi River. During this respite, the Miami had invited the Shawnee, old Iroquois enemies, to settle among them.

The Iroquois threatened the Miami for their perceived lack of loyalty. The frightened Miami, fearful of Iroquois retribution, switched their allegiance to the French side. This turn of events provided an opportunity for the French to broker a peace with the Illiniwick.

By 1683, the Native population in the vicinity of Fort St. Louis had grown to more than twenty thousand persons. Threatened by such a large population in territory the Iroquois believed to be theirs by right of conquest, they attacked Fort St. Louis.

The Iroquois attacks did not succeed and they laid siege to the fort. Iroquois war chiefs were reluctant to be bogged down in a stalemated campaign. The Iroquois were never comfortable with siege warfare, perhaps due to their preference for a mobile shock and awe mode of combat. Growing frustrated and restless, the Iroquois abandoned the siege and retreated. This was a significant event and a turning point in the *Beaver Wars*.

The Iroquois retreat from the Fort St. Louis siege gave encouragement to the French. They began to build alliances with regional tribes that had been threatened or suffered losses to the Iroquois. Many of the aggrieved tribes saw an alliance with the French as a path to enable them to strike back at the Iroquois.

By the 18th Century, devastated by European disease epidemics and Iroquois raiding, only five of the principal confederacy tribes remained. The surviving tribes were: the Kaskaskia; Cahokia; Peoria; Tamaroa; and Michigamea.

The *Indian Removal Act, 1830*, forced the surviving Illiniwick population from their ancestral lands to modern-day Oklahoma. Today, the remnant of the once strong Illiniwick are known as the *Peoria Tribe of Indians of Oklahoma*.

Denonville's Treachery

The French Crown appointed Jacques-Rene Denonville (1637-1710) as Governor of New France. His tenure was 1685-1689. Denonville embarked on an ambitious initiative. He began the construction of new strategically located forts, strengthened old forts, and began to supply firearms, powder and ball to the Great Lakes Algonquin.

Denonville built a French alliance with the Ojibwe; Ottawa; Wendat; Potawatomi; Mississauga; Fox; Sauk; Miami; Winnebago; Menominee; Kickapoo; Mascouten; and the Illiniwick Confederacy. In 1687, this powerful alliance would begin their offensive against the Iroquois.

Covertly, Denonville began to implement his plans to attack the Iroquois territory. Lumber to build flatboats to transport soldiers and supplies across Lake Ontario was assembled at Fort Frontenac, present-day Kingston, Ontario.

Fearing that someone from the small number of Iroquois families living in the vicinity of Fort Frontenac would send word of his plans to the Haudenosaunee on the south shore of Lake Ontario, Denonville decided to round-up the local Iroquois. He declared the local Iroquois as hostiles and captives would be treated as prisoners of war. There were two groups of local Iroquois. One group lived at the village of Kente, present-day Quinte. The second group lived at Ganneious, present-day Napanee, where the Sulpician missionaries of Montreal had established a mission.

Parkman (1877, pg.140) writes that Denonville's real motive for taking the Iroquois prisoners was not a matter of mission security. Rather, it was Denonville giving the appearance of being an obedient and faithful servant of the French Crown by following the orders of the French court that *"as the Iroquois were strong and robust, as many as possible should be captured and sent to France as galley slaves to serve with convicts and Huguenot prisoners."*

Iroquois captives were in short supply. Unless grievously wounded, warriors never allowed themselves to be captured. So Denonville, his moral compass apparently knocked askew by thoughts of a gratuitous French court, moved to comply with the King's command by entrapping unsuspecting relatives of the southern Iroquois.

In June, 1687, Denonville put his plan into play. He sent out word that a peace council would be held at Fort Frontenac. The intent of the meeting was to discuss and find agreement on settlement of past grievances between the Iroquois and the French. Unaware of the treachery at hand, Jesuit priest Father Jean Lamberville was tasked with bringing the message to the Iroquois. The invitation was simple: *'come to the fort for a feast.'*

Denonville believed that deceiving the Jesuit priest was justified. If Father Lamberville knew the truth of his intent to capture prisoners and invade the Iroquois homeland, the Jesuit would be justifiably angered and refuse his part in the ruse. Denonville had put Father Lamberville into grave danger with the Iroquois.

Thirty men and ninety women and children from the village of Kente turned up at the fort to attend the council and feast. No one from the mission of Ganneious showed up for the council.

Met at the Fort's gate by Intendant Jean Bochart de Champigny, the Iroquois were welcomed and began to enter the fort. Once inside, the Iroquois were surrounded by French soldiers.

The prisoners were badly treated. Baron Lahontan, a French soldier, wrote in his 1709 journal that some of the men had their hands and feet tied to posts. The bindings were restrictive and painful. The tied men where in pain and could not sleep. The captives could not defend themselves from mosquitos that plagued them in swarms throughout the night. Christian Indians allied with the French added to the prisoners suffering by pushing the finger tips of the bound captives into the burning tobacco in their smoking pipes. Many of the trussed Iroquois men began to sing their death songs.

The captives held in the fort were not part of the Iroquois who were fighting the French. They were all baptized Christian Iroquois who had settled in the area.

The Christian Iroquois families earned part of their living by keeping the French at Fort Frontenac supplied with fish and game and agricultural crops surplus to their needs.

Denonville sent a party of Canadiens [French settlers born in New France] and Christian Indians to the Ganneious mission to take prisoners. A few more Iroquois were captured along the river. The Iroquois captured along the river were fishing and gathering in family groups. The families were certainly not hostile Iroquois on the warpath. Iroquois war parties did not travel with their women and children.

During captivity, a prisoner escaped from the fort and reached the Onondaga on the south side of Lake Ontario. Warning was given of the French treachery and plans for invasion.

Denonville's treachery resulted in the capture of 51 men and 150 women and children. During their captivity, some of the Iroquois died *"partly from distress, and partly from a pestilential disease"* (ibid, pg. 141).

Women and children survivors were baptized and distributed among the mission villages throughout the French colony. The men were sent to Quebec. At Quebec, a few prisoners were claimed by Christian relatives and released from their captivity. The remaining prisoners were *"baptized and sent to France to share with common convicts and Huguenot prisoners the horrible slavery of the royal galleys."* (ibid pg. 142).

The story of Denonville's treachery often includes the suggestion that all the Iroquois Confederacy hereditary royaner (chiefs) had been captured at the Fort Frontenac council. The truth of the matter is not one hereditary Haudenosaunee royaner was captured as a result of Denonville's treachery and subsequent prisoner roundup. The story of a massive roundup of Iroquois chiefs was a crude attempt at demoralizing propaganda.

Father Lamberville was spared by the Iroquois. After the Denonville treachery, Father Lamberville was summoned by the Haudenosaunee to a council of chiefs. At this council, Father Lamberville was told: *"We know you too well to believe that you meant to betray us. We think that you have been deceived as well as we; and we are not unjust enough to punish you for the crime of others."* On the direction of the council, a group of experienced Iroquois warriors took the priest away and hid him before the furious younger warriors could get their hands on him. (ibid, pg. 142)

In 1687, Denonville began a well-planned campaign against the Seneca. On June 13, 1687, the French left Montreal to begin their campaign. The French force consisted of 832 colonial regular soldiers, 900 Canadian militia; and more than 400 Native allies. This impressive force travelled up the St. Lawrence River in a flotilla of 200 bateaux and 200 canoes.

The invasion force landed in Iroquois territory on the south shore of Lake Ontario at Irondequoit Bay. The invaders invested time and resources to build a palisade to protect the beached flotilla. Once defenses were completed, the force began their march to Ganondagan. Along the route of March, the invading army began their attack on Seneca and Onondaga villages. The French had invaded the Iroquois homeland.

On July 13, 1687, the French were attacked by a force of 800 Seneca. After a short violent engagement, the Seneca retreated. Arriving at the Seneca village of Ganondagan the following day, the French found it burnt. The French killed a large number of abandoned pigs and burnt an estimated 1.2 million bushels of stored and standing corn. After a brief respite, the invading army moved west and destroyed the village of Totiakton, the largest of the Seneca villages, at present-day Mendon, Monroe County, New York State. The French army then returned to their flotilla and embarked for new adventures. The Seneca and Onondaga, bruised and vengeful, replaced their crop loses and built new villages.

The Iroquois were furious over this invasion of their ancestral lands. In August of 1689, a military force of some 1,200 Iroquois warriors struck back. The Iroquois raided the French settlement of Lachine, a short distance west of the present-day city of Montreal. More than two hundred French settlers were killed. The following year the French and their Sokoki allies retaliated with a raid on Schenectady. During 1690 and 1692, the Mohawk attacked the Sokoki at their St. Francois settlements.

Denonville travelled west along the shore of Lake Ontario and established Fort Denonville where the Niagara River meets Lake Ontario. The site, named Fort

Conti, had been used by La Salle during the years 1678 to 1679. The site would later become Fort Niagara.

Continental tensions between England and France had been festering for some time. War was inevitable. The Iroquois Confederacy, now allied with the English, initiated sustained hit and run guerilla warfare against *Canadien* settlements. At the time, the term *Canadien* was applied to persons of French ancestry born in New France. Denonville petitioned the King of France for more soldiers. The French had no spare troops to send to New France. Hostilities between the Imperial powers of Britain and France broke out in 1688.

For months, in the vicinity of Montreal, 1,500 Iroquois warriors had been raiding and skirmishing with farmers. On August 4, 1689, the Iroquois attacked Lachine adjacent to Montreal, killed 24 people, and took an estimated 70 to 90 prisoners. The attackers burned Lachine to the ground. The Iroquois continued to raid Canadien farms near Montreal. The raiding warriors destroyed 56 farms and killed or captured more than 100 settlers.

In 1688, Louis XIV, the King of France, ordered Louis de Buade, Comte de Frontenac et de Palluau, back to New France to resume his role as Governor of New France. The French King realized he had to replace Denonville. Louis de Buade, Comte de Frontenac et de Palluau (1622-1698), was a French soldier and Governor General of New France during the years 1672-1682 and again in 1689 until his death in 1698.

Frontenac understood Denonville's Iroquois captives being held in France served no good purpose. Frontenac knew the entire business of the Denonville treachery was exceptionally counter-productive in terms of any hopes of reconciliation with the Iroquois.

Frontenac, resolved not to leave France without the Iroquois, searched and found 13 surviving Iroquois captives. The surviving Iroquois returned to New France with Frontenac. The Iroquois had been prisoners in France for 12 years. Their captivity conditions had been harsh.

Iroquois tension was not high on the French list of chores to tackle. For the first time, the fur market in Europe had more supply than demand. With the competition for furs cooled, the French Jesuits took up their old cry that the New

France fur trade had brought great harm to the tribes of the region and social destruction to eastern North America in general.

The Jesuits, skilled in the application of political agitation when the need arose, convinced the French Monarchy to make change. The unprofitable state of the fur trade meant reduced revenues for the monarchy. This situation provided favorable economic conditions to argue for the Jesuit strategy to curb the fur trade. The Jesuits convinced the French monarchy to issue a proclamation terminating the French fur trade.

With the Jesuit success, a Royal Proclamation was issued that curtailed the fur trade in the western Great Lakes Region. However, it would seem that a good deed in the eyes of one was not such in the eyes of another.

Frontenac, when he received the Royal Proclamation, recognized unacceptable consequences if the terms were enforced. Frontenac knew the proclamation would be a disaster for the French and Algonquin alliance. He delayed implementing the proclamation. His delaying tactics angered the French monarchy and Frontenac was removed from office in 1682.

Frontenac's second term, 1689 until his death in 1698, involved defence of the large and growing town site of Quebec from British invasion during *King William's War, 1689-1697*. Frontenac planned and implemented French raids against Iroquois and English settlements. Early on, he replaced the formal European military approach to war fighting with guerilla tactics disdained by the British. His war fighting tactics were borrowed from the Iroquois. Attacks involved carefully scouted and quiet approaches to apply hit and run tactics using small groups of skilled and experienced soldiers. He would engage the enemy with sudden and brief ferocity and then fade back into the wilderness to prepare for the next skirmish. Unlike the British, who were disdainful of opposing forces who refused to stand and fight, Frontenac was not reluctant to adopt fighting tactics from the Iroquois.

Frontenac's brazen raiding played a significant role in neutralizing the Iroquois threat to New France. Frontenac is responsible for bringing about the expansion of the French fur trade. He instituted the use of courier-des bois, the fearless long distance paddlers, to go into the wilderness of the northern Great Lakes Region, and far beyond.

In 1689, Frontenac was the Governor General of New France when France authorized the importation of slaves to Quebec from the West Indies.

The 1693-96 campaigns launched by Frontenac brought the war to the Iroquois homeland villages. In 1696, Frontenac led 2,000 fighters to Onondaga. The people, knowing of Frontenac's advance and intentions, burned their town and disappeared into the forest. The soldiers destroyed the Onondaga corn, beans and squash fields.

Meanwhile, Frontenac received a visitation from the neighbouring Oneida asking to negotiate a peace. Frontenac sent Philippe de Rigaud de Vaudreuil with 600 men to the Oneida village. Many of the Oneida had fled. However, Vaudreuil made the remaining Oneida promise to move, as soon as they could, to a *Canadien* mission village along the St. Lawrence River. Then Vaudreuil burned the Oneida village. (Parkman, 1877)

The French offensive was far from passive in terms of initiating a friendlier relationship with the Iroquois. On the fur trade routes along modern-day lake St. Clair and Lake Erie, great battles between large canoe fleets were fought.

This was a time of intense military action and social upheaval. A smallpox epidemic broke out among the Iroquois villages. By 1694, the Iroquois had been so weakened by raiding and disease that they approached the French to negotiate a peace. The Iroquois, obstinate in the face of military defeat, refused to accept the French condition that a peace with the Iroquois be extended to French tribal allies. The French turned away from the Iroquois overtures for a peace. Matters could not have been worse for the Iroquois.

By 1696, the Mississaugas had forced the Iroquois to abandon most of their villages in present-day southern Ontario. Except for parts of modern-day eastern Ohio and Pennsylvania, the Iroquois had been pushed back to their ancestral homeland.

King William's War between New England and New France ended in 1697 with the *Treaty of Ryswick*. As a term of this treaty, the Iroquois gained the protection of the English. Although saving the day for the Iroquois, this treaty condition was not something the Iroquois had asked for or wanted. However, the French, concerned that their long war with the Iroquois would now lead to more conflict with the English, changed their tune and began to give greater attention to Iroquois approaches for a peace.

Frontenac, Governor General of New France, was a man worthy of note. In his first term as Governor General, he encouraged the expansion of the fur trade. In order to secure the lower Great Lakes Region trade, he built Fort Frontenac at Cataraqui, present-day Kingston, Ontario. Against the opposition of his Bishop, Francois de Laval, Frontenac supported the trade of brandy with Native people. Laval looked upon this as a mortal sin. Frontenac was told his soul was in peril if he continued to trade alcohol with the Natives. This was not an idle threat in a time of significant religious influence. Although his soul was forfeit, Frontenac did not relent. Frontenac was 76 years old when he participated in his last raid against the Iroquois. Governor General Frontenac was a temperamental, turbulent, fearless, decisive soldier and citizen who was loved by his people and feared by the Iroquois.

Frontenac's successor, Louis-Hector de Calliere, 1698-1703, was obedient to the French Monarchy and their wishes with regard to the fur trade proclamation. The new Governor General of New France was eager to put the Royal Proclamation terms into play. He closed strategically placed French forts and trading posts throughout the western Great Lakes Region. This action erased the source and supply of trade goods to trading partners and allies alike. By doing this, the French worked hard to weaken their alliances with numerous tribal partners. The simple matter was that trade and the supply of sufficient quantities of trade goods was France's singular source of regional influence on allies and enemies alike. Now, what they had built was being squandered by royal decree. A great folly on the part of the French monarchy.

Tribes allied with the French grew suspicious when they learned of French interest to establish a peace with their old enemies the Iroquois. The Algonquin, with proven cause given their history with the duplicitous French, were suspicious that the French would abandon them for a separate peace with the Iroquois. In the meantime, the Iroquois were busy extending trade offers to the Ottawa who were the current allies of the French and Algonquin.

A stumbling block for the French and Iroquois peace negotiations was the matter of a return of prisoners adopted by the Iroquois. The Algonquin were aware of the reduced ability of the Iroquois to field a strong military force, and seeing a chance of an Iroquois collapse, were insistent about the return of captured Algonquin. The Algonquin decided that continuing the war with the Iroquois might give them a victory. The fighting continued until 1701.

The Grand Settlement of 1701

The Iroquois Confederacy had not been having a good time of it. Threat from combative neighbours; a shrinking empire; and disrupted trade with the imperial European powers were taking their toll on the Iroquois Confederacy.

Iroquois ambassadors had been busy during the period 1699 through 1701. The Lords of the Grand Council of the Iroquois Confederacy understood that new solutions had to be found for the problems facing the Confederacy. As old threats festered and new threats bubbled to the surface, factionalism began to simmer within and among the Five Nations of the Confederacy.

To secure a peace and a return of stability and harmony, the Lords of the Iroquois Confederacy understood that an economic strategy was preferred to costly military campaigns.

Iroquois ambassadors moved among the Iroquois communities, the French in New France, and the English in the eastern seaboard colonies. Led by Teganissorens, the experienced and respected Onondaga statesman, the Iroquois ambassadors worked to implement strategy to find solutions to the disputes and conflicts that were tearing the Iroquois Confederacy apart.

The Iroquois Confederacy began to implement their strategy on three fronts: the July 19, 1701 council with Lieutenant Governor John Nanfan, Province of New York (1698-1702), at Albany; the Montreal council with Louis-Hector Calliere, Governor General of New France (1698-1703), commencing August 4th, 1701; and the negotiations with English colonists in Philadelphia, Commonwealth of Pennsylvania, completed in 1704. This was a lot of balls to keep in the air by the ambassadors of the Iroquois Confederacy.

The Nanfan Council:

The economic strategy of the Iroquois Confederacy consisted, in part, of forging new alliances that would serve Iroquois objectives. In 1701, representatives of the Iroquois Confederacy and John Nanfan, the Colonial Governor of New York, representing the British Crown, met at Albany, New York. The meeting brought about the July 19, 1701, *Nanfan Treaty*. This treaty, amazingly, was a deed from the Iroquois Confederacy to the King of England for the Iroquois *Beaver Hunting Grounds*.

The council with Governor General John Nanfan was completed around the same time as the beginning of the Montreal council. The Iroquois council with John Nanfan had resulted in unsettling mixed outcomes.

The *Nanfan Treaty, 1701,* was scandalous for the Iroquois and one must wonder what possessed the Iroquois negotiators to agree to terms. The *Nanfan Treaty* text indicates that the Iroquois Confederacy formally deeded to King William of England, the lands the Iroquois claimed as their western lands. Those lands are described as extending from western boundary of present-day New York State to Chicago, Illinois. This was territory that the Iroquois Confederacy had taken by right of conquest in the 1670s during the later part of the *Beaver Wars.*

It is difficult to understand what the Iroquois Confederacy was thinking. What kind of strategic value for the Iroquois could come from such a generous outcome for England?

The Iroquois Confederacy granted " *after mature deliberation out of a deep sense of the many Royal favours extended to us by the present great Monarch of England King William the Third"* an extensive land area covering the greater part of present-day mid-western United States and southern Ontario, and as far west as Quadoge, present-day Chicago. These were the lands, called by the Iroquois the *Beaver Hunting Grounds*, that the Iroquois had claimed by right of conquest during the *Beaver Wars* of the 17th Century.

A large territory of the *Beaver Hunting Grounds* described in the *Nanfan Treaty*, was also claimed by New France, and also her Algonquin allies. The French did not recognize the *Nanfan Treaty*.

The existing state of affairs was misleading at best. By 1701, the Iroquois had lost effective control of the western lands to the Algonquin, who were allied with the French. As the Albany council began to conclude, the attending Iroquois ambassadors counseled John Nanfan that the Montreal Conference, being conducted simultaneously with their meeting with Nanfan, was of no consequence. The Iroquois agreed that they were allied with the English. The Iroquois position was that trade was the heart of the Iroquois and New York relationship. In view of this, the Iroquois agreed to allow traders from the western tribes to pass through Iroquoia on their way to Albany, New York. For their part, the British promised to defend Iroquois hunting rights on Iroquois ceded lands.

It is interesting that twenty-five years after the *Nanfan Treaty* was signed, the 60-mile-wide strip of land joining Lake Erie and Lake Ontario, starting at Sandusky Creek, was reserved for continued Six Nation occupation and use, with the permission of the British owners under the *1701 Nanfan Treaty* with the King of Great Britain.

The Montreal Council:

Delayed by their meeting with John Nanfan, a delegation from the western Iroquois (Cayuga and Seneca) accompanied by Mohawk representatives, arrived late for the Montreal council.

The August 4, 1701, Montreal council brought together a full array of leaders. Louis-Hector Calliere, the Governor General of New France (1698-1703), met with a gathering of ambassadors and tribal leaders representing an amazing array of allies and antagonists. The Oneida, Onondaga, Cayuga and Seneca attended the beginning of the council. At the start of the council, the Oneida represented the Mohawk. Leaders of all the tribes allied with the French also attended: Wyandot, Algonquin, Abenaki, Nipissing, Ottawa, Ojibwa, Sauk, Fox, Miami, and Potawatomi. Representation for the imperial powers of France and Britain participated.

Leadership for all the Indigenous tribes, confederacies, and alliances struggling for influence and resolution for trade and settlement disputes made their needs and wants known. The shrewd and persistent effort of the Iroquois ambassadors enabled the groundwork for truce negotiations and mutually agreeable trade agreements.

In the early stages of the council, the participants ratified the previous year's agreements which had introduced a general peace among the various factions. Although vague in description, boundaries for the western hunting territories had been agreed to. The prickly Iroquois had agreed to remain east of Detroit. If disputes arose, the agreement stipulated the Governor of New France would arbitrate to find peaceful resolution. Arbitration was accepted as a preferred alternative to the bloodletting of armed conflict.

A key resolution was reached between the Iroquois and Governor General Calliere of New France. Specific terms of understanding were settled particular to Iroquois access to Detroit and French trading posts further west. The Iroquois agreed to a peace with the French and all the tribes allied with the French. For the French, this was immense. The French celebrated the Iroquois promise of neutrality in any future French-Anglo wars.

The achievements accomplished at the 1701 Montreal council would become known as the *Grand Settlement of 1701*.

In the meantime, Iroquois ambassadors had begun a third set of negotiations in Philadelphia, the Commonwealth of Pennsylvania. The Philadelphia negotiations took some time, but by 1704, the Iroquois had secured an informal trade agreement with Pennsylvania. This set of negotiations were separate from the *Grand Settlement* negotiations.

In retrospect, the Iroquois treaty terms with Governor General Calliere of New France represented a defeat for the Iroquois. The Iroquois Confederacy had lost the war and agreed to treaty terms dictated, in a large part, by Calliere. In accepting this, the Iroquois conceded that they could not prevail militarily against the French with their tribal allies.

However, on the other hand, the shrewd and brilliantly implemented strategy and diplomacy of the Iroquois ambassadors did secure five critically important objectives.

The five accomplishments were: 1) The *Grand Settlement* allowed the Iroquois a reprieve from the devastating warfare of the 1690s. 2) Hunting rights on the western territory were ceded to the Iroquois. 3) The Iroquois agreement to allow the western tribe traders to move through Iroquois lands on their way to the Albany trading center presented profitable trade opportunity for the Iroquois. 4) The agreements solidified access to a broad geography of trade markets in New France, New York, and Pennsylvania. 5) The Iroquois had won a promise they would not be forced to be a proxy military force for Britain or France in any future imperial war - which the Iroquois knew to be inevitable.

For the Iroquois, the *Grand Settlement of 1701*, and concurrent agreements with the Province of New York, and the Commonwealth of Pennsylvania, were accepted as victories.

The *Grand Settlement* brought peace to the northern and western Iroquois borders allowing for a stable economy based on guaranteed western territory hunting access. The agreement also held out promise that the Iroquois would not be dragged into European conflicts as a proxy military asset. These benefits, combined with diverse access to European markets, reduced warfare intended to ensure Iroquois economic power and survival to an unnecessary and obsolete strategy.

In 1724, an Iroquois spokesman explained to a delegation from Massachusetts how the treaties of the *Grand Settlement* – restrictive to Iroquois military and political options as they may be – were acceptable to the Iroquois Confederacy. The spokesman said:

"Tho the Hatchett lays by our side yet the way is open between this Place and Canada, and trade is free both going and coming."

When the American colonists attempted to incite the Iroquois to attack New France, the spokesman replied:

"If a War should break out and we should use the Hatchett that layes by our Side, those Paths which are now open would be stopped, and if we should make war it would not end in a few days as yours doth but it must last till one nation or the other is destroyed as it has been heretofore with us. We know what whipping and scourging is from the Governor of Canada." (New York Col. Docs., V, 724-725)

The *Grand Settlement* was valued by the Iroquois and they worked diligently to stay within its parameters and make use of the assurances given by the European powers. The Iroquois used this relatively peaceful period to build trading relationships with the western tribes. From time to time, skirmishes broke out between Iroquois and western tribe hunting parties encroaching too close to French trading posts for the Iroquois liking. Skirmishes presented an opportunity for hot-blooded young Iroquois warriors, eager to prove their mettle in combat, to conduct mourning-war raids to seize captives.

Iroquois leaders were not hesitant to use Canadian arbitration when the need arose. The chiefs also worked assiduously to curb their eager young warriors from lighting war fires among the western tribes. For the veteran Iroquois leaders, the challenge of controlling hot-blooded young warriors, eager to prove their mettle, must have been taxing to the limit.

The Iroquois Confederacy strived to set warfare aside and use diplomacy and negotiation to navigate through the perils of Anglo-French imperial enmity and the subtle economic contests of the fur trade.

The legerdemain of Iroquois diplomats during this time was seldom recognized and less often understood by the French and English.

The *Grand Settlement of 1701* is an amazing and complex diplomatic triumph of Iroquois ambassadors who enabled the process required for treaty ratification. For a time, the *Grand Settlement* served to bring harmony and peace between the Iroquois, the French, the British colonists, and the western tribes.

Little Stays the Same Forever.
The Resumption of Hostilities.
Queen Anne's War, 1702-13

By late 1701, the hard-won French alliances in the Great Lakes Region had begun to crumble. The Iroquois, seeing diminished French influence - and in a weakened state themselves - moved to take advantage of the new situation with an economic rather than military strategy. They would attack the French with trade. The Iroquois were down, but a long way from being out of the game.

The inevitable fires of the 'future war' were soon kindled.

Queen Anne's War (1701 - 1713) was the North American theatre of the *War of Spanish Succession, 1701-14*, which was fought primarily in Europe. *Queen Anne's War* was was fought for control of the North American continent. This was the second of four *French and Indian Wars* fought in eastern North America between France allied with Spain, their foe England with each countries respective Native allies.

The Iroquois kept themselves informed about the New England and Maritime skirmishes of *Queen Anne's War, 1702 – 1713*, which were occurring on their eastern borders. Shrewd Iroquois statesmanship allowed the Iroquois Confederacy to keep their promise of neutrality during the New England and Maritime campaigns. However, the Iroquois began to grow anxious about developments on their western borders.

The French focus had shifted to the territory of Ohio Valley Region. Claiming the territory as an extension of New France, the French overlooked the need to first extinguish Iroquois claims in favor of their own claim to the region.

The French knew conflict was on the horizon and were eager to secure an Iroquois neutrality. The Mississaugas, a French ally, were expanding their territory with incursions into present-day southern Ontario. The Iroquois protested the Mississaugas trespass to the French. The French ignored the Iroquois. The French response did little to encourage the Iroquois to seriously consider an alliance with the French.

The Iroquois Confederacy considered the French claim of the Ohio Valley Region an invasion of their territory.

The British had also recognized the future critical importance of the Ohio Valley Region. The British claimed the Ohio Valley Region at a time when the French were in disarray.

The British interpreted the *1697 Treaty of Ryswick* to mean the Iroquois had been put under British protection. This interpretation allowed the British to assume the Iroquois claim by right of conquest to the Ohio Valley Region was in effect, a British claim. The Iroquois did not see matters in the same light as the British.

By 1713, the Iroquois were preparing for a war campaign against the French in retaliation against Mississaugas seizure of Iroquois territory. Before the Iroquois could embark on their adventure, *Queen Anne's War* ended with the ceding of the French territories of Hudson Bay; Acadia; and Newfoundland to Britain. France kept Cape Breton and a few other islands in the Gulf of St. Lawrence, notably the islands of St. Pierre and Miquelon. This lull in war gave the French the incentive to negotiate a temporarily peaceful resolution to the Iroquois and Mississaugas tensions.

The Assassination of Alexander Montour and Samuel Vetch's Plans for the Invasion of Canada

The years 1709 and 1711, presented high risk events that threatened to pull the Iroquois into war with the Europeans and their allies.

In 1709, Governor General Pierre de Rigaud de Vaudreuil de Cavagnial of New France, ordered the murder of Alexander Montour, a French trader who had successfully built a trade between the western tribes and Albany. Vaudreuil believed the assassination was a necessary response to the escalating diversion of French western trade to the Iroquois and the English. The assassination had unintended consequences for the French. Pro-French Iroquois changed their allegiance from the French to the British.

Matters disintegrated further. English colonists Samuel Vetch with Francis Nicholson began their planning for an invasion of Canada. The majority of Mohawk and Oneida warriors with some Onondaga and Cayuga, supported the invasion plans. In the west, the Seneca were not shy in making it known that they would sit this one out. Their close proximity and dependence on trade with tribes allied with the French made the choice of neutrality a wise one.

In the end, the invasion army of Iroquois warriors and British colonists never landed in Canada. Refusal of the British government to commit the Royal Navy to blockading the St. Lawrence river and commencing an attack of French Canada from the east put an end to invasion plans.

In 1711, Vetch and Nicholson put together a second plan to invade Canada. The Iroquois were now primed to join in hostilities against the French. In 1710, the

Seneca had been attacked by western tribes. The Seneca believed the attacking tribes had been incited by the French. In the spring of 1711, a party of French had arrived in Onondaga, threatened the Onondaga of the consequences of Iroquois hostility, and attempted, unsuccessfully, to build a blockhouse in an Onondaga village. These events, and the promise of a fight with the French, ensured that all the Five Nations of the Iroquois Confederacy lined up with Vetch and Nicholson and their Canadian invasion plans.

However, once again, the critical support for the invasion by the Royal Navy was withheld. Doubtless frustrated and disheartened, the Iroquois warriors and the soldiers of the colonial land invasion army returned to their villages and towns.

A downside of this entire affair is that French and Iroquois relations could not pull out of the downhill slide that started with Vaudreuil's assassination of Alexander Montour and the consequent invasion planning.

Iroquois-British relations also cooled. The sabotaged invasion plans of 1709 and 1711 convinced the Iroquois that the British military was strong on spit, polish, and discipline, but their promises were hollow and they had no heart for the fight. For a time, after all of that, Iroquois diplomats succeeded in maintaining neutrality with France and England during their imperial Anglo-Franco wars.

The Iroquois continued to control access to British and Dutch traders at Albany. When the French began to implement the fur trade restrictions of the *Royal Proclamation*, the Iroquois watched and refrained from interference. Their strategy would let the French and their allies beat themselves up with internal grievances. While this civil unrest bubbled, the Iroquois would gradually re-enter the fur trade as a neutral non-combatant, offering fair trade with ample quantities of lower priced but superior quality trading goods.

The Iroquois remained obedient to their *Great Peace* that forbade internal strife among the Iroquois Confederacy of Five Nations. This unity among the Iroquois allowed them the internal stability to began to make inroads into the traditional territories of the French fur trading empire while their competition bickered and fought amongst themselves. In 1717, the Ottawa, an old French trading partner and ally, began to trade with the Iroquois. Other French allies soon followed.

Iroquois Strategy of Economic Warfare against the French

In order to shorten the travel distance to trading posts for the Great Lakes tribes, the Iroquois allowed the British to build Fort Burnet (1727). The original fort, a stone blockhouse, is in the Iroquois ancestral homeland at present-day City of Oswego, Oswego County, New York State. The stone blockhouse, later known as Fort Pepperrell (1745), and finally as Fort Oswego, was strategically located to attract fur traders to the English trading hub at Albany, the present-day capital of New York State. By 1728, an estimated 80% of the beaver on the Albany market was coming from tribes that had once supplied the French fur markets.

After 1701, the British had accepted Iroquois neutrality. However, this did not mean that the neutral Iroquois were left in isolation. The British saw the Iroquois as a buffer between themselves and New France. Now, with the French alliance collapsing, the Iroquois found themselves the balance of power between the British and the French in North America.

The Iroquois manoeuvred through the pitfalls of this situation and were successful in keeping both power and independence. This was a notable Iroquois achievement in terms of diplomatic skills. Their statesmanship was the equal of, and at times superior to, any of their European counterparts.

The Iroquois strategy of weakening the French with economic warfare had been successful. The Iroquois, without force of arms, using economic warfare alone, had recovered their place as the dominant fur trade middleman between the British, the French, and their respective trading partners. Recognizing this, the French rescinded the *Royal Proclamation* that had banned fur trading. It was, however, too late for the French.

At the same time as the Iroquois economic strategy against the French was having effect. The Iroquois used British fear of French influence among the Native tribes in the British colonies along the eastern seaboard to gain support for the Covenant Chain. The British encouraged tribes to seek membership in the Covenant Chain. Membership moved back and forth among the Shawnee; Miami; Delaware; Conestoga (Susquehannock); Nanticoke; Saponi; Tutelo; Munsee; Mahican; Conoy (Piscataway); Cherokee; Creek; Choctaw; Catawba; and Chickasaw.

However, matters were not always smooth running for the Covenant Chain members. The Iroquois Confederacy position of influence and power as sole spokesman for Covenant Chain members was not accepted by all member tribes. With such a culturally diverse membership, it would indeed be a challenge to find common interest and consensual resolution to issues.

The Chickasaw; Creek; Cherokee; Catawba; and Choctaw resisted Iroquois authority. These groups, with other less vocal tribes, saw the Iroquois placing their own interests and the interests of the British above the interests of the Covenant Chain tribes. Under terms of the Covenant Chain, the Iroquois Confederacy was supposed to speak for and defend member tribes.

The Iroquois knew that rebellious members threatened the foundation of the Covenant Chain. They pushed back. The tension sometimes resulted in warfare between the Iroquois and rebellious tribes.

There were exceptions. The Iroquois could, when they considered the cause worthwhile, stand strong in protecting the integrity of the Covenant Chain. Support for the oppressed Tuscarora is an example of Covenant Chain cohesion.

The Carolina colonists had been fighting to displace the Tuscarora who resisted encroachment on their ancestral lands by the English settlers. The *Tuscarora War, 1712-1713*, had devastated the Tuscarora. Recognizing that if the war went on much longer, the Tuscarora would be annihilated, they petitioned the Iroquois Confederacy for protection. The Oneida Nation sponsored the Tuscarora, and in 1722, the Confederacy accepted the estimated 1,500 Tuscarora as the sixth member of the Iroquois Confederacy. The Iroquois assisted the Tuscarora dispersal from the Carolinas to the Iroquois homeland in modern-day western New York State. They settled on lands between villages of the Oneida and the Onondaga.

By 1722, the Tuscarora, now formally adopted by the Iroquois Confederacy, were given a place to sit with the Haudenosaunee during confederacy councils. The Haudenosaunee would allow the Tuscarora to sit at council, but they would not have the privilege of influencing the decision-making process in matters of governance. With the adoption of the Tuscarora into the Iroquois Confederacy, the British began to call the confederacy the *Six Nations*.

The Tuscarora were not about to be side-lined. William Andrews, an Anglican missionary working among the Mohawk, described the Tuscarora relationship:

"The Tuscarora have an implacable hatred against the Christians in Carolina."

Andrews was not kind to the Tuscarora. He wrote:

"the Tuscarora were a great Occasion of Our Indians becoming so bad as they are, they now take all Occasions to find fault and quarrel, wanting to revolt." (Schoolcraft, 1846, pgs. 147-148)

The Tuscarora had certainly become a handful for the Five Nations.

The Iroquois had long memories. Years after the Tuscarora adoption, Iroquois raiding parties would travel south to bring vengeance to the Catawba who had helped the Carolina settlers devastate the Tuscarora in their ancestral lands. The Catawba would suffer from the Iroquois mourning-war raids to secure captives for revenge and adoption.

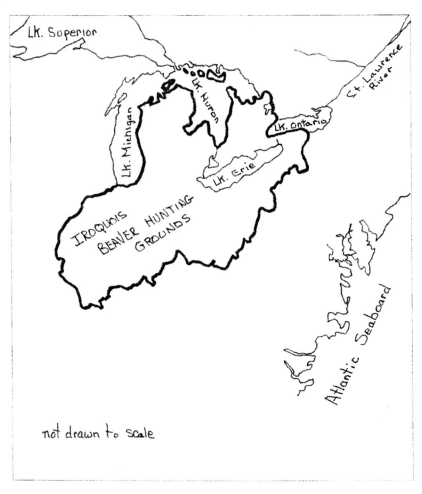

Iroquois Beaver Hunting Grounds

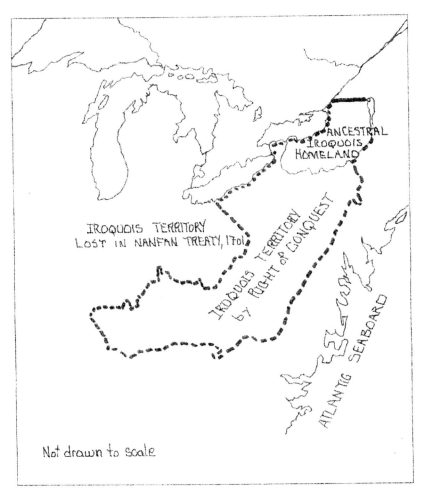

Iroquois Empire, 1701

Chapter 13

The Jesuit Influence

The Iroquois Confederacy armistice brought about the political union of the five Iroquois tribes. The Great Binding Law, the constitution of the Iroquois Confederacy, was the source of the Confederacies unity, political strength, and military power.

As good as it was, the union was not perfect. Fractures between groups within the Confederacy began with internal differences about religion. With the arrival of the French, the Iroquois had two spiritual beliefs on their doorstep: the Great Binding Law and animist spirituality of the Haudenosaunee longhouse people; and the Christian religion introduced by the Jesuit priests of the French Catholic religious order, the Society of Jesus.

European arrivals to North America called the land undiscovered. For the Europeans, this new land fell under the influence of the Papal *Doctrine of Terra Nullius*. The Latin translation for Terra Nullius is *nobody's land* or *land unoccupied*. This Christian doctrine set out that if a land was unoccupied it could be claimed for a sovereign.

This new land was certainly not unoccupied. The land was home for numerous and populous tribes with their own distinct cultures. Each group of Indigenous people had their own unique language, culture, history and spirituality.

The Europeans needed a justifying rationale to seize the land and its riches for their own. The rational flowed from religious doctrine. If the land's occupants were not Christian, then they were pagans without souls. The Church position was that until a person was baptized as Christian, they had no soul. If they had no soul they were, as the French said, *savages*, and as the English said, *Godless heathens*. Therefore, they were not people. Ergo, the land was not occupied and therefore prime for the taking. Terra Nullius declared the ancestral lands of the North American Indigenous tribes open for the taking. And taken they were.

The *Doctrine of Terra Nullius* and its application remains relevant in modern times. The *Doctrine of Terra Nullius* is applied to frozen lands of Antarctica. For a time, the Doctrine also applied to the huge expanse of the vacant Western Sahara Desert region. That is, until the nomadic Bedouin, who seasonally crossed those lands, satisfied concerned parties that those vast sand lands were not *nobody's land*.

The priests had much work to do among those they saw as savages and heathens. French explorers, who were the first Europeans to explore the St. Lawrence River Region, Great Lakes Region, and Ohio Valley Region, arrived first as soldiers. In close pursuit, came Christian missionaries. The soldiers claimed territory for their sovereign. The priests claimed souls for their God.

The Jesuit priests of the Society of Jesus have a long history in the New World.

Following are the early missions in New France. The First Jesuit Mission was established on Penobscot Bay in 1609. The Penobscot mission, in present-day Maine, was part of the French colony of Acadia. In 1611, a second mission was established at Port Royal, in present-day Nova Scotia. The third mission in 1613, brought a mission to Mount Desert Island, in present-day Maine. The fourth mission was established at Habitation, present-day Quebec City, in 1625. Not long after, another Jesuit mission was established at Trois Rivieres, on the St. Lawrence River, between present-day Montreal City and Quebec City.

The Jesuits, through their courage, influence, persistence, faith in God, and the driving force for saving souls through baptism and conversion to Christianity, were the shock troops of the Catholic Church. The Jesuits were respectful of the way of life of the Indigenous people and tribes they lived among.

19th Century Protestant historian Francis Parkman wrote: *"Spanish civilization crushed the Indian, English civilization scorned and neglected him, French civilization embraced and cherished him."* (Parkman. 1867)

Fortunate for all who have an interest in history, the Jesuits kept meticulous journals of their travels and experiences. Jesuit writing provides a historical narrative for their time. Indeed, Jesuit writing particular to the Indigenous people they encountered provides the only cultural anthropologies we have today for the people they encountered and lived with. The Jesuit journals are presented in the many volumes of *Jesuit Relations* for the years 1610 through 1791.

The Jesuits embraced pain and suffering as acceptable, even desirable, as a matter of course in the conversion of *pagans* to Christianity. At the same time, they expected their Native flock would also *'suffer for their own good.'*

After the French began to settle and trade in the St. Lawrence River Region, the killing and suffering associated with Iroquois raiding of Algonquin villages was relentless. The Jesuit missionary view of this violence was that it was the price the Algonquin had to pay for the gift of conversion to Christianity.

Hessel (1993, pgs. 61-62) writes: *"The missionaries were willing to endure the most unspeakable hardships, even torture and agonizing death for the glory of God. They regarded their missions as external, benefiting the pagan Indians; and internal, benefiting their own souls."*

Father Lalemant, Society of Jesus, writes in the Jesuit Relations: *"We shall die, we shall be captured, we shall be burned. Granted: but the bed does not always make the most glorious death."* (JR vol. 30, pg. 251)

In the beginning, the spiritual culture and world view of the European and Indigenous people conflicted and caused unease and social tension. The indigenous people the Jesuits encountered had their own deeply rooted animistic spirituality that embraced religious beliefs, ceremonies, and practices. The

Jesuits did not, at first, accept this reality. If you were not a Christian, how could you have a soul, regardless of what other spirituality you might have.

The Jesuits tried to destroy the ancient spiritual beliefs of those they called pagans. In the beginning, the Jesuits struggled to overcome the skepticism of the Indians; to convince them to adopt ideas of heaven and hell; soul and sin; prayer and penance. These things, all of them, were totally alien to the Natives. Words did not exist in Native languages for biblical terms and the concepts of Christian theology.

Hessel (1993, pg. 62) explains the Jesuit and Native people relationship very well when he writes: *"The Jesuits and other missionaries after them regarded the Algonquin and other tribes as barbarians, savages whose minds were almost completely blank, ready to absorb the teachings of Christianity like dry sponges."*

The Jesuits were tireless in the efforts to become fluent in Native languages. After a time and for the most part, the Jesuits began to be more accepting of the cultures of the Indigenous people they encountered. Perhaps to the extent of becoming, themselves, assimilated into the culture of the people they lived with.

Jesuit missionary Jerome Lalemont wrote: *"a missionary must have penetrated their thoughts, adopted himself to their manner of living and, when necessary, been a barbarian with them."* (Cave. 2004)

The Jesuits, in their teachings to bring converts to Christianity, saw parallels between Catholic catechism and Native animistic spirituality. To their credit, rather than reject differences and rebuke the Natives, some Jesuits did not hesitate to build upon spiritual similarities in their missionary work. Building trust and confidence in this manner, the Jesuit success in winning converts to Christ began to gain momentum.

> *An afternoon in Akwesasne. I recall talking with a young Mohawk woman who had rejected Christianity and returned to the Haudenosaunee spirituality of her ancestors.*
>
> *"You have called the onkwehon:we cannibals because the stories say that we ate parts of warriors captured in raids. We did this in honour of their courage as a warrior and to honor their courage in*

death. We wanted to have some of that warrior's courage as our own. This was our belief.

The Prophet Jesus was condemned and mocked by his own people. He was whipped, beaten, and his head pierced by thorns. Then he was nailed to a wooden cross to die.

In the Catholic belief, during your mass, the bread and wine on the alter is transformed into the body and blood of Jesus Christ. At communion, you eat His flesh and drink His blood. You believe this with all your heart and soul. It is your spirituality. We too have our beliefs that we accept with all of our heart and soul. Are they not similar?"

Between 1632 and 1665, forty-six French Jesuits arrived in New France to 'bring God to the savages.' In 1634, Jesuits, under the direction of Father Jean de Brebeuf, established a mission in Huron-Wendat territory in present-day Simcoe County, Ontario. The mission, called Mission de Sainte-Marie, at present-day Midland, Ontario, thrived and was soon recognized as the 'jewel of the Jesuit missions in New France.' A little more than a decade after being built, the mission was destroyed by the Iroquois raids of 1648 and 1649.

This was a dangerous time for the Jesuit priests at their mission at Sainte-Marie Among the Huron. At various times and places during the period 1642-1649, eight Jesuits were captured, tortured and killed by the Mohawk.

The martyred Jesuits were canonized by the Catholic Church in 1930. The names of the eight Jesuit priests and the year of their death follows: Rene Goupil (1642); Issac Jogues (1646); Jean de Lalonde (1646); Antoine Daniel (1648); Jean de Brebeuf (1649); Noel Chabanel (1649); Charles Garnier (1649); and Gabriel Lalemant (1649). Today we know of these adventuring missionaries as the *North American Martyrs.*

This was a time of war between the Iroquois and Huron-Wendat and brutal hit and run raiding of villages of tribes allied with the Huron-Wendat. Refugees roamed the land looking for safe sanctuary.

The Jesuits provided safe sanctuary by establishing *reductions*. A reduction is a village established by the Jesuits for the protection of the people. Residents of a reduction where under the authority of the Jesuits. The intent of a reduction was to provide a safe refuge on neutral ground. For the most part, this neutrality was observed by the Iroquois. But not always.

The first Jesuit reduction was established at Sillery, now a suburb of present-day Quebec City. In 1645, there were an estimated 167 Native residents at Sillery. In 1646, in spite of the declared neutrality of the settlement, the Iroquois raided the reduction at Sillery. Disaster struck again in 1670, when a measles epidemic spread through the population. Soon after, the Montagnais left the reduction. The Jesuits abandoned Sillery in 1698.

A second reduction was established at Trois Rivieres on the St. Lawrence River between present-day Montreal and Quebec City. Additional reductions at Notre-Dame-de Foy; Lorette; and Prairie de la Madeleine were built adjacent to present-day Quebec City. The expansion of reductions was necessary to provide refuge for the displaced Huron-Wendat, and their allies the Montagnais and Algonquin.

Jesuits priests began visiting Iroquois villages in the 1640's. The priests were persistent and courageous. Theirs was a perilous co-existence with the Iroquois, the Mohawk in particular.

The Iroquois were suspicious of the French, and the Jesuits were French. A particularly perilous time for the Jesuits was when epidemics of European smallpox began to infect villages. In their fear and confusion, the Iroquois would accuse the Jesuits of witchcraft. The accusation carried the risk of being maimed by torture or killed.

The Jesuits persisted. They continued to preach their religion to the Iroquois. Slowly, the priests began to make converts. In 1642, the Mission of St. Marie was established at the Mohawk village of *Teatontaloga*, present-day upper New York State. The mission was wiped out three years later by a smallpox epidemic.

The passionate Jesuits, undeterred by constant threat of torture and death, had managed to gain a foothold among the Iroquois. In 1654-56, they established a mission among the Onondaga. This was a strategic success for the Jesuits. The Confederacy Fire was symbolic of the unifying Great Law of the Iroquois. Protecting the fire had been entrusted to the Onondaga by the Peacemaker. Two years later, Father Rene Menard, built the mission of Etienne for the Cayuga. Separate missions for the Oneida and Seneca followed in 1656.

The Iroquois had their own animistic spirituality. For the Haudenosaunee, inanimate objects and creatures all had a soul - the wind, the rain, the thunder, animals and birds. The Haudenosaunee spirituality embraced monotheism. The Iroquois accepted that the universe was organized and watched over by one supernatural power, the Creator.

The Haudenosaunee celebrated the Creator with a sophisticated and intricate system of spiritual ceremonies that gave thanks to the Creator for all the gifts he bestowed upon the people. It was enormously helpful for the Jesuits that the Iroquois, similar to the Jesuits, believed in one true God, the Creator. Both religions had their holy prophets. The Jesuits brought the teachings of the Prophet Jesus Christ, the Son of God. The Jesuits shared the messages of the Holy Bible. The Iroquois already had their own prophet, Dekanawida. The messages from Dekanawida, given to him by the Creator, were shared in the *Kaianerenko:wa*, the Great Binding Law.

The gradual acceptance of the new religion by the Iroquois was, in a great part, due to the Iroquois Confederacy adoptions of large numbers of converted Huron-Wendat; Tionontati, and Neutral during the 1650s. This helped to open the doors for the Jesuits among the Iroquois Nations. Over the next thirteen years, the Jesuits established missions among all five Nations of the Iroquois Confederacy.

> *I recall an afternoon of discussion with Mohawk elder Ernie Kaientaronkwen Benedict, on his porch in Akwesasne. I had asked about the Catholic Church in St. Regis, the Quebec territory of Akwesasne, and the story I had heard that the St. Regis church was older than the church built at Quebec City. Ernie thought that this was very likely. We each sipped from a cool glass of good well water, and after a time Kaientaronkwen told the story of how the Jesuits came to build their church in Akwesasne. Ernie's story follows.*

"After a time, the Jesuits came and met with the chiefs. The priests asked for permission to build their church in Akwesasne. The chiefs said they would think about it.

After a time, the chiefs called the priests to meet with them. They told the Jesuits that they could build their church with two conditions. The first condition was that the priests must learn to speak the language of the people so that the people would know what they were being told. The second condition was that the first rows of seats in the church would be for the chiefs. In this way, the chiefs would know what was happening between their people and the Jesuits.

The Jesuits agreed. They learned to speak our language. They built their church. The church today is not the same church. It was burnt. But the new church sits on the stone foundation of the first church. There is a Jesuit priest living in St. Regis today as there has always been. This priest speaks fluent Mohawk. If he couldn't, he wouldn't be there."

I had occasion to visit with the Jesuit at St. Regis and we had a long discussion about things historical and things contemporary. His view of the teachings of the Catholic Church and the teachings of the Great Law were that in many ways they were not so different. His summary for me was: " there is only one God and He is the Creator of all things. For the Haudenosaunee, it is the same."

Now, today, there is no longer a Jesuit at the Akwesasne parish. The Parish is shared by two Catholic priests. They are not Jesuit. They are from Africa.

The relationship between the French Jesuits and the Iroquois had always been uneasy. Nagging suspicion over the Jesuits existed among Native villages. Distrust festered because of the Jesuit relationship with the Huron and their allies. This was interpreted to mean the *blackrobes* were duplicitous in their relations with the Iroquois.

With the introduction of European disease epidemics, the Jesuits were seen by some Iroquois as 'witches.' Always considered firm allies of their ancient Huron-Wendat enemies, the Jesuits felt the brutal reprisal of the Iroquois on many occasions.

Chapter 14

Religious tensions among the Iroquois

A fracturing of the Great Binding Law

As the number of Iroquois converts to Christianity increased, friction between converts and followers of the Haudenosaunee ideology began to emerge.

For the Iroquois, the Jesuits appeared to be partisan to French interests. This was a time when the French had agreed to a peace with the western Iroquois - Onondaga, Cayuga, Seneca - but refused to resume trade with them. Instead, the French preferred to trade with the Ottawa. The French, acknowledging the influence the Jesuits had earned with the Iroquois, approached the priests and demanded that they act as mediators.

In 1658, a Jesuit serving as a French ambassador to the Iroquois was murdered. The peace, always fragile between the French and Iroquois, ended. Christian Iroquois allied themselves with the French.

The defection of the Christian Iroquois to the French began a rift within the Iroquois Confederacy. The emerging friction between the Haudenosaunee and the Christian converts would, in time, have incontrovertible consequences for the Confederacy.

Renewed hostilities caused the Haudenosaunee Iroquois to wonder about where the allegiance of the Christian Iroquois lay. Tensions mounted as Haudenosaunee pressure on the Iroquois converts to return to their traditional ways became more intense. Many converts renounced their new religion and returned to the Haudenosaunee. Many more did not. Among the eastern Iroquois, those who refused to renounce their Christian beliefs were forced from their homes. They moved closer to the French and settled in villages along the St. Lawrence River.

The first of these settlements was at La Prairie, a little to the north of Ville Marie. By 1667, the Jesuits had persuaded some Oneida Christians to relocate to the settlement. Christian Mohawk families soon followed. The soil at the settlement proved to be poor and unable to produce crops of corn, beans, and squash sufficient to meet the needs of the growing population. By 1673, the people had begun to relocate to the area of Sault St. Louis at present-day Lachine, Quebec. The new settlement was called Caughnawaga. The Mohawk name Caughnawaga is translated as *praying Indians* which reflects the Christian orientation of the residents. This settlement would later be named Kahnawake, as it is known today.

The majority population of this new settlement were Christian Mohawk. There was a scattering of Huron-Wendat who had moved from Notre-Dame-de Foy. By 1680 there were more Mohawk warriors living at Caughnawaga then there were in the Mohawk homeland.

The Caughnawaga Mohawk had been forced to leave their ancestral homeland over religious differences - the Great Binding Law of the Haudenosaunee versus Christianity. However, the so-called *praying Indians* of Caughnawaga remained steadfast in their observance of the teachings of the Great Binding Law that forbade any of the Five Nations from taking up arms against another member. The Caughnawaga Mohawk population worked hard in their attempts to remain neutral in future wars between the French and the Iroquois Confederacy. But good intentions are sometimes put aside in the heat of events.

Tensions were escalating. In 1689, the Iroquois Confederacy raided the French settlement at La Chute. This was not a local skirmish but a well-planned attack by a large Iroquois force. Now, the Caughnawaga Mohawks were forced to enter the war as French allies.

Caughnawaga Mohawk joined with the French in retaliatory raids against Albany and Schenectady, in present-day New York State. They also participated as guides in French attacks on the Iroquois homeland. Through all of this, and as difficult as it must have been to avoid confrontation where raids and skirmishes could result in Iroquois killing Iroquois, the Caughnawaga Mohawk and Haudenosaunee warriors observed the Great Peace. Even so, war casualties were high. Caughnawaga paid dearly for their support of the French in *King William's War, 1689-1697*. By 1696, half of the Caughnawaga warriors had been killed. The French war with the Iroquois ebbed and flowed until 1701.

The warring parties were exhausted. The Caughnawaga had a meaningful role in negotiating the terms for a cessation of hostilities in 1701. The Haudenosaunee agreed to remain neutral in any future war between England and France. However, no conditions particular to neutrality were placed upon the Caughnawaga.

By the time *Queen Anne's War (1702 - 1713)* had been declared, the Caughnawaga Mohawks had allied with the Abenaki as French allies. War parties raided English settlements in New England. In 1704, Deerfield, present-day Massachusetts, was raided and destroyed with 59 killed, and 109 captured. In 1710, Groton, Massachusetts, was burned to the ground.

Two young boys, John and Zachary Tarbell, along with their sister Sarah, were captured during the Groton raid, and taken to Caughnawaga for ransom. Taking ransom in exchange for prisoners of war was a lucrative and thriving business during the French and English wars. John and Zachary were adopted by an Akwesasne Mohawk family. The boys grew up as Mohawks, married into Mohawk clans, and became community leaders. Later in life, the two men were among the founders of the Akwesasne Mohawk community adjacent to present-day Cornwall, Ontario. Sarah was ransomed by a French family, converted to Catholicism, and entered an order of Catholic Sisters in Montreal. (Demos, 1994, pgs. 196 and 224)

This is only one of hundreds of such stories of capture, adoption, and assimilation into a Nation of the Iroquois confederacy. Indeed, there are stories of women captives who had been adopted and assimilated into an Iroquois family and clan and who refused repatriation when offered. The reality was that

Haudenosaunee women enjoyed more family and community influence and authority, and more freedoms, than European women.

The original Caughnawaga settlement had by now grown so populous that a part of the settlement relocated south, across the St. Lawrence River, to start a second village which became known as Kahnawake. Christian converts, referred to as the *praying Indians,* continued to ally with the French. After 1701, in terms of numbers, there were more Iroquois warriors fighting for the French than for the English.

French and Iroquois relations were deteriorating. The Jesuits decided that it would be prudent to begin to close missions until a time when it would be favorable for their return. During the period 1708 through 1718, all the Iroquois missions were closed. Many of the baptized Iroquois moved to the Jesuit mission at Kahnawake, across the St. Lawrence River from present-day Montreal.

By 1720, the Lake of Two Mountains mission was established and would become the town of Oka. Oka is famous for cheese and the 1990 *Mohawk Crisis*. The Sulpician mission (Society of Priests of Sulpice) was established on lands that were the ancestral lands of the Algonquin. The Sulpician Mission was heavily focused on agriculture.

Nomadic hunters and gatherers, the Algonquin found it difficult to adapt to the staid life of a farmer. They grew increasingly restless. The priests were frustrated with this undependable work force which preferred to be away hunting and fishing rather than tending stock and crops. Gradually, the Mohawk moved to the mission to fill the labour gap left by the truant Algonquin. The Mohawk, with their agrarian culture, were satisfied as members of a farming community. A hard working and reliable people, the Mohawk soon earned the respect of the Sulpician priests. The mission became known as Kanesatake.

In the meantime, new settlements along the St. Lawrence River were established as the population of pro-French Iroquois continued to increase. Sault Recollect, located on the Riviere des Prairies, Montreal Island, was established in 1721. In 1748, Oswegatchie, present-day Prescott, Ontario; and the La Presentation Mission at present-day Ogdensburg, New York State, were settled for the Onondaga, Oneida, and Cayuga. St. Regis, part of the present-day Mohawk

Territory of Akwesasne, began to take Mohawks from the overcrowded conditions at Kahnawake, adjacent to present-day Montreal.

In the east, the Haudenosaunee continued to lose population through migration to Christian settlements in Lower Canada (Quebec).

Estimates for Iroquois population vary. The most reliable Iroquois population estimates are recorded in the journals of the *Jesuit Relations*. The *Jesuit Relations* records have put the Iroquois population at the time of Jesuit arrival in New France to have been 17,000 persons.

At its peak in 1660, the estimated Iroquois population was 25,000 persons. In 1722, the Tuscarora, sponsored by the Oneida, were adopted into the Iroquois Confederacy. This addition of some 1,500 people did not compensate for the loss by migration of 1,000 Susquehannock, Cayuga, and Seneca to Ohio and another 2,000, mostly Christian Mohawks, to Caughnawaga, present-day Kahnawake.

By 1740, as a consequence of war and epidemics, the Iroquois population was estimated to be 14,000 persons. One estimate of Iroquois population in 1774, is from 10,000 to 12,500 persons. In 1911, an estimate established a population of 16,000 Iroquois persons.

Defection by Iroquois converted to Christianity to French settlements in Lower Canada was destabilizing the political influence, military power, and unity of the Iroquois Confederacy.

Chapter 15

The Western Campaign

Shifting Iroquois Fortunes in the Ohio Valley

The French and the English were aware of the erosion of Iroquois military capability. However, the tribes in the Covenant Chain, as disgruntled as some may have been, continued to represent a potentially formidable military coalition.

Decades of war and European disease epidemics had depleted the Iroquois population. The Iroquois had always used adoption as a strategy for replenishing their population.

The massive adoptions of the 1650's may have resulted in the clan populations of the Iroquois becoming a minority within the Confederacy. The Haudenosaunee wanted to ensure the political power of the 'real' Iroquois was protected. Confederacy council chiefs were selected only from the *royaner*, the Haudenosaunee Lords who had their ancestral origins in the original clan system of the Five Nations.

In practice, this system of civil governance ensured that adoptees were excluded from positions of political influence. Doubtless, this two-tier system created a second-class citizenry. This development would have been the source of much dissatisfaction and resentment among the people. Ever mindful of the military power and vengeful will of the 'clan' Iroquois, many dissidents chose to separate themselves from the Confederacy rather than take on the risk of rebellion. And so, in accordance with the Haudenosaunee *philosophy of the corn*, the migration had begun.

Numbers of Iroquois, largely Seneca and Cayuga descendants of the adopted Huron-Wendat, Susquehannock, Neutrals and Erie, began to move to the wilderness Ohio and western Pennsylvania regions in the 1720s. The Ohio Valley Region was a territory the Iroquois claimed by conquest. Land was cleared, crops were sown, and permanent villages were established outside of the ancestral Iroquois homeland. Life was good, there was peace and stability. The population flourished.

By 1730, the British had begun calling the relocated Susquehannock, Cayuga, and Seneca *Mingo*, a corrupted pronunciation of the Algonquin word *Mingwe*. And so, the migration of Iroquois away from their ancestral homeland became known as the *Mingo Migration*.

The migration was a concern to the Iroquois Confederacy. There was little political influence or military threat could do about it. The movement of Iroquoian people had always been recognized as an eventual necessity. For the Haudenosaunee, the movement of people is known as the *philosophy of the corn*. When soil grew infertile after numerous crops, villages and towns moved to new areas with soil having the capacity to provide a sustainable living for the people.

The Iroquois Confederacy saw the migration as something of a strategic development in their favor. With Iroquois settling the Ohio region, a buffer was being established to prevent the French and their Algonquin allies from claiming territory.

The Confederacy did not object when a part of the adopted Wyandot migrated from the present-day Detroit area and settled along the Sandusky River in northwest Ohio. The Iroquois Confederacy seized the opportunity this presented to pull the Wyandot away from the Great Lakes French alliance and bring them into the Covenant Chain agreement. Wyandot statesmen began to speak at Confederacy councils and began to be seen by other tribes in the region as the Iroquois representative for Ohio. Inter-group relations had come a long way from the time of the *Great Pursuit* and the relentless and punishing Iroquois war against the Huron.

By 1740, an estimated 1,000 Mingo settled in western Pennsylvania and eastern Ohio. As long as the Mingo acknowledged the authority of the Iroquois Confederacy, there would be no interference. However, the Mingo had become confident in their new identity and authority. They began to think and act as an independent tribe, outside the influence of the Iroquois Confederacy. The binding ties to the Iroquois Confederacy imposed by Covenant Chain membership was not high on the Mingo list of allegiances.

The inclination for the Iroquois to look after their own interest first and above the interest of other Covenant Chain tribes is demonstrated by the Iroquois support of the *Walking Purchase, 1737*. Pennsylvania had found an old treaty with the Lenape Delaware that was interpreted by the British colonists to have ceded a large area of the remaining Lenape Delaware homeland to the British. The British, through fraud and deceit, enlarged the claim to include most of the remaining Lenape Delaware land. The Lenape Delaware were members of the Covenant Chain. They turned to the Iroquois for help.

The Lenape Delaware request for intervention on their behalf was turned away by the Iroquois. The Iroquois believed the stories that the Lenape Delaware had sold land without Confederacy permission. The Iroquois supported the Colonist claim. The Lenape Delaware persisted but were silenced in 1742. During a meeting with the governor of Pennsylvania, when the Lenape Delaware spokesman *Nutimus* stood to voice complaint, the Iroquois representative *Canasatego* told *Nutimus* the Lenape Delaware were women and ordered the delegation to leave.

The landless Lenape Delaware, along with some Shawnee, had exhausted their avenues for grievance. The Iroquois ordered them to relocate to the upper Susquehanna in north-central Pennsylvania where the Iroquois had established a settlement for Covenant Chain tribes displaced by the spread of British settlement. The Iroquois strategy in giving land to displaced groups was not solely one of generosity to Covenant Chain tribes. They saw this as building a reserve of warriors should war with the French begin again. But the conditions in the Susquehanna villages were growing ever more crowded and the land's resources were growing scarce. Disease flourished and became widespread.

The Shawnee were the first to leave Susquehanna for better opportunities in western Pennsylvania and Ohio. The Mingo did not resist the Shawnee migration and shared their villages with the newcomers. After a time, the Shawnee considered themselves permanent residents and invited the Lenape Delaware to join them. During 1742 and 1749, large numbers of Delaware moved west to live in mixed populations of Mingo, Shawnee and Delaware. This mixed population became known as the Ohio tribes.

The Iroquois did not object to this movement of Covenant Chain people. The settling of the people in western Pennsylvania strengthened the Iroquois claim to the region and weakened the claim of the French and their allies. Soon, the Wyandot invited the Shawnee and Delaware to settle in Ohio. The Mingo, cousin to the Iroquois, had already established a presence in the region. The mixed Mingo, Delaware, Shawnee villages were outside the French alliance and were viewed as republics by the British.

The Iroquois and the British had made a mistake with the Indigenous groups the British had begun to refer to as republics. What the British and Iroquois Confederacy had failed to grasp was that they had lost influence and control over the established 'republic' villages and populations. By 1750, the Shawnee, Delaware and Mingo republics numbered an estimated 10,000 migrants of which some 2,000 were capable warriors.

The republics had become a military asset that had to be included in the power equation for the region. The nation winning the alliance of the 'republics' would gain a significant force multiplier. Such an alliance, in principle at least, could be a game changer for a regional power balance.

The Ohio Region was becoming a contested area. The Iroquois claimed the area by right of their 1650s and 1660s conquest. The French claimed the area by right of discovery. The British claimed the area by right of the *Treaty of Ryswick, 1697*, which, in the British interpretation, had put the Iroquois under British protection.

The *Treaty of Ryswick* was a diplomatic bind for the European powers and the Iroquois Confederacy. The treaty settled none of the issues that provoked conflict among the French, British, and the Iroquois Confederacy. The question of who had jurisdiction over the Iroquois and their territory remained unsettled.

Was it the French or the British? The Iroquois position that the Iroquois Confederacy was an independent sovereign Nation seems to have been misplaced, most certainly conveniently forgotten, by the European powers.

Frontenac, the Governor of New France, and his successor, Louis-Hector de Calliere, worked against including the Iroquois in the British treaty. They wanted the Iroquois, whom they referred to as *unruly French subjects*, to enter a separate treaty with New France. The British argued equally aggressively that the Iroquois had been listed as British subjects in the *Treaty of Ryswick*. The British worked hard to prevent the Iroquois and French from negotiating.

While the Iroquois Confederacy, French, and English were working to find a solution satisfactory to all, the tribes allied with New France continued to attack the Iroquois. In the later part of the 1690s, the Ojibwa led an offensive against the Seneca. The conflict resulted in significant Seneca casualties. Within a year of signing the *Treaty of Ryswick*, the Onondaga suffered more than ninety warriors killed. The Seneca suffered as great a casualty cost as the Onondaga. The Iroquois experienced defeats in 1700 when the Seneca dealt with over fifty deaths in skirmishes with the Ottawa and Illinois. During this time of defeat, the British at Albany strenuously counselled the Iroquois not to strike back. The British pleaded for time to negotiate with the French on behalf of the Iroquois.

By 1700, Iroquois culture and war strategies had arrived at a precipice. Until the period around 1675, warfare had a functional purpose that outweighed its costs. This changed with the onset of the French-English struggle for dominance in North America. The European struggle that pulled tribal alliances into the fray was disastrous for the Iroquois Confederacy. Iroquois forays in the west were intended to secure fur supplies. Instead, western conflict had stopped the supply of furs from reaching Albany. This meant that the Iroquois suffered economic hardship from a lack of fur to trade compounded by the wartime shortages of trade goods available for trade.

Economic hardship was one thing, but the physical toll among all the Five Nations of the Iroquois Confederacy was shocking. Invading armies had destroyed villages and crops throughout Iroquoia. The exception was the Cayuga Nation.

Famine, disease, and causalities of war had greatly altered Iroquois demographics. Colonial records suggest that between 1689 and 1698, half the fighting strength of the Iroquois Confederacy had been lost. Always difficult to establish population census in this period, the estimate is probably less than accurate. However, by 1700, it is believed that as many as 500 of the 2,000 warriors the Iroquois had available in 1689, had been killed, or had deserted to the French missions in Canada. Young warriors were not available to replace veteran warriors. A conservative estimate of Iroquois losses is 1,600 from a total population of more than 8,600 persons.

Iroquois warrior population estimates are really all over the map. The number of Iroquois Confederacy warriors fluctuates depending on the source. In 1685, the warrior population was estimated to be 2,050. The warrior population was believed to be 1,400 in 1691; 1,750 in 1700; and 1,200 by a French cabinet paper issued in 1701. Colonial documents refer to a total population of Iroquois warriors to be 2,550 in 1689. This population had been reduced to 1,230 by 1698. Colonial documents estimate that if a figure of 1,750 warriors is correct, the total Iroquois population in 1700 would be an estimated 7,000 persons.

In terms of military strength, the above estimates are based on the clan population. The clan Iroquois, persons with the birthright of having been born into one of the clans of the Five Nations are described as the 'real' Iroquois of the Five Nations of the Iroquois Confederacy. Given this, the estimate does not include the large number of young men captured in mourning-wars and assimilated into the Iroquois Confederacy as citizens, with all the rights and duties that entailed. The warrior estimate does not include the hundreds of Iroquois warriors who had converted to Christianity and moved to one of the seven settlements scattered along the St. Lawrence River in New France. These largely Christian Iroquois settlements would become known as the Seven Nations, or League of Seven Nations. Also to be considered are the hundreds of warriors who left the ancestral lands of the Iroquois and migrated west to later identify as Mingo. Add to this the warriors of the Covenant Chain tribes who could be called upon to pick up arms for the Iroquois Confederacy.

When the full potential roster of Iroquois warriors is considered, the Iroquois Confederacy represented a very strong and capable military force.

War on Many Fronts
The Continuing Struggle for Alliance and Advantage

This was a time of fractional alignments among the Five Nations of the Iroquois Confederacy.

War weariness and the pressures placed upon the Iroquois Confederacy by the imperial struggle between France and England presented a source of friction. One Iroquois faction sided with the argument that the best way forward was a separate peace with the French. The opponents of this view favored a continued reliance on their alliance with the English. This division among Iroquois cut across lineages, clans, and religion. Social instability brought about by tension of factional alignments was eroding the social unity that was the most important binding aspect of the Iroquois Confederacy. The growing disunity was approaching the unmanageable for the Grand Council of the Iroquois Confederacy.

What the French, British, and Iroquois were slow to recognize was that the real control over present and future trade lay in the western territory and the Ohio region tribes. The French woke up to this new reality and initiated contacts to build an alliance. But the Ohio tribes, anxious not to have a repeat of the tragic experiences of past years, were not about to enter an alliance with the French. Nor, for that matter, did they trust the English or the Iroquois Confederacy.

The French persisted. They offered promises of lucrative trade and protection. Some Shawnee and Cayuga Mingo shifted to the French side. The British were alarmed at these shifts and pressured the Iroquois to order the Shawnee and Delaware to return to the Susquehanna region. The Iroquois Confederacy agreed to the British demand. They sent out ambassadors to demand Shawnee and Delaware acquiescence with the Confederacy command. A shock was in store for the Iroquois delegation. The Shawnee, Delaware, and Mingo told the Iroquois ambassadors to go home. The Ohio tribes weren't going anywhere. The Iroquois Confederacy and their Covenant Chain strategy had begun to show cracks.

Except for the Mohawk, the Iroquois Confederacy remained neutral during *King George's War, 1744 – 1748,* between Britain and France. Winning Iroquois Confederacy neutrality was a near thing for the British. The Iroquois were angry and frustrated with the British, whose colonists in Pennsylvania and Virginia had interpreted the *Treaty of Lancaster, 1744,* as Iroquois cessation of Ohio to the British. What the Iroquois had intended and believed they had accomplished with the *Treaty of Lancaster* was a far cry from the colonist interpretation. The Iroquois intent was to give the British permission to build a trading post at the forks of the Ohio River at present-day Pittsburgh, Pennsylvania State. Nothing more.

The Iroquois Confederacy protested the British treaty interpretation. Pennsylvania and Virginia ignored the protests and both moved forward with their claim of Ohio territory. Pennsylvania's claim was less brazen and extended only into eastern Ohio. Virginia, on the other hand, claimed the entire Ohio River Valley west to the Illinois River. The Virginia claim included Kentucky and lower Michigan. The region under control of the Iroquois Confederacy was rapidly shrinking. So to was the influence of the Confederacy itself.

The western front was tense. The eastern front was at war. Similar to the earlier *Queen Anne's War,* most of the fighting in *King George's War* was conducted in New England and the Canadian Maritimes. During this time the Kahnawake Mohawk remained allies of the French and also allied themselves with the Sokoki and Abenaki. When *Drummer's War, 1722-1726,* broke out between the eastern Abenaki and New England settlers, it was followed by *Grey Lock's War, 1723-1727,* a separate conflict in western New England. The French, aside from supplying weapons to the Abenaki and Sokoki, did not involve themselves in either war. However, the Kahnawake Mohawk joined the Sokoki in their raids against western New England settlements.

Fearful of developments, the British asked the Iroquois Confederacy to intervene. The Confederacy declined, having grown tired of being proxy policeman for the British. Certainly, the Confederacy did not want to fight with the Kahnawake warriors and break the covenant of the Haudenosaunee Great Binding Law. The Confederacy did hold out one olive twig and asked the Abenaki to stop raiding. They also offered to mediate a cessation of hostilities.

There was tension across the region. Twenty years after *Grey-Lock's War,* the Kahnawake warriors - claiming western Vermont as part of their homeland - formed war parties with the Sokoki and Abenaki and began to raid British settlements in Southern Vermont and New Hampshire. Over the next four years, much of the New England frontier was abandoned. In August, 1746, Fort

Massachusetts on the Hoosac River was captured. This led to abandonment of much of the settled territory east of the Hudson River in New York.

The Mohawk continued to fight as allies of the British. In 1747, after a Mohawk raid struck settlers just south of Montreal, the Kahnawake warriors and other groups of New France Iroquois declared war on the British colonies. This war ended with the *Treaty of Aix-la-Chapelle, 1748*.

In the Ohio Valley Region and Great Lakes Region, fighting was sporadic. The pro-French Mingo and Shawnee attacked British traders. The French sent their allies, the Ottawa, Menominee, Winnebago, Illinois, Saulteur, Mississauga Ojibwe, Potawatomi, and Wyandot east to Montreal to defend New France against an expected British attack.

The war became a disaster for the French when the British began a naval blockade of New France in 1745. The blockade was successful in preventing badly needed French trade goods from reaching Quebec. Unable to supply their allies with trade goods, the French tribal alliance crumbled. The British moved quickly, entering the Ohio Valley Region, and began trading with old French allies, the Wyandot and Miami.

These developments favored the English and Iroquois who strived to keep the French out of the Ohio Region and western Pennsylvania. The Iroquois were still rankled by the Shawnee and Delaware refusal of the Iroquois Confederacy demand for them to move back to the Susquehanna region. During the *1744 Treaty of Lancaster,* negotiated by the British with the Iroquois, Shawnee, Delaware and Mingo; Pennsylvania urged the Iroquois Confederacy to restore the Ohio tribes to the Covenant Chain coalition. If this could be done, a strong barrier against the French would be created.

Seeing a barrier to French expansion as advantageous, the Iroquois Confederacy adjusted by creating a system of special Iroquois emissaries to represent the Ohio tribes at the Iroquois Confederacy Grand Council. Still mindful of the need to maintain a Haudenosaunee hereditary clan leadership, the emissaries were called *half-kings*. The emissaries consisted of one Shawnee, and one Delaware. Both *half-kings* were appointed from the Mingo. With this Iroquois concession and adjustment, allegiance to the Covenant Chain was renewed.

In 1749, the French sent Pierre-Joseph Celoron to expel British traders from the Ohio Region and survey the territory for the French. Celoron was met with a hostile receiving party and sent packing. Two years later, Chabert de Joncaire arrived in the region and demanded that British traders be sent out of the Ohio region. The Mingo, calmly asked by what authority the French were claiming Iroquois land. Joncaire was also sent packing. So ended the Joncaire mission along with any French hope for a reversal in fortune.

Chapter 16

The French and Indian War, 1755-1763

New England and the Ohio Valley
Changing Iroquois Alliances

The New England colonies considered the Ohio Valley Region up for grabs. After the *1747 Treaty of Lancaster,* Virginia chartered the Ohio Company to begin settling the lands around present-day Pittsburgh. Pennsylvania had similar plans.

Investors and land speculators came from most of the influential families of Virginia, including Lawrence Washington, the older half-brother of George Washington.

The Iroquois, dismayed but not surprised given their histories, saw the two colonies as thieves fighting over Iroquois land. To add insult to injury, the Iroquois also continued to be peeved about the reduction in gifts given to them by the British after *King George's War*. The French, for their part, knew they were losing Ohio and understood to secure a turn-around in their favor, they needed to take action.

In 1752, Frenchman Charles Langlade, leading a war party of 250 Ottawa and Ojibwe from Mackinac, a Lake Huron island in present-day Michigan, attacked and destroyed a Miami village and the important British trading post at Pickawillany, present-day Piqua, Ohio. After apologizing to the British, the tribes ceased their trade with the British and rejoined the French alliance. To impede British access to the Ohio Region the French and their allies began constructing a series of forts across western Pennsylvania.

However, very little goes exactly as planned in war or peace. The Mingo, Shawnee, and Delaware, shunned the idea of French control and turned to the Iroquois Confederacy. After consideration, the Iroquois Confederacy decided that the French were an immediate threat and allied themselves with the British. The Iroquois signed the *Logstown Treaty, 1752*. The treaty confirmed their earlier cessation of the Ohio Region in the *Lancaster Treaty, 1744*. The Iroquois also granted permission to the British to build a blockhouse at Pittsburgh. Before this fortification was completed, the French attacked, forced the defending force to surrender, and burnt the half-finished structure to the ground.

In December, 1753, Governor Dinwiddie of Virginia, sent young militia Major George Washington to Fort Le Boeuf. Major Washington had orders to demand the French abandon their forts and leave Ohio. The French commander graciously received Major Washington, listened to governor Dinwittie's demands, refused, and sent Major Washington on his way with a warning not to come back.

In May of the following year, Washington was sent west again. This time he had 130 militia soldiers guided by Mingo warriors under half-kings Tanacharisson and Monacatoocha. Washington's commission was to bring about the surrender of Fort Duquesne, located at the forks of the Ohio River.

Washington never arrived at his destination. While marching, the militia skirmished with 50 French soldiers commanded by Joseph Villier de Jumonville. Monsieur Jumonville was killed in a brief, furious engagement. With the furious French in hot pursuit, Washington beat a hasty retreat. Washington decided to ignore the Mingo advice to keep moving until he reached Virginia. He stopped, and invested valuable time, material, and manpower in building Fort Necessity. The Mingo argued with Washington, decided he was a fool, and left him to his fort building. The French, not quite believing their good fortune, surrounded the small, hastily built fort, and forced Washington's surrender. Washington now found himself a prisoner of war. However, after unknowingly signing a confession to murdering Jumonville, who the French were now calling a French ambassador on a mission of peace, Washington was paroled. This incident started the *French and Indian War (1755 - 1763)*.

In May, 1754, the Iroquois Confederacy and representatives of the English colonies met in Albany, New York, to prepare for war with the French. The Iroquois knew they needed English help to defend the Ohio Region from the French. The Iroquois Confederacy had, to their chagrin, apparently ceded the Ohio Region to Pennsylvania. They intended to hold the Wyoming Valley and Susquehanna Valley for the Covenant Chain tribes.

At the Albany meeting, a land speculator used alcohol to get several minor Iroquois emissaries drunk enough that they unknowingly signed an agreement with Connecticut land companies to open the Wyoming and Susquehanna Valleys to settlement. The treaty meeting ended badly. Rather than achieving unity in the war with the French, matters spiralled off in different and deadly directions.

The Iroquois were furious with the British for making a fraudulent treaty. Pennsylvania threatened violence over Connecticut's attempt to claim its territory. The Delaware living on the upper Susquehanna threatened to kill any white man who tried to settle in the Wyoming Valley.

In spite of this dramatic turn of events, there were some successes for the English at the Albany Conference. Representatives from Kahnawake, despite their long history as French allies, attended the conference and agreed, on behalf of the Sokoki and Abenaki, to remain neutral in the coming war. They would be unable to keep this promise.

The French, knowing war was on the horizon, had been busy preparing. They had organized a coalition of predominantly Christian Iroquois living in settlements along the lower St. Lawrence River. The coalition members would become known as the *Seven Nations of New France*. The alliance was also called the *League of Seven Nations*, and the *Seven Fires of Caughnawaga*. The coalition included: the Mohawk of Akwesasne (St. Regis); Kahnawake (Caughnawaga); Mohawk and Anishinaabeg (Algonquin and Nipissing) of Khanesatake;

Abenaki of Odanak and Becancour (now Wolinak); and the Huron of Jeune-Lorette (now Wendake). (McLeod, 1996)

Although the coalition was dominated by Caughnawaga, after the outbreak of war they were often over-ruled in decision making by the pro-French majority. The Caughnawaga were not as active in this war as in past conflicts. However, in 1758, the Onondaga from Oswegatchie attacked the British settlement at German Flats, present-day Herkimer, New York.

The Ohio tribes, after learning about the Iroquois cession of the Ohio region to the British at the Albany Conference, must have been devastated. The Ohio tribes included the group referred to by the English as *Mingo*, a corruption of the Algonquian name *Mingwe*, who had migrated west into the Ohio region. As previously described, this Iroquoian speaking group was made up of primarily Seneca and Cayuga. Later, the Mingo assimilated refugees from the Shawnee, Delaware, Wyandot, and Susquehannock tribes.

In general, the Mingo now saw the British as enemies. They also considered the Iroquois Confederacy to be untrustworthy. A few Mingo remained loyal to the British. Even with a population made up of many Caughnawaga who had moved in with the Mingo in the 1750s, and had a history of loyalty to the French, the Mingo did not formally switch allegiance to the French. The French were having difficulty supplying their chain of forts, and finding allies willing to fight with them against the British. And all the while, British General Edward Braddock was assembling his army.

The policy of the Mingo, Shawnee, and Delaware in Ohio was to maintain a belligerent neutrality with both the French and the English. Braddock was ready. With his assembled army of 2,200 soldiers, militia, and Native allies, Braddock began his march towards Fort Duquesne. The threatened French brought in 600 Native allies from New France. The French defenders with their newly arrived Native allies proved more than adequate to repel the British army. General Braddock, with typical British disdain for his Native allies, refused to use his Native warriors to scout ahead of his army. On a day in July, just south of Fort Duquesne, present-day Pittsburgh, General Braddock marched into an ambush. Braddock and half his command were killed. (Pargellis, 1935, pgs. 253-69)

The colonies were shocked when they learned of the stunning defeat of their army. Shock turned to anger. A Delaware and Shawnee delegation could not have picked a worse time to travel to Philadelphia to protest the Iroquois cession of Ohio. Pennsylvania seized the delegates and hanged them. The Shawnee and Delaware struck back with a vengeance. War parties raided frontier settlers and settlements in Pennsylvania, Maryland, and Virginia. Some of the Delaware on the upper Susquehanna River, pressured by the Iroquois Confederacy not to become involved, did not join the raiding. However, by 1775, they had defied the Iroquois Confederacy and their war parties began raiding. In August, 1756, the Susquehanna Delaware sued for peace. However, rebellious Delaware, Shawnee and Munsee continued their hit and run raids. By the end of 1756, more than 2,500 colonists had been killed. (Waddell et al, 1996)

Loses were mounting for the Colonists. In October, 1758, a peace conference was held with the eastern Delaware at Easton, Pennsylvania. The *Treaty of Easton, 1758*, paid for Delaware lands taken by New Jersey. Pennsylvania renounced all claim to land west of the Appalachian Mountains that had been ceded by the Iroquois Confederacy at Albany in 1754. News of the treaty reached Ohio. In November, English General John Forbes moved to capture Fort Duquesne. With the continued neutrality of the Shawnee and Delaware, the French fort was taken by General Forbes.

The shock waves of Braddock's defeat in 1755, continued to feed acts of reprisal by the British colonists. Bad things happened. A Seneca war party travelling to attack Catawba in the Carolina had been massacred by Virginia militia. This event, coupled with the fraudulent land cessions taken by treaty at the Albany Conference, resulted in many of the western Iroquois - the Seneca, Cayuga, and Onondaga - allying with the French. This was a huge development. For the first time in two centuries, the Iroquois found themselves at war on different sides. At this time, only the Mohawk under Chief Soiengarahta Hendrik and the Oneida remained British allies. This allegiance was due largely to a man named William Johnson who would play a critical role in future events.

Sir William Johnson (1715-1774) was an Irishman who had immigrated to New York in 1734. Johnson established himself as a planter and fur trader in the Mohawk Valley. William Johnson married Molly (Mary) Brant, a Mohawk woman, the sister of Mohawk war chief Joseph Brant. Molly Brant was also known by her clan names *Konwatsi'tsiaienni* and *Degonwadonti*. Molly Brant was an intelligent, educated woman with all the personality traits of a Mohawk warrior. Molly Brant enjoyed great influence among the Iroquois and plantation owners and used her influence to support the work of her husband William Johnson.

William Johnson became known among the Iroquois for his honesty in his dealings with them. He learned the Mohawk language, and with diligent observation and practice, he became proficient with the ritual courtesies of the Iroquois Confederacy councils. The Mohawk called him *Waraghiyaghey*, their word for *big business*. (Hamilton, 1976)

The Mohawk were infuriated by the drunken cession of the Wyoming Valley to Connecticut at the Albany Conference. However, because they trusted Johnson, they agreed to help the New York and New England militias capture the French fort at Crown Point on Lake Champlain. Chief Soiengarahta Hendrik was killed while leading 200 Mohawk warriors into battle.

The Caughnawaga were with the French defenders at the fort. They recognized Mohawk warriors fighting beside the English, and retired from the battle to sit it out. Despite the anger at losing Chief Hendrik, the Mohawk, acknowledging the Caughnawaga warrior presence with the French, also retired from the fighting to leave the French and English to battle it out between them. The Great Binding Law of the Five Nations of the Iroquois prohibiting war between the Confederacy Nations would not be dishonored that day.

Matters between the French in New France and the English of the eastern seaboard colonies had reached a boiling point. Raiding, skirmishes, and sieges of fortifications increased in number and scale. The *Battle of Carillon*, also known as the *Battle of Ticonderoga* was fought on the shore of Lake Champlain on July 8th, 1758. The location of Fort Carillon was strategic in all ways. The fort was a natural point of conflict between French forces moving south from New France and the St. Lawrence River to the Hudson Valley, and the British forces moving north towards New France from Albany, New York. (Chartrand, 2000)

The battle lines consisted of a combined French force of 3,600 regular soldiers, militia and their Native allies, led by General Lois-Joseph de Montcalm and the Chevalier de Levis. The English forces comprised 6,000 regular troops, and 12,000 militia, rangers, and Native allies, and were led by British General James Abercrombie.

General Abercrombie, frontally assaulted the opposing French forces who had dug in and fought from a line of trenches. The English attacked without the benefit of a field artillery barrage to soften up the defenders before musket, bayonet and sword were put to work. The British and their allies ran into a wall of musket fire. The battle was a brief and bloody affair. Indeed, the battle was the bloodiest of the *French and Indian War*. The French suffered 400 casualties while the English forces suffered more than 2,000 casualties. Some estimates put the battle's butcher list at more than 3,000 casualties all told. (Anderson, 2000. Chartrand, 2000)

Examining how the battle unfolded, American historian Lawrence Henry Gipson wrote of General Abercrombie's campaign: *"No military campaign was ever launched on American soil that involved a greater number of errors of judgement on the part of those in positions of responsibility".* (Gipson, 1965, pg. 232)

A year later, with the French in retreat towards the St. Lawrence River Region to defend Montreal and Quebec from the growing English threat of invasion, Fort Carillon was captured by the British and renamed Fort Ticonderoga.

The British campaign to defeat the French and win control of the Great Lakes and Ohio Regions moved forward. The Mohawk fought as allies of the British at the *Battle of Fort Niagara*. After a twenty-day siege, the fort was captured on July 26, 1759. The capture of Fort Niagara by the British occurred on the same day that French forces had begun their retreat from Fort Carillon. Fort Niagara was a major French military post and supply depot servicing the Ohio Valley Region. Strategically placed between Lake Ontario and Lake Erie, the fort was well designed and supplied.

The defending French forces consisted of 200 French regular soldiers, 20 artillerymen, and about 300 provincial troops and militia with a few Iroquois allies. The British forces were much larger. Brigadier General John Prideaux led the expedition, which also included Sir William Johnson, the British agent who led an allied force of approximately 600 Iroquois.

When the British arrived to begin their siege, the approximately 100 Iroquois allied with the French decided that they would not break the covenant of the Great Binding Law of the Iroquois Confederacy by fighting against their Iroquois brothers. They left the fort.

The French commander, Captain Pierre Pouchot, conducted a vigorous defence of the fort. The British commander, Brigadier General John Prideaux, was killed by shrapnel from one of his own artillery pieces. Command now fell to Sir William Johnson. Johnson was not in the regular army. He was a provincial officer who, as commander of the Iroquois warriors, held a royal commission as Colonel. Similar to present times, the regular army officers questioned a militia officer's right to command His Majesty's forces in a war campaign. But Johnson was a bulldog, and even after a lower ranking regular army officer, Lieutenant Colonel Frederick Haldimand, arrived at the battle, Johnson kept his role as campaign commander. (Dunnigan, 1996)

The French surrendered the fort to Colonel Johnson on July 26, after a relief force was defeated at the *Battle of La Belle-Famille*, two miles distant from Fort Niagara.

The *Battle of La Belle -Famille* was a short vicious engagement involving a column of 800 regular French troops and militia, and 500 Native allies led by Captain Francois-Marie Le Marchand de Lignery. Lignery had been unsuccessful in his attempt to recruit an estimated 1,000 Iroquois to his cause. The British force of 350 regular army troops, 100 New York militia, and 450 Iroquois, was led by Lieutenant Colonel Massey. Massey set up a blockade across the road the approaching French troops were marching on, and using flanking tactics, raked the French with volleys of musket fire followed up with the bayonet. The French will to continue the fight collapsed. The retreating French were pursued back along the road for some five miles. French causalities were high. Captain Lignery was killed. Lieutenant Colonel Massey was wounded. (ibid, 1996)

The Iroquois, caught in a bad place as allies of both the French and the English, were ever mindful of the Great Binding Law that cemented the unity of Iroquois Confederacy. Before the action, Iroquois allied with the British got word to their brother Iroquois who were allied with the French, that they did not intend to fight in the coming battle. They asked their brothers to do the same. Many of the Iroquois who had allied with either the French or the British, walked away from the coming battle.

Now, the British began to concentrate their planning and forces on the final French strong points of Montreal and Quebec City.

On the night of Sept 12 and throughout the pre-dawn hours of Sept 13, 1759, British soldiers under General James Wolfe (1727-59) ascended the cliffs fronting the City of Quebec. By first light, General Wolfe had his forces arrayed, in proper British regimental fashion, on the Plains of Abraham. The French garrisons were taken by surprise. As the sun rose, French sentries were greeted with ranks of British soldiers on their front lawn.

The French forces were commanded by experienced General Louis-Joseph de Montcalm (1712-59). The battle commenced and lasted less than an hour. General Montcalm was killed on the field. General Wolfe was sorely wounded and died the following day. (Mathieu, 1992. Wood, 1911. Toporoski, 1998)

The French settlement at Montreal surrendered to British forces the following year. With the English capture of Quebec and the surrender of Montreal, the war in North America was over. The French in North America were defeated. French imperial ambitions for a New World empire were frustrated.

In Europe, the war between France and England was known as the *Seven Years War (1756-1763)*. The people of New France and New England thought of the war as the *French and Indian Wars*. These years of conflict were the first global war of our time. And now it was finished.

The beginning of this epic war had its start with the French expansion into the Ohio River Valley. This initiative brought France into armed conflict with the British colonies and their Native allies. This had been a war fought by all the major European powers of the time, and in theatres of a world-wide scope.

The ending of war was formalized with the signing of the *Treaty of Hubertusburg* and the *Treaty of Paris* in February, 1763. By way of the *Treaty of Paris*, France lost all claims to her lands known as New France. The treaty gave French Louisiana to the Spanish, while Great Britain took Spanish Florida. The regions of the Lower Great Lakes and the St. Lawrence River Valley along with various other French overseas holdings were also secured by the British. The *Treaty of*

Paris gave Great Britain colonial and maritime supremacy and strengthened the thirteen American colonies by removing their French rivals to the north and to the south. (Marston, 2002. Galloway, 2006)

Fifteen years later, festering French anger and frustration over the loss of most of their colonial empire provided some New France French a reason to intervene on the side of the patriots in the *American Revolutionary War, 1775-1783.*

The English Period, 1763-1783

Chapter 17

The English Period, 1763-1783
Unravelling of the Iroquois Empire

The Iroquois Confederacy was being squeezed on all sides by the seemingly endless arrival of land hungry Europeans. The Iroquois must have recognized that they were now in a position growing more untenable by the year.

The Five Nations Council of the Iroquois Confederacy was battered by the demands for intervention by the Covenant Chain tribes. The hereditary royaner must have been confused and disheartened by the refusal of Covenant Chain tribes, including some Iroquois factions, to obey the commands of the Council of the Iroquois Confederacy.

The Five Nation hereditary royaner were keenly aware that they would be sorely challenged to hold unto what was left of Iroquois Confederacy power and influence in rapidly changing times.

> *This story was given to me by Mohawk Elder Ernie Kaientaronkwen Benedict, one of the last of the Rotinonkwisere Long Hair Chiefs of Akwesasne.*

In sharing this story with me, my friend Karientaronkwen gave permission for it to be shared with others. And so now I will.

This is what I remember:

"A long time ago when your ancestors came to this land, they asked to sit with us on our log bench. We moved a bit and made room. We were comfortable with one another. We honored the Two Row Wampum and respected each other as sovereign nations. We paddled our canoes on the same waters, side by side, without interference.

After a time, another of your ancestors asked to sit on our bench. We moved to make room.

Over time, others joined us and asked for a place to sit. Finally, there was no more room on the bench.

If we moved again to make more room for the newcomers, we would fall off our bench and sit on the ground.

So, we stood to make room.

And then we walked away.

Niawen'ko:wa "

Sometimes, at a serious gathering, a young person in the audience would be angered about what had happened to the Iroquois in the years since the arrival of Europeans. The person would stand, sometimes fumble with their words, express anger, pause in silence, and show quiet grief. There would be a silence among the people while these things were contemplated.

On another occasion, Haudenosaunee Elder Tom Sakokwenionkwas Porter shared a little humour with a historical anecdote.

" You know, the Seneca, our elder brothers, keepers of the western gate to our Confederacy, are not happy with their Mohawk younger brothers who are the keepers of the eastern gate. Our younger

brothers were too lenient with the immigration policy of the Iroquois Confederacy. They were too nice. They let in too many Europeans."

If people were in a good mood, a Mohawk was sure to fire off a final remark.

"Yes, we Mohawk, as keepers of the eastern gate, are nice people. We should have told those Europeans that we didn't mind them coming, but we preferred they make reservations first."

And so, it still goes on today. What else can you do. Grieving lost empire never brings it back.

Pontiac's Rebellion, 1763-1766

After the French capitulation at Montreal and Quebec, and the ensuing *Treaty of Paris, 1763,* surrenders of French territory to the English, matters concerning the spread of European settlers and the subjugation and dispersal of Native tribes escalated.

British garrisons occupying the surrendered French forts in the Ohio Valley stayed on as an occupying army. Fort Duquesne was rebuilt and renamed Fort Pitt. The fort was garrisoned with two hundred soldiers. The newly appointed British Indian Agent, Sir William Johnson, recommended that the French practice of maintaining good relations with the region's tribes through trade and an annual gifting of presents to tribal leaders be continued by the British. However, in keeping with the British tradition of holding their Native allies in disdain, such was not to be. (Pound,1930)

The new British commander, Lord Jeffrey Amherst, despised 'Indians' - whether allies or not. In 1760, Amherst brought an end to the annual gift presentation to tribal leaders; increased the price of trade goods; and restricted the supply of rum, firearms, powder and ball. The Natives were infuriated. By 1761, the Seneca were calling for an uprising against the British. Only the Shawnee and Delaware showed support for the Seneca call to arms.

Sir William Johnson learned of the Seneca plan from a Wyandot delegation during a meeting at Detroit with tribes from the now defunct French alliance. Other calls to arms were sent out by the Caughnawaga and the Illinois. It would take the religious movement of Neolin, the Delaware prophet, to establish the unity needed for a general tribal uprising.

Neolin encouraged rejection of the white man's trade goods, especially rum and whiskey. He promoted a return to traditional tribal ways. Chief Pontiac, an experienced and respected leader of the powerful Ottawa, and an old ally of the French, used this opportunity to begin to bring substance to the plans for an uprising. During this time the Delaware, Shawnee and Mingo warriors also raided along the Pennsylvania frontier and killed more than 600 colonists.

Chief Pontiac wanted the task of capturing Fort Detroit for himself. Pontiac's strategy for taking the fort was based entirely on a surprise attack. The rebellion started on May 7, 1763, when Pontiac and 300 warriors attacked Fort Detroit.

Had the fort commander, Major Henry Gladwin, not been forewarned of the pending attack, the attack would have caught the British completely off-guard. Gladwin, with the short notice he had received, was able to beat back Pontiac's attack.

During May, Pontiac, with more than 900 warriors from a half-dozen tribes, laid siege to Fort Detroit. As word spread of Pontiac's rebellion, warriors began to attack British forts and English settlements throughout the region. At its peak, the rebellion had captured nine of the eleven British forts west of the Appalachian Mountains. In July, 1763, Pontiac overwhelmed a British force at the *Battle of Bloody Run* but was unable to capture their fort.

The British forts not captured by Pontiac's forces in the initial attacks continued to hold. The secured British forts served as a rallying point and allowed the British to plan their response to the insurgency. The British, their balance restored, began to counter attack and the rebellion began to falter. The short-lived rebellion was now doomed to failure. (Peckham,1947)

Weakened by desertion, Pontiac had lifted the siege of Fort Detroit in October. He retreated west to Illinois where he had sympathizers among the Kickapoo and Illinois. Pontiac began to recruit and motivate warriors for another campaign. He approached the French at Fort de Chartres, on the Mississippi River, for help. The commandant of the fort refused to give aid and tried to convince Pontiac to cease his revolt.

During Pontiac's rebellion, the exhausted Iroquois kept the peace and healed their war wounds. The Iroquois Confederacy preferred to remain neutral. However, the Seneca, not wanting to be a bystander, attacked Fort Niagara on Lake Ontario, present-day Youngstown, New York State. The Seneca ambushed a British relief column trying to reach the fort, and the vicious fighting included a Seneca massacre of prisoners and wounded soldiers. Fort Niagara held. A combined force of Mingo and Wyandot captured Fort Venango in northwest Pennsylvania. (Dunnigan, 1996)

However, the siege by the Delaware, Shawnee, and Mingo of Fort Pitt, present-day Pittsburgh, Pennsylvania, dragged on. The British desperately wanted to break the siege. They turned to germ warfare. The British managed to get smallpox infected blankets among the opposing forces. A smallpox epidemic broke out. In spite of sickness, the warriors somehow kept Fort Pitt locked up. The siege of Fort Pitt was finally broken in August, 1763, after Colonel Henry Bouquet, in a three-day battle at Bushy Run, broke through the forces arrayed outside the fort. The Delaware, Mingo, and Shawnee, having had enough of the static nature of siege warfare, began to leave. (Fenn, 2000)

In November, Lord Jeffrey Amherst was replaced by Thomas Gage. Gage was a willing supporter of Sir William Johnson's position of resuming the French practice of generous and fair trade with Natives and gift giving to tribal leaders. Gage soon restored the availability of trade goods to the rebellious tribes in generous quantity, at reduced prices. Relations began to improve.

The Pontiac revolt had been entirely unexpected. The revolt proved to be a defining shock for the British. The British brought forward the *Royal Proclamation of 1763*. The Proclamation stopped all new settlement west of the Appalachian Mountains. The Seneca had ended their siege of Fort Niagara after signing a surrender.

Pontiac was disgraced when he signed a peace in 1765. In 1766 Pontiac moved to Illinois, never to return to his ancestral lands in the Detroit region. In 1769,

Pontiac was murdered by a Peoria (Illinois) during a visit to the Illinois village of Cahokia. (Middleton, 2007)

Sir William Johnson survived the Pontiac rebellion and became the official responsible for British Indian policy in North America. Johnson had not lost his influence among the Iroquois Confederacy councils. Indeed, his influence was so great among the Mohawk that some would say the Mohawk were his private army. (O'Toole, 2005)

Johnson encouraged the Mohawk to attack the Delaware in reprisal for their support of Chief Pontiac. In 1763, the Mohawk attacked and destroyed the Delaware village of Kanhanghton. By the end of the rebellion, most of the Delaware in the Susquehanna Valley had moved west to Ohio.

The Covenant Chain is Broken

Settlement of the Ohio Valley and failure of the Iroquois Confederacy

The westward movement of frontier settlement, greed driven land speculation, and escalating conflict with Natives threatened by relentless encroachment of white settlers on ancestral lands, was turning a vast wilderness region into a battlefield.

Settlers from Connecticut, seizing on the advantage presented by the treacherous 'drunken' treaty signed by the Iroquois at Albany in 1754, began to pour into the Ohio Valley Region. In 1768, white settlers began to kill white settlers over land claims in the vicious skirmishes between Connecticut and Pennsylvania frontier militias. With the whites fighting among themselves, this was no place for 'Indians'.

The Covenant Chain tribes of Nanticoke; Saponi; Tutelo; Munsee; Delaware, and a few Iroquois left the Wyoming Valley in Pennsylvania to begin their trek to the crowded and shrinking Iroquois homeland is eastern New York State.

The *Pontiac Rebellion* had consequences across a broad region. On the eastern front, with the French rendered powerless by their defeat at Quebec City, the

Caughnawaga lands along the lower St. Lawrence River were being overrun by settlers.

During the *French and Indian War,* Roger's Rangers, a group of British militia, had attacked and destroyed the Sokoki village at St. Francois in 1759. The Sokoki had been given refuge by the Caughnawaga. By 1763, white settlement had seized a great part of the Sokoki and Caughnawaga lands along the shores of Lake Champlain.

The Caughnawaga had ample reason to ally with the 1763 *Pontiac Rebellion.* However, they remained neutral and became advocates for peace. If they thought that their neutrality and advocacy would earn favor, they were wrong. Sir William Johnson supported a few of the Caughnawaga claims to the upper Champlain Valley. However, Johnson's interpretation of the *Royal Proclamation of 1763* did not apply to the lands claimed by the Sokoki in Vermont and New Hampshire.

Johnson was aware of the huge resentment the *Royal Proclamation of 1763* had caused among the English settlers. Indeed, the anger the Proclamation stoked among the colonists is one of the major factors that brought about the *American Revolution.* Settlers ignored the Proclamation and continued to push west. Vast stands of old growth forest were felled. Forests were slash cut and burned to clear land for planting. All of this on lands the *1763 Royal Proclamation* protected for the Natives.

The British were in an awkward situation. They were fully aware of resentment in the colonies, and also the fact that waves of settlers continued to encroach upon Native lands in clear contravention of the *Royal Proclamation*. To avoid fomenting a colonial rebellion, the British rescinded the *Royal Proclamation* in 1768. The next move would be negotiation of a new treaty with the Iroquois to address the Ohio claims.

Sir William Johnson was tasked with managing the Ohio negotiations for the British. Johnson, with his knowledge of the workings of the Iroquois Confederacy Grand Council, invited only representatives of the Haudenosaunee to attend. The French, no longer a regional military or political power, and their Caughnawaga Iroquois allies were excluded.

The Iroquois Confederacy had lost some its influence and advantage. With the flood of settlers encroaching on their lands, the Iroquois could see where things were headed. They were at a real disadvantage in terms of any hope of stopping settlement. Johnson, a land speculator himself, met with little opposition when he convinced the Haudenosaunee that it was in their best interest to give up their claim to the Ohio. In exchange, the Iroquois would get a clear metes and bounds description of the boundaries for their remaining lands. And so, it came to be.

Treaty of Fort Stanwix, 1768

The *Treaty of Fort Stanwix*, was signed in 1768 at Fort Stanwix, present-day Rome, New York State. The treaty saw the Haudenosaunee cede to Great Britain a good part of western Pennsylvania and the entire Ohio Valley Region.

The treaty was self serving on the part of both signatory partners. Neither party had control over the groups they represented, the British for the Americans and the Iroquois for the Covenant Chain Ohio tribes. The land deal contained in the *Treaty of Fort Stanwix* was the match that lit the fire for various wars over the next fifty years. In the end, the conflict had cost more than 30,000 lives. (Marshall, 1967)

The treaty was negotiated by Sir William Johnson on behalf of Great Britain, and Haudenosaunee representatives of the Iroquois Confederacy. The treaty objective was to adjust the boundary line dividing 'Indian' lands and British settlements that had been defined in the *Royal Proclamation of 1763*.

Great Britain wanted a treaty agreement that set out a boundary that could be enforced in order to end the growing violence between Natives and frontiersmen. The affected Native groups held the hope that a clearly defined boundary would stop British colonial expansion. (Billington, 1944)

Sir William Johnson was supported by colonial representatives from New Jersey, Virginia, and Pennsylvania. The Iroquois representatives received gifts and cash in the impressive amount of 10,460 pounds sterling, present-day US $15,173.00. This treaty payment would be the highest ever made by the New England colonists to an Indigenous tribe.

The treaty established a boundary line that ran from Fort Pitt and followed the Ohio River as far as the Tennessee River. The treaty ceded the Kentucky portion of the colony of Virginia to Great Britain along with most of the land known today as West Virginia. (Marshall, 1967).

During the negotiation proceedings, the British learned that the Iroquois Confederacy continued to defend a claim over much of Kentucky. The Shawnee, contesting colonial Virginia settlements between the Alleghenies and Ohio, did not agree to the treaty terms. Although consensual agreement was difficult to secure, it would come with the *Treaty of Camp Charlotte, 1774*.

The Iroquois Confederacy had earlier recognized the British settlement rights southeast of the Ohio River at the *Treaty of Logstown, 1752*. However, the Haudenosaunee did not relinquish their claim of ownership by conquest of all the land as far south as the Tennessee River. The Iroquois considered this territory a reserve for hunting and trapping. The Iroquois maintained their position that the Tennessee River was their boundary with the Cherokee and other southern tribes.

Representation from the tribes who occupied these lands, mostly Shawnee and Lenape Delaware, were present during the treaty negotiations at Fort Stanwix. However, they were not included as signatories. Accordingly, representatives of the attending tribes were excluded from any role in the treaty negotiation. They could do little but watch as the Iroquois Confederacy relinquished their homeland to the British. The Iroquois strategy revolved around the belief that by ceding the Ohio lands, pressure would be taken off their own ancestral homeland territories in Pennsylvania and upper New York State. (Taylor, 2006)

For the Iroquois, the *Treaty of Fort Stanwix* destroyed their credibility as representatives of the Ohio tribes. The treaty decision also allowed many Iroquois to believe that the Iroquois Confederacy Grand Council could no longer make responsible decisions. For the Iroquois, this was a time of confusion and grief.

The Shawnee protests to the Haudenosaunee were greeted with the threat that if they opposed the agreement the Shawnee would be wiped out. Shocked, the Shawnee turned to other affected tribes and formed the *Western Alliance*. The Shawnee brought tribal representatives together to meet at Shawnee villages along the Sciota River in Ohio. Members of the western Alliance included: Shawnee,

Illinois, Kickapoo, Wea, Piankashaw, Miami, Potawatomi, Wyandot, Ottawa, Delaware, Mascouten, Ojibwe, Cherokee and Chickasaw.

Sir William Johnson was also busy. Fearful of consequences if the alliance was able to become an organized, well led coalition, Johnson used threats of war with the Iroquois Confederacy to intervene. Johnson succeeded in delaying the formation of the Western Alliance. When the Western Alliance failed to coalesce, the option for affected tribes to express coordinated violent defiance evaporated.

With no barriers and minimal threat to oppose them, frontiersmen and land speculators streamed across the Appalachian Mountains into the Ohio lands. By 1774, the estimated population of whites in the Ohio region was 50,000, with more coming every year. The British began to close their forts and withdraw their garrisons, saying their retreat was an 'economy measure.'

Lord Dunmore's War, 1774

The inflammatory state of frontier affairs brought about *Lord Dunmore's War* in 1774. The war was essentially a conflict between the Colony of Virginia and the Shawnee and Mingo people.

At first, much of the new colonial settlement was situated along the Ohio River between Pittsburgh and Wheeling, West Virginia. The Shawnee, Delaware, and Mingo were now isolated. They tried to manage their affairs as non-confrontationally as they could with the Virginia and Pennsylvania frontiersmen. However, tension was building. Things got worse after treaties signed with the Cherokee opened up settlement in Kentucky. The Shawnee skirmished with Virginian survey teams sent to the region in 1773. In 1774, the Virginia militia moved into abandoned Fort Pitt. The fort would be used as a fortified command and supply center in the event of war.

There was skirmishing the following spring. Believing that war had started with the Shawnee, Michael Cresap and a group of vigilantes attacked a Shawnee trading party near Wheeling, Virginia. A Shawnee chief was killed. The next month, a group of frontiersmen attacked and massacred a band of Mingo at Yellow Creek, modern-day Stuebenville, Ohio. The attack killed the wife, brother, and sister of Logan, a Mingo war chief.

Chief Cornplanter, an experienced and respected Shawnee leader, visited Fort Pitt. Cornplanter's intention was to avoid more bloodshed. He asked the Virginians to 'cover the dead'. In the meantime, a grieving and furious Logan approached the Shawnee and Mingo village of Wakatomica and formed a war party.

Logan took his revenge by killing 13 settlers near the mouth of the Muskingum River. In June, 1774, the war known as *Lord Dunmore's War*, or *Cresap's War*, began. By July, Chief Logan assured the colonists that the fighting was finished. By then the settlers had gathered in the region's forts to await help. Lord Dunmore turned away from Iroquois and Delaware offers to negotiate a peace. Instead, he ordered an army of American militia to the Ohio Region. (Randall, 1902. Skidmore et al, 2002)

The Iroquois and most of the Delaware elected to remain neutral. The Detroit tribes were sent a wampum war belt by the Shawnee and their Mingo allies. The call to war was rejected. Sir William Johnson, still hard at work playing both sides, kept the Miami and other possible allies from declaring war by using the threat of Iroquois Confederacy involvement if they took up arms as allies of the Shawnee. By now Dunmore's militia army had destroyed Wakatomica and five other Shawnee and Mingo villages.

By October, Lord Dunmore had gathered his forces at Point Pleasant, present-day west Virginia, in preparation for a second campaign. As preparations were being made, the Shawnee and Mingo attacked. The battle lasted most of a day and there were heavy casualties on both sides. The Shawnee and Mingo withdrew from the fight. A month later, they agreed to surrender all their land claims south of the Ohio River.

Kentucky was now opened for settlement. The first Kentucky settlements were established at Harrodsville and Boonesborough.

The *American Revolutionary War* had begun.

Chapter 18

The Beginning of the End of the Iroquois Empire

The Iroquois Confederacy – From Princes of Empire to Refugee; the Council Fire of the Iroquois Confederacy is extinguished.

The *American Revolutionary War (1775-1783)* began with fighting at Lexington and Concord in Massachusetts.

A largely overlooked campaign of the *American Revolutionary War* involves the capture of the British Province of Quebec; the occupation of Montreal; and the siege of Quebec City by the American Continental Army.

The leadership of the rebellious American colonies believed that the predominantly French Catholic Canadian population of the Province of Quebec would ally with the Americans against British rule. The Americans also believed the Christian Mohawk in the Seven Nation settlements along the St. Lawrence River would ally with their rebellious cause against Britain. For the most part, this was a miscalculation on the part of the Americans. The Americans did not have a full appreciation for the sympathies of the Province of Quebec Canadians among whom they had hoped to foment discord and rebellion against the British.

The British had won control of the Province of Quebec in the *French and Indian War, 1760*. British governance had stirred animosity between the local French Catholics and Protestant English speaking British military and civilian administrators. However, the *Quebec Act, 1774*, condemned by the rebellious American colonies, had restored land and civil rights to the French Canadians. Administration of the Province of Quebec by the British did not impose upon the influence of the Catholic Church. The French Canadians, encouraged by their priests, decided not to ally with the Americans in their campaign of conquest and occupation. (Black, 2009)

The Continental Army's invasion of the Province of Quebec began in September of 1775. Montreal was captured on November 13, 1775. The invading army was under the command of Major General Philip Schuyler. Later, command of the occupying American force would be taken over by Brigadier General Richard Montgomery. (Smith, 1907)

Major General Philip Schuyler stated the goal of the Continental Army was to *"drive away, if possible, the troops of Great Britain that under orders of a despotic ministry aim to subject their fellow citizens and brethren to the yoke of a hard slavery."* (ibid, 1907)

At Fort Niagara, Loyalist Captain John Butler had worked hard to recruit Iroquois support for the British in their pending push against the Americans in the province of Quebec. Butler used liquor and stories of glorious combat in an attempt to break the Iroquois promise of neutrality in the war between Britain and the American rebels. Butler may have recruited as many as fifty Seneca, Cayuga, and Onondaga to the British cause.

British Indian agent Claude de Lorimier of Montreal, succeeded in recruiting an estimated 204 warriors from the Seven Nations communities of Akwesasne and Oswegatchie, present-day Prescott, Ontario. The warriors would have been predominantly Mohawk. In May of 1776, a British force composed of regular troops, militia, and Iroquois allies skirmished with Continental Army units in and around an area known as The Cedars. The Cedars was about 45 km (28 mi) west of Montreal.

Brigadier General Benedict Arnold was the commanding officer of the Continental Army units occupying Montreal. On May 19, 1775, the Continental

Army garrison posted at The Cedars surrendered to a combined force of British troops and Iroquois led by Captain George Forster, British Army. On May 20, American reinforcements on their way to The Cedars from Montreal were intercepted and captured after a brief skirmish.

Matters were particularly messy for Captain Forster after the Battle of The Cedars. Charles Carrol, a member of an American Congressional delegation in Montreal at the time of the battle, wrote in his dispatches that *"a hundred or more Americans were barbarously murdered by savages."* (Kingsford, 1893)

Evidence of grievous barbarous treatment of American prisoners by the Iroquois is dubious, to say the least. General Arnold's report refers to unsubstantiated allegations that two American prisoners were killed by the Iroquois. Other accounts of the battle, such as the 1882 history written by Charles Jones, suggest that atrocities were committed by Forster's Iroquois allies. There is insufficient evidence to suggest that Iroquois atrocities against American prisoners occurred.

The 1775 *Battle of The Cedars* was the first defeat experienced by the Continental Army in the *American Revolutionary War*.

Negotiations between Captain Forster and General Arnold secured the release of all the captured Americans with the promise from General Arnold that an equal number of British prisoners would be released. The American Congress was not pleased with General Arnold's agreement. The agreement to release British prisoners was retracted by order of the American Congress.

Relations between the Americans occupying Montreal and the population was unravelling. For the most part, for economic reasons, Montreal citizens were less than supportive of the occupying force of Americans. Believing trade goods would be used to support British garrisons, the Americans had embargoed the prosperous Canadian trade with various Indigenous fur trading partners of the upper St. Lawrence River and Great Lakes Region. The fur trade was a mainstay of the livelihood and prosperity of Montreal. The embargo was a stress point among both the supporters and opponents of the American occupation. In terms of whether to support or agitate, realpolitik was a deciding factor.

Although suffering defeat from the effective British resistance at the *Battle of The Cedars*, General Benedict Arnold refused to retreat. He began the siege of Quebec City.

The American siege of Quebec was a brutal affair for the Americans. The Continental Army soldiers had scarce provisions to support itself and were ill equipped to live in hastily built military camps during the harsh Quebec winter.

Sir Guy Carleton, British Governor of the Province of Quebec, realizing the potential of weakening the American siege, condoned the practice of releasing smallpox infected civilians from the besieged city. This strategy had an impact on the Americans. Smallpox took a heavy toll of General Arnold's soldiers.

Governor Carleton, with a manpower advantage on his side, refused to leave the city to attack the American camp. Carleton had served under British General James Wolf during the 1759 siege of Quebec, and knew that French General Louis-Joseph de Montcalm had paid dearly for leaving the defences of Quebec City and engaging the British in the *Battle of the Plains of Abraham* where Montcalm was defeated and killed. (Smith, 1907)

On May 6, 1776, a British fleet, the vanguard of a much larger relief fleet, arrived at Quebec City with reinforcements and provisions. The Americans realized the siege was impossible to sustain. In a state of disorganization, they began to pack up their camp in preparation for retreat. Governor Sir Guy Carleton, choosing his moment, left the city and attacked the Americans. The Americans, suffering the ravages of smallpox and the debilitating results of a long winter camp, were routed. The American retreat did not stop until the Continental Army reached Fort Ticonderoga on Lake Champlain. (Fraser, 1907)

By late summer of 1776, the American Continental Army had been driven from the Province of Quebec.

The Western Campaign

The *Quebec Act of 1774* had made the Ohio Valley Region and Great Lakes Region a part of British Canada. This territory concession had brought Pennsylvania and Virginia to the brink of revolution. The straining and snapping dogs of rebellion were finally being let lose.

The British had been a bystander in the wars of colonial westward expansion. With the outbreak of war between the rebellious colonies and Great Britain, Britain embarked on a strategy to incite the Shawnee and Mingo into renewing their attacks on the American rebels.

Many tribes decided that remaining neutral would be best for them. However, the British worked hard to spread fear that the Americans were on the march to take over tribal land. The British agent provocateurs convinced the Detroit tribes, and the Potawatomi and Ojibwe, to ally themselves with Britain against the Americans. The alliance was strengthened when war factions of the Shawnee and Cherokee (Chickamauga) joined. In July, 1776, the Chickamauga attacked two forts in the Carolinas. The Americans were furious. They retaliated against all Cherokee, peaceful or not, it did not matter to the Americans bent on retaliation. On the Kentucky front, Shawnee and Chickamauga war parties were busy attacking Americans.

Meanwhile, the relentless crusader Sir William Johnson, using his fiery oration to incite the Mohawk to fight the Americans, suffered a stroke and died several days later. Johnson's duties as Britain's Indian Commissioner passed to his son-in-law, Guy Johnson. Sir William Johnson's personal wealth - a 100,000-acre estate - was willed to his son, John. Both John and Guy Johnson were loyalists. Neither had the influence with the Mohawk that Sir William Johnson had earned. However, what they did have was the support of Sir William's good friend, the charismatic Mohawk leader Joseph Thayendanega Brant (1743-1807).

With the start of the American Revolution, both the Americans and the British worked to gain the allegiance of the Iroquois Confederacy. The Iroquois Confederacy recognized the new United States, but, after listening to both the Americans and the British, the Iroquois Confederacy decided to remain neutral in the war. The Confederacy ordered the Shawnee to stop attacking the Americans in Kentucky. The Shawnee refused and continued to raid. By this time, the Iroquois Confederacy was no stranger to incidents when their commands to Covenant Chain tribes were ignored.

Had the Iroquois Confederacy been able to remain neutral throughout the *American Revolutionary War*, they might have been able to come through this tumultuous time with some of their old influence intact. Possibly, they may have been able to secure a great deal more territory than the final war outcome would leave them. Certainly, there would have been far less human tragedy among those engaged in the vicious rebellion, victors and vanquished.

But this would not be the case. The *Great Binding Law*, the cement that held the Five Nations of the Iroquois Confederacy together in unity and armistice faltered in 1777. Two years later, the Iroquois Confederacy was a defeated shamble and a mere shadow of its once powerful political and military self. The Iroquois Empire, in decline for some decades, was now in disarray.

How did the Iroquois Confederacy fall from their strong position of political influence and military power? The answer rests in a great part with the dynamics associated with expansion of European settlers unto the ancestral lands of the numerous Indigenous tribes and allied tribal coalitions. The imperialist policies and strategies of the European powers struggling for control of eastern North America, and the onslaught of war brought about by the rebellious Thirteen Colonies, are certainly no small part of the cause of the collapse of the Haudenosaunee empire. The unstoppable migration of Europeans onto tribal lands and territories is the defining reason for the empire collapse. Just as it is a subtle cause for the *American Revolutionary War*. Unfair taxes without representation certainly. But unmanageable migration into the wilderness, unhindered by social or legal barriers, coupled to unscrupulous greed for land and resources, is the defining cause of the collapse of the Haudenosaunee empire.

The breaking point was the overwhelming, uncontrollable migration of European settlers into the ancestral lands of pre-European Native confederacies. The flood of land hungry settlers combined with the inability of governments – British and American – to regulate the overwhelming human tide was the death knoll for any chance of peaceful regional coexistence. Haudenosaunee statesmanship, diplomatic skill, military power and brilliant strategy were neutralized by the Machiavellian manoeuvrings of greedy land developers, and the onslaught of uncontrollable European migration. Neither the British nor the American governments could influence the inevitable outcomes.

Perhaps some clarity can be found from the precursors to the loss of the Iroquois Confederacy empire. To start, we need to look at the Mohawk settlement of Kahnawake.

The settlement population consisted of mostly Mohawk converted to Christianity. Due to this, the village was originally called Caughnawaga, which in Mohawk meant *praying Indians*. The Caughnawaga and other members of the *Seven Nations of Canada* had been drawn into the conflict. Over time, Caughnawaga warriors fought on both sides of the *American Revolutionary War* - for the British and for the Americans.

The *Seven Nations of Canada,* sometimes referred to as the *League of Nations,* were a group of seven predominately Christian Native settlements along the St. Lawrence River, French Canada. The settlements included: The Onondaga of Oswegatchie; the Mohawk of Akwesasne; Mohawk of Caughnawaga (Kahnawake); Mohawk and Anishinaabeg (Algonquin and Nipissing) of Kanesetake; Abenaki of Odanak; Abenaki of Becancour (now Wolinak); and the Huron-Wendat of Jeune-Lorette (now Wendake).

The *Seven Nations* was founded around 1667 as an alliance of mutual protection after the French raided Mohawk villages in the Iroquois ancestral homeland of upper New York State. The difference between this group of tribes and the Haudenosaunee of the Five Nations Iroquois Confederacy flows from religious beliefs. The *Seven Nations of Canada* were largely Christian converts; the Haudenosaunee were not Christian. Their spirituality is animistic. The Haudenosaunee followed the teachings of the Great Binding Law brought by the Peacemaker.

The communities that made up the Seven Nations mirrored the communities of the Five Nations of the Iroquois Confederacy in terms of custom. The clan system of traditional governance remained firmly established. Clan mothers nominated men for positions of leadership. The nominees, with consensual agreement, became hereditary Rotinonkwisere, or Longhair Chiefs. The chiefs represented all the clans and were not restricted to the dominant Wolf, Turtle, and Bear clans of the Mohawk Nation.

An early reference to the *Seven Nations* was made in a record of a 1755 encounter between Iroquois warriors and their French allies at an ambush site on a canoe portage between present-day Lake George and the Hudson River, New York State.

A Kahnawake Mohawk observed Mohawk warriors moving with the British troops. He called out asking them to identify themselves. The Mohawk with the British replied *'we are Mohawk and Five Nations.'* The Mohawk accompanying the French replied *'and we are Mohawk of the Seven Confederate Nations of Canada.'* The meeting was recorded by Daniel Claus, who was employed by Sir William Johnson as a British Indian Agent. (MacLeod, 1992)

Sir William Johnson, and his brother-in-law Joseph Brant, played significant roles in the Iroquois Confederacy decisions concerning Iroquois neutrality in the American Revolution.

Joseph Thayendanegea Brant (1743-1807), a Christian Mohawk and younger brother of William Johnson's wife Mary Brant (1736-1796), was a charismatic leader of Iroquois warriors during, and after, the *American Revolutionary War*.

Joseph Thayendanegea Brant was educated at an English school in Connecticut. Brant gradually became an influential person among the Mohawk. He believed the Iroquois would lose their lands and independence if the Americans were successful in their rebellion against British rule. Joseph Brant was strongly opposed to the decision of the Grand Council of the Iroquois Confederacy to remain neutral during the conflict. He defied the Haudenosaunee of the Grand Council by choosing to ignore their decision that the Confederacy remain neutral in the coming war between the rebellious Thirteen Colonies and Great Britain.

Joseph Brant accepted a Captain's Commission in the British army. In 1775 he sailed to England, and after returning home he was in time to participate in the *Battle of Long Island, 1776*. The Americans had arrested Sir William Johnson's son, Sir John Johnson, for pro-loyalist activities. Angered by the arrest, Brant defied the Iroquois Council and led warriors loyal to him north to help the British defend Canada against an American invasion planned for the winter of 1776-77. The members of the Iroquois Council opposing Brant were the Oneida and the Tuscarora. Both Nations, as a consequence of the influence of the American missionary Samuel Kirkland, favored supporting the Americans in their rebellion.

The involvement of the Tuscarora in Iroquois Grand Council decision making is telling in itself. The Tuscarora had been adopted into the Confederacy in an act of generosity when the Tuscarora, decimated by settler attacks, asked the

Confederacy for refuge. The adoption of the Tuscarora as the Sixth Nation of the Iroquois Confederacy was by name only. The Iroquois Confederacy allowed the Tuscarora a council seat in the longhouse. However, they were not given the privilege of speaking or decision making in matters before the council. Now, with the Tuscarora no longer silent, signs of the fracturing of the Iroquois Confederacy were showing.

The crunch began to unfold in 1777. The British planned their campaign around a strategy to cut New England off from the other more southerly colonies. The campaign strategy would engage three British armies. The armies would march to Albany, New York. General William Howe would arrive from his headquarters in New York City. General John Burgoyne marched south from Montreal. Colonel Barry St. Leger would move east through the Mohawk Valley. In order for Colonel St. Leger to achieve his orders, he would need to move his army through the ancestral homeland of the Iroquois.

The British needed to approach the Grand Council of the Iroquois Confederacy for consultation on how to proceed. Matters were complicated. An epidemic had sickened several important Iroquois royaner. Opposed by the Oneida royaner Skenandoah, Joseph Brant persisted and convinced the Seneca and Cayuga that an alliance with the British was best for the security and future of Iroquois Confederacy.

Differences between Council members hardened. A consensus decision could not be found. The Onondaga, keepers of the Haudenosaunee council fire, extinguished the fire of the Haudenosaunee Confederacy. The Onondaga joined the majority who had decided to ally with the British.

When the Confederacy fire was extinguished, the Five Nations of the Iroquois Confederacy were no longer bound in a united confederacy. Each of the Five Nations was now free to go its own way. The Great Binding Law that had made the Great Peace and brought unity among the Iroquois was ended. Now with the armistice ended, Iroquois would fight Iroquois. Centuries of political influence and unified military power ended when the Onondaga extinguished the Confederacy fire. The unity that had given purpose, strength, and passionate nationalism to the Iroquois Confederacy had drifted away with the smoke of the last Iroquois Confederacy council fire.

The August 6th, 1777, *Battle of Oriskany* was a grievous tragedy for the Iroquois Confederacy. Colonel St. Leger, now joined by Iroquois and other Native allies, moved through the Mohawk Valley toward Fort Stanwix - called Fort Schuyler by the Americans. British and American forces clashed.

Oneida warriors fought beside the Americans and Mohawk and Seneca warriors fought beside the British. Everybody killed everybody else. Colonel St. Leger failed to capture Fort Stanwix and his defeat forced him to abandon his part in the campaign. He retreated back to Canada. In October, the Oneida scouts led the Americans to victory over British General Burgoyne at the *Battles of Saratoga*, September 19 and October 7, 1777. The battle outcome earned the Americans a decisive victory over the British forces. This victory was the turning point in the *American Revolutionary War*.

That winter, the Oneida again helped the Americans by bringing food to General George Washington's starving army encamped at Valley Forge. (Foote, 1998. Glatthar, 2006. Watt, 2002)

The American victory at the *Battles of Saratoga* in the fall of 1777, changed the tactics of warfare for the British army. The traditional regimental lines of battle gave way to guerilla frontier war of ambush and hit and run raids.

In May, 1778, the Oneida, under the command of Continental Army Officer Marquis de Lafayette, fought in the *Battle of Barren Hill*. This was a minor skirmish in the war. The British had attempted to surround Lafayette's militia; but the soldiers were able to break through the British encirclement and escape capture. During the summer and fall of 1778, despite setbacks, the British raided frontier settlements putting the Americans on the defensive in New York and Pennsylvania.

Loyalist Colonel John Butler had recruited a regiment of Loyalist militia. John Butler was the commander of British forces engaged in the hit and run guerilla warfare along the northern and western borders of the Thirteen Colonies. His regiment was called Butler's Rangers. (Cruikshank, 1893)

Butler was supported by Seneca warriors recruited by Seneca war chiefs Sayenqueraghta and Kaiiontwa'kon (Cornplanter). Joseph Brant added to this force by recruiting Mohawk warriors. This combined force of British irregulars,

Seneca and Mohawk warriors, engaged in vicious raids and skirmishing against frontier settlers and American militia. (Barr, 2006)

Throughout 1778, the Seneca raided settlements along the Allegheny and Susquehanna Rivers. In early June, Butler's Rangers, along with Seneca and Mohawk raiders, met at the village of Tioga, New York State. Butler, with the Seneca chiefs Cornplanter and Sayenqueraghta, made plans to attack the Wyoming Valley.

Joseph Brant and his Mohawk warriors continued to raid settlements further north. They had successfully raided Cobleskill, present-day Warnerville, New York, on May 30, 1778.

The *Battle of Cobleskill* is also known as the *Cobleskill Massacre*. The raid involved 200 to 300 Iroquois warriors and Loyalist Militia. The plan was efficiently brutal. A small number of Iroquois would harass to get settler attention, then retreat. The plan was to draw the settlement militia towards a larger party of Loyalists and Iroquois who waited in ambush. The assaulters were under the command of Joseph Brant. The ambush was a success. Twenty-two militia soldiers were killed. The settlement was burned. Later that same year, American militia attacked and destroyed Iroquois villages in upper New York State. (Halsey, 1902. Barr, 2006)

On July 3, 1778, the *Battle of Wyoming*, also known as the *Wyoming Massacre*, was fought in the Wyoming Valley, in and around present-day Wyoming, Pennsylvania. The area was home to two American forts, Forty Fort and Jenkins Fort. On the day of the battle, Butler ambushed an advancing party of Connecticut Militia. The battle is reported to have lasted 45 minutes. The American militia panicked and the Seneca set off in pursuit. Butler reported that 227 American scalps had been taken. The butcher's bill for the engagement was an estimated 340 American militia killed and from 5 to 20 captured. Butler's forces suffered 3 killed and 8 wounded. (Cruickshank, 1893, pg. 47)

The morning after the battle, Colonel Denison, American Continental Army, surrendered Forty Fort and his surviving soldiers. Colonel Butler paroled the American militia soldiers on the condition that they not fight for the remainder of the war. However, all the soldiers were back in the fight before the end of the year.

With the surrender of the forts, non-combatants were spared and few inhabitants of the settlement were injured or molested. In his after-battle report, Colonel Butler wrote:

"But what gives me the sincerest satisfaction is that I can, with great truth, assure you that in the destruction of the settlement not a single person was hurt except such that were in arms, to these, in truth, the Indians gave no quarter." (ibid, pg. 49)

A settlement farmer, witness to the battle's aftermath wrote: *"Happily these fierce people, satisfied with the death of those who had opposed them in arms, treated the defenceless ones, the women and the children, with a degree of humanity almost hitherto unparalleled."* (Commager, 1958, pg. 101)

On November 11, 1778, Joseph Brant's 321 Mohawk and Seneca warriors, with 150 Butler's Rangers, and 50 soldiers of the British 8th Regiment of Foot, attacked the log wall fort at the village of Cherry Valley, New York. The engagement was under the command of Captain Walter Butler, son of Colonel John Butler. The fort, hastily built after Joseph Brant's raid on Cobleskill, was garrisoned by 300 soldiers of the 7th Massachusetts Regiment of the Continental Army commanded by Colonel Ichabod Alden. The Cherry Valley raid would become known as one of the most horrific raids of the frontier war. (Murray, 2006, pg. 64)

The Mohawk raiders were led by Joseph Brant. Within the raiding party there was simmering grievance and animosity. Captain Walter Butler treated Brant badly. This served to undermine Brant's authority over Mohawk and Seneca warriors. The Seneca were furious about accusations that they had engaged in atrocities during the *Battle of Wyoming*. Also, the Seneca thirst for a revenge raid was fed by the American reprisal destruction of Seneca villages at Unadilla, Onaquaga, and Tioga after the *Battle of Wyoming*.

Although the defenders of the Cherry Valley settlement had received warning from Oneida scouts of a pending attack, the warning was not heeded.

Captain Walter Butler, aware of the tensions among his command, held a council the night before the attack. At the meeting, Butler insisted that the Seneca and Mohawk warriors under his authority promise that they would not harm non-combatants. (Graymont, 1972, pg. 186)

The attack began early on the morning of November 11, 1778. The fort walls were high and strong and the attack on the fort faltered. After putting a guard around the fort, the attackers turned on the settlement. A fortified building known as Wells House became a focus of attack. A Seneca warrior, Little Beard, surrounded the house with his warriors. Colonel Ichabod Alden and 16 officers and troops were killed at the house. Lt. Colonel William Stacey, second in command, was taken prisoner. The house was entered and hand-to-hand fighting ensued. The Seneca killed most of the remaining soldiers in the house and then killed the entire Wells household of twelve persons. (Barr, 2006. pg.154)

The Seneca moved through the settlement, setting fire to all the houses. The rampaging Seneca are reported to have killed any person they encountered. Butler and Brant struggled to contain the rampaging Seneca and Mohawk but matters had taken on a momentum of their own. (ibid, pg. 154)

In the aftermath of the battle, Joseph Brant was shocked and grieved to learn that a number of the families whom he had counted as friends had been savaged by the Seneca rampage. Among the slaughtered families and friends were the Wells, Campbell, Dunlop, and Clyde families. (Swinnerton, 1906, pg. 24)

Joseph Brant is credited with saving Lt. Colonel Stacy when he intervened just as Stacy was about to be killed. *"Brant saved the life of Lieut. Col. Stacy, who was made prisoner when Col. Alden was killed. It is said Stacy was a freemason, and as such made an appeal to Brant, and was spared."* (Beardsley, 1852, pg. 463)

The morning after the battle, Walter Butler sent Brant and some Rangers into the village. The raiders found 70 survivors, mostly women and children, and took them prisoner. Butler managed to release 40 of the prisoners. The remainder were taken to their captor's villages and held until their eventual exchange. (Graymont, 1972, pg. 189)

Lt. Col. Stacy was taken to Fort Niagara as a prisoner of the British. (Campbell, 1831, pgs. 110-111, 181-182)

The fighting at Cherry Valley was a brutal and merciless affair. Feeling anger and resentment, a Mohawk chief wrote to an American officer and said: *"You Burned our Houses, which makes us and our Brothers, the Seneca Indians angry, so that we destroyed, men, women, and Children at Chervalle."* (Graymont, 1972, pg. 190)

The Seneca *"declared they would no more be falsely accused, or fight the Enemy twice"* [meaning they would refuse quarter (mercy) in the future] (ibid, pg. 190)

Captain Walter Butler, in his after-action report, wrote: *"Notwithstanding my utmost Precaution and Endeavours to save the Women and Children, I could not prevent some of them falling unhappy Victims to the Fury of the Savages."* (Kelsay, 1986, pg.231-232)

Quebec's governor, Frederick Haldimand, was distressed and infuriated by Walter Butler's inability to control his forces.

Haldimand wrote to Butler and expressed his feelings: *"Such indiscriminate vengeance taken even upon the treacherous and cruel enemy they are engaged against is useless and disreputable to themselves as it is contrary to the dispositions and maxims of the King whose cause they are fighting."* (Wrong, 2009, pg. 119)

The killing at Cherry Valley branded Joseph Brant *Monster Brant*. The moniker may have been undeserved. Most of the Cherry Valley killing is believed to have been done by members of Butler's Rangers. Their appetite for killing and waging war was demonstrated to be far more vicious than Brant's Mohawk. The suggestion that Butler was the true monster has been met with skepticism. However, historian Barbara Graymont has called Butler's command and leadership of the Cherry Valley episode *'criminally incompetent.'*(Graymont, 1972, pg. 186)

Following the Cherry Valley attack, Joseph Brant led a raid on Minisink Island on the Delaware River between New Jersey and Pennsylvania. Several farms were burnt. Brant inflicted heavy casualties on a pursuing American militia force. Setting an ambush, 120 of the militia were killed and another 30 escaped. In September, Joseph Brant raided the settlement of German Flats in the Mohawk Valley. The Americans had been warned of the attack and most escaped to the safety of forts at Dayton and Herkimer.

Two weeks later the Americans struck back at Brant. They succeeded in destroying villages at Unadilla and Oquaga on the Susquehanna. In November, Brant again joined forces with Walter Butler and his Butler's Rangers and attacked Cherry Valley for the second time. The attack took the Americans by surprise. Homesteads were burnt, 30 settlers were killed and another 71 taken prisoner. The American fort was attacked and 16 soldiers were killed. American reinforcements arrived the next day and Brant's Mohawk and Butler's Rangers withdrew. (Goodnough, 1968)

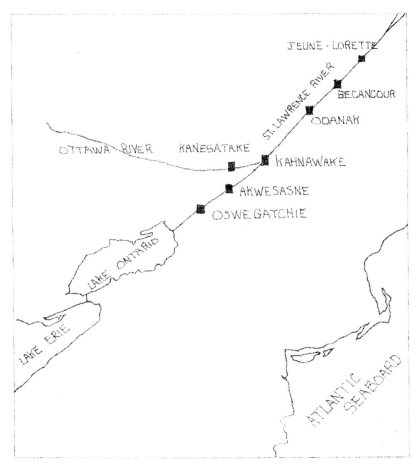

Seven Nations of Canada

The Sullivan Expedition, 1779
Scorched Earth and Refugees

Joseph Brant's 1778 raids targeting frontier settlements would have a devastating consequence for the Iroquois. The Continental Army would soon be sent to neutralize the Iroquois in their ancestral homeland.

The *1779 Sullivan Expedition* was about to be unleashed on the Iroquois by General George Washington. Washington's orders for this campaign laid out a virtual scorched earth campaign of reprisal and final defeat of the Iroquois in their ancestral homeland. The devastation wreaked by the scorched earth campaign of the *Sullivan Expedition* ordered by General George Washington would turn the Iroquois ancestral homeland into a scorched wasteland of refugees.

In the summer of 1779, General George Washington sent three armies to destroy the Iroquois homeland in upper New York State. General John Sullivan advanced from the south and marched up the Susquehanna with 4,000 soldiers. General James Clinton moved his army west through the Mohawk Valley; and Colonel Daniel Brodhead advanced up the Allegheny River from Fort Pitt.

Oneida scouts guided the American armies. At the second *Battle of Oriskany*, the American forces quickly overwhelmed Joseph Brant's 500 Mohawk warriors and Colonel John Butler's 200 Rangers. In September, the Americans captured the Iroquois Confederacy's capital, the Onondaga village of Kanadaseagea.

In this campaign to erase forever the threat of the Iroquois Confederacy, the Americans burned more than 40 towns. At one point in the campaign, General Washington, in dispatches, criticized General Sullivan for his slow advance. General Sullivan replied, describing the number of villages and the expanse of crops that had to be destroyed as so great in number and acreage that he was unable to advance at a faster rate. The Iroquois gave General Washington the name *Caunotaucarius*. Translated, the word means *town destroyer*.

With their homes and crops destroyed, the Iroquois had a cold, hungry winter ahead. Those who remained near their destroyed towns and villages were destitute. Many Iroquois, terrorized by the destruction brought by the Continental Army, journeyed as refugees to the vicinity of the British Fort Niagara at present-day Niagara-on-the-Lake, Ontario. There was more war and turmoil to come.

> *I have another story to share. The Chief responsible for the environment portfolio of the Mohawk Council of Akwesasne, invited me to attend a meeting with a group of landowners on the St. Lawrence River west of the City of Cornwall.*
>
> *The landowners were in agreement that a small parcel of their land would be given to the Akwesasne Mohawks. The land was*

a combination of rock, a few mature white pine trees, and some cedar swamp. The idea was that land would be used for walking trials and a place of quiet and reflection. Wonderful. Generous.

On the arranged evening, the Chief and I sat with a number of gentleman farmers and exchanged greetings. The land transfer intention was explained. This was a good meeting.

Business having been completed, we enjoyed an evening coffee. The Chief, a Haudenosaunee, graciously declined the offer of 'black water' and accepted a glass of cold well water.

One of the landowners told us that his ancestors were United Empire Loyalists. The landowners present had a common family history, they were all descendants of United Empire Loyalists. Their ancestors had all come to Canada during the American Revolutionary War. Upon arriving, they received the 200-acre King's land grant given to the Loyalists.

Having shared this bit of history, a landowner mentioned that a condition attached to the land grant was that the larger white pine trees could not be cut down. The prime trees were reserved for the Royal Navy as masts for the fleet.

The Chief, listening to all of this, coughed into his hand, and seized the attention of all attending.

After a quiet pause, he said: "You know, the war had not gone well for your ancestors. They were sorely persecuted by the rebels. Most were sick and hurt. They asked for help. My people, old friends of the British, walked many days to their places and we brought them back. Some were too sick to walk. We carried them on our backs. When they arrived, the King gave them our land to settle as a reward for their loyalty. Today, our home is a small place we call the 'land where the partridge drums.' You know it as Akwesasne. The good news is, tonight we Mohawks got a little more land back."

Civil War Among the Iroquois

Washington's Continental Army had brought destruction and defeat to the Iroquois.

Joseph Brant, the charismatic war leader, was not about to bury the war hatchet. Even in the midst of social disintegration, the charismatic Brant managed to bring together a large war party. Brant wanted vengeance. He embarked on a relentless and vicious guerilla war against the Americans.

That winter, Brant and his warriors attacked Oneida villages. The Oneida had allied themselves with the Americans. They had been an effective alley of the Americans as they pursued their war of punishment against the Iroquois. Hundreds of Oneida were killed. The surviving Oneida fled to the Americans at Schenectady for protection. This was now an Iroquois civil war.

For the rest of the war the Oneida lived in poverty and misery. They did, however, continue to serve as army scouts for the Americans.

Joseph Brant was a persistent and vengeful warrior. He successfully disrupted attempts by the Seneca Chief Red Jacket to make peace with the Americans. Brant continued to attack settlers along the frontier. The sons of Sir William Johnson, Guy Johnson and John Johnson, led raids into the Mohawk Valley in the summer and fall of 1780.

Butler's Rangers continued to be active. Captain Walter Butler was killed by an Oneida warrior near Johnson Hall in October, 1781. The Americans hated Walter Butler with a true passion. They refused to bury his body and left it, uncovered, to be ravaged by scavenger birds and animals.

Joseph Brant continued to fight in the Ohio Valley throughout 1781. In August of that year, he ambushed a Pennsylvania militia patrol near the mouth of the Miami River in present-day Cincinnati, Ohio. Later that season, Brant attempted to ambush the exploration and survey party of George Rogers Clark on the Ohio River. Clark avoided the ambush and escaped to Fort Nelson at present-day Louisville, Kentucky. Brant turned east. His final skirmish with the Americans was at Johnstown in 1783, the last year of the American Revolutionary War. (Eckert, 2003. Graymont, 1983. Kelsay, 1984)

The Iroquois Confederacy
From Empire to Refugee

At the end of the American Revolution, Joseph Brant entered Canada accompanied by an estimated 2,000 followers. Mostly Mohawk and Cayuga, Brant's war refugees included members of all six of the Iroquois Confederacy Nations. British allies including the Delaware, Munsee, Saponi, Nanticoke, and Tutelo, were also represented.

Canadian Governor Frederick Haldimand pledged Joseph Brant 675,000 acres of land along the Grand River, south western Ontario, adjacent to modern-day Brantford. This land gift was in compensation for the Iroquois lands lost in New York. The land was given *in honor of the Crown* as recognition of the support the Iroquois and allied tribes had given to the British during the *American Revolutionary War*.

However, tragedy continued to pile upon tragedy. Governor Haldimand's term of office expired before he could secure legal land title. In 1785, Joseph Brant sailed to England with the intention of establishing clear title to the Grand River lands. The matter remains contentious and unsettled to this present day.

The war refugees who followed Brant to Canada had lost everything. They had what they could carry with them, and little else. They were demoralized and destitute. In order to secure funds to purchase food and supplies for the war refugees, Brant, under significant duress, sold an estimated 300,000 acres of the Six Nation land grant. Much of the land sale at that time, and since, is disputed. Today, what is left of the original Haldimand land grant is called the Six Nations Reserve. Of the original 675,000 acres, the Six Nation Reserve is now 45,000 acres in size. In addition to the Grand River land grant, a second group of Iroquois refugees settled at Tyendinaga, on the north shore of Lake Ontario adjacent to present-day Deseronto, Ontario.

At the beginning of the *American Revolutionary War*, the Iroquois population in their upper New York State ancestral homeland was estimated to have been 8,000 persons. Fewer than 5,000 Iroquois had survived the war and of those survivors, an estimated 2,000 persons had moved to Canada.

The fall from influential political and military power to refugee had been a long and tragic journey.

On the Six Nations Reserve at Grand River, Joseph Brant used his influence to rekindle the Iroquois Confederacy fire which had been extinguished in 1777 at Onondaga. While Brant was working to pull together the fractured and demoralized Confederacy, a second group of Iroquois lit the Council fire at Buffalo Creek, New York State. The lighting of two Iroquois Confederacy council fires was a source of contention over which fire represented the original Confederacy and their claim to the Ohio Valley. Today, this remains a contentious issue.

The successful exploration and survey by George Rogers Clark of the Illinois country in 1778, had pushed the boundary of the United States west to the Mississippi River. The Americans, because it served their land claim interests, had no doubt that the New York State Council fire was the genuine item, not the Canadian fire at Six Nations.

The Iroquois in New York were told by the Americans that they were a conquered people. This was followed up with a forced signing by the New York Iroquois of a second treaty at Fort Stanwix, located at present-day Rome, New York, in 1784. This treaty ceded much of the Iroquois ancestral homeland and confirmed the earlier cessation of Ohio made to the British in 1768.

Joseph Brant's Mohawk followers and other Canadian Iroquois did not attend the treaty signing. The Iroquois Confederacy had split into two parts. As time passed, the Canadian and American Iroquois grew further apart. By 1803, the Canadian Iroquois had stopped being invited to American Iroquois councils.

The Iroquois Confederacy had fallen far.

The American Treaty Period,
1783-1830

Chapter 19

The American Treaty Period 1783-1830 Struggle for the Ohio Valley, an undeclared War

The war fought in the Ohio Valley was, in many ways, separate from the war being fought at the same time in the region east of the Appalachians Mountains. Fighting in the Ohio Valley continued after the *1783 Treaty of Paris*. The British would supply arms and ammunition to any tribe who would ally with them. The British also began paying a bounty for American scalps.

The Chickamauga (Cherokee) and Shawnee were particularly active in raiding. Raiders selected the least risky targets, regardless of allegiance. Paying bounty for scalps tends to blur the distinction between the scalp of a man, woman or child whether ally, foe or friend.

More tribes began to enter the fray against the Americans. The Mingo joined the Shawnee and Cherokee and would remain a part of the British alliance until 1794.

Many of the anti-American raids used Pluggy's Town, a Mingo village located near present-day Delaware, Ohio, as their assembly point. In September, 1777, a force of 400 Shawnee, Mingo, and Wyandot attacked Fort Henry, present-day Wheeling, West Virginia. The settlement adjacent to the fort was burnt, and half the fort's 42 soldier garrison was killed.

The Americans built Fort Laurens in the eastern Ohio in 1778. A Mingo and Wyandot war party surrounded the Fort and kept it under siege until August, 1779, when the garrison abandoned the fort as indefensible. Next, in 1782, a Mingo war party burnt Hannastown, Pennsylvania.

Throughout 1783, raids and counter raids ebbed back and forth throughout the Ohio region. During this time the Mingo and other British allies began to relocate their villages into northwest Ohio to provide a wilderness buffer between them and the Americans along the Ohio River.

The Ohio Valley Region, 1783

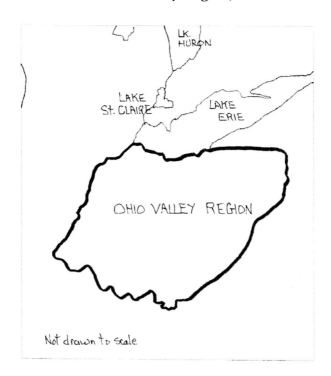

For the British, and certainly for the American frontiersmen, the question of who managed the Ohio territory had not been satisfied.

In 1782, Simon De Peyster, a British agent at Detroit, had been encouraging the regional tribes to form an alliance to resist the Americans moving into the Ohio. In 1783, De Peyster invited Joseph Brant to attend a meeting of the Ohio tribes at Sandusky. The British were absent from the meeting. However, Brant's influence and persuasiveness resulted in the formation of a western alliance of tribes. The first alliance council fire was at the Shawnee village of Waketomica. The Americans burned Waketomica in 1786. The alliance moved their council fire to Brownstown, a Wyandot village south of present-day Detroit, Michigan.

The British, procrastinating until the Americans paid the Loyalists for property losses incurred during the American Revolution, refused to comply with the conditions set out in the *1783 Treaty of Paris*. They continued to hold onto their remaining forts in American territory.

A problem was that the Americans simply could not pay their *Revolutionary War* debts to the Loyalists until they began to sell land in the Ohio Valley.

The British were fully aware of the American situation. They understood pressure needed to be kept on the Americans. The British moved quickly to spread word among the alliance tribes that they would have the full support of the British if they raided the Americans.

When the alliance tribes learned that a second treaty had been signed at Fort Stanwix by the New York Iroquois in 1784, the intention of the Americans became very clear - they were going to seize the Ohio Region. They would achieve this using whatever it took to succeed. By this time the western alliance tribes recognized the capacity of the Iroquois Confederacy to represent their interest was a shoddy promise at best. Consequently, the influence of Joseph Brant and the Canadian Iroquois was strengthened.

Several tribal alliances and confederacies were at play in the Ohio Valley Region and the Northwest Territory. The confederacies, and sometimes nonaligned tribes, were originally formed as a strategy of resistance to Iroquois Confederacy expansion into the northwest of the lower Great Lakes Region. As events moved forward, the tribal confederacies switched their mission to addressing the threat of expanding European settlement from the east.

The tribal confederacies aligning themselves to resist the expansion of American settlement into the Ohio Region included the following groups:

Anishinaabe
Council of Three Fires

The *Council of Three Fires,* often referred to as the *Three Fires Confederacy,* was an Anishinaabe Confederacy consisting of the Ojibwe [Chippewa]; Ottawa [Odawa]; and Potawatomi. The formation of the Confederacy is dated 796 CE.

In the council, the Ojibwe are called the *Older Brother;* the Odawa are called the *Middle Brother;* and the Potawatomi are the *Younger Brother.* The Ojibwe are the *Keepers of the Faith;* the Odawa are the *Keepers of the Trade;* and the Potawatomi are the *Keepers of the Fire.*

The principal meeting place for the *Three Fires Confederacy* was at Michilmackinac located on the strait between Lake Huron and Lake Michigan. The French visited the area in 1612 and established a trading post. In 1671, Jesuit missionaries established the mission of St. Ignace at the site. In 1715, the area became known as Fort Michilimackinac, also called Ancient Fort Mackinac.

The Great Pursuit of the Wendat by the Iroquois forced Wendat, Tobacco, and Neutral refugees north to the Michilmackinac area. It was here that the relentless pursuit by the Iroquois of the defeated Wendat and their allies ended. Taking on the Anishinaabe in a war was not included in the Iroquois list of things to do.

The Anishinaabe were a very large population group able to gather significant powerful military power when need arose. This potential for a strong military response to threat, presented an effective barrier to Iroquois northward expansion. The Iroquois knew when and where to pick their wars of expansion.

The Anishinaabe enjoyed a mostly peaceful coexistence with neighbours. The strength of their confederacy and their skills as fair trading partners assured a peaceful existence. When the need for arms arose, the Anishinaabe where not shirkers. They fought against the Iroquois who advanced from the south and the

Sioux who posed a threat from the west. Indeed, the Sioux were a ferocious and expansionist tribe. The Jesuit missionaries referred to the Sioux as the *Iroquois of the west.*

During the *Seven Years War,* the Three Fires Anishinaabe Confederacy fought against England. In the *Northwest Indian War* and the *War of 1812,* the confederacy fought as allies of the English against the Americans.

In 1776, after the *American Revolutionary War,* the Anishinaabe became the principal member of the *Western Great Lakes Confederacy.* This alliance was also known as the *Western Confederacy.* The confederacy consisted of an alliance of Wyandot, Algonquin, Nipissing, Sac, and Meskwaki tribes.

Illinois Confederacy

The Illinois Confederacy, also referred to as the *Illiniwek* or *Illini,* were a group of tribes living in the upper Mississippi River Valley. Their ancestral lands included a triangular shaped territory moving from present-day Iowa to the shores of Lake Michigan at present-day Chicago, then south into present-day Arkansas.

The name *Illinois* was not the name the Natives gave themselves. *Illinois* is a French transliteration of *ilinwe.* This word comes from the Odawa language *irenweewa,* meaning *he-who-speaks-the-common-way.* The Confederacy word for themselves was *inoca* or *inoka* [unknown meaning].

The Illinois Confederacy included the following member tribes: Kaskaskia; Cahokia; Peoria; Tamaroa; Moingwena; Michigamea; Chepoussa; Chinkoa; Coiracoentanon; Espeminkia; Maroa; and Tapouara. At the time of European contact, the population of this alliance was estimated to be more than 10,000 people. The tribes spoke a variety of dialects of the Algonkian languages family.

During the 17th Century, the Illinois were devastated by epidemics of European diseases. The Illinois were forced into warfare by the expansion of the Iroquois into the western Great Lakes Region as they sought to secure productive trapping and hunting territory for the fur trade. By the mid 18th Century, European disease epidemics and warfare had reduced the Illinois Confederacy to five principal tribes: Cahokia; Kaskaskia; Michigamea; Peoria, and Tamaroa.

A final tragedy for the Illinois was inflicted by the *American Indian Removal Act, 1830*. The Illinois were forced to relocate from eastern Kansas, where they had been driven by the Iroquois wars, to Oklahoma. Today, the remnants of the Illinois live in Ottawa County, Oklahoma, and are known as the *Peoria Tribe of Indians of Oklahoma*.

Western Confederacy (Post 1776)

The *Western Confederacy*, also referred to as the *Western Indian Confederacy*, the *Miami Confederacy*, and *Western Great Lakes Confederacy*, came together to resist the expansion of the Americans into the Northwest Territory after Great Britain ceded the region to America in the *Peace of Paris (1783)*.

The confederacy was established at the Wyandot town of Upper Sandusky. The confederacy goal was to form a common front to deal with American expansion. Many of the members of the Native tribes that formed the confederacy had fought as British allies against the Americans in the *American Revolutionary War*. However, Britain gave no recognition or consideration to their Native allies in the *Treaty of Paris*. Mohawk war leader Joseph Brant, one of the primary architects of the confederacy, was not reluctant to say that the British had *sold the Indians to Congress*.

The Confederacy included membership of tribes gathered from a broad geography. Members included: Anishinaabe [Council of Three Fires]; Iroquois Confederacy; Seven Nations of Canada [the Christian Mohawk of Caughnawaga and associated villages along the St. Lawrence River]; Wabush Confederacy [Wea; Piankashaw]; Illini Confederacy; Wyandot; Mississauga; Menominee; Shawnee; Lenape [Delaware]; Miami; Kickapoo; Kaskaskia; Chickamauga Cherokee [Lower Cherokee]; and Upper Muscogee.

Most of the groups who participated as members of the Western Confederacy were not united political units. Membership in the confederacy was based on the independent decision of individual villages.

Tribal resistance brought about the *Northwest Indian War, 1785-1795*. The war ended with an American victory at the *Battle of Fallen Timbers, 1794*.

Northwest Indian War, 1785-1795

The *Northwest Indian War*, also referred to as the *Ohio War*, and *Little Turtle's War*, was a war between the new United States of America and confederacies of Native tribes allied with the British. The war was fought for control of the Northwest Territory.

The Americans continued to be uncertain about how much influence and strength the New York Iroquois retained in the Ohio Region. The Americans needed to break any alliance the Iroquois might have with the western alliance tribes. The Americans knew the western tribal alliance was a British initiative, but the problem for the Americans was that they could only approach the tribes individually, and not the leaders of the alliance as a whole.

Knowing they could not gain security through treaty with the western alliance as one entity, the Americans embarked on a strategy involving a grab bag approach to treaties – take what you can where you can. This was a strategy of divide and disrupt the friends of your enemy.

The treaties the Americans did manage were not with the western alliance leadership. Specific treaties with distinct tribes such as the Wyandot, Delaware, Ottawa, Ojibwe, and Shawnee were weak documents. In terms of treaty credibility and unity, treaties were sometimes made with a village of a tribe. The treaties the Americans secured were useless because the terms did not reflect the consensus of the alliance leadership. The treaties did not reflect any sense of tribal unity. In many cases, the treaties did not reflect a consensus within a village or within a tribe. None of this bothered the Americans. In fact, their strategy was a success. The scrabble of treaties caused dissension and weakening of unity among the tribes of the western alliance opposing the Americans. This American subterfuge also weakened the coalition strength of the British in the region.

The frontier settlers were also at odds with the American idea of boundary. Most of the alliance warriors were fighting to secure the Ohio River, not the Muskingum River, as the boundary of settlement. The frontiersmen had an entirely different agenda. They would only be satisfied with the entire Ohio Valley Region. It seems, now, that the tribal intent to enforce a boundary to halt American expansion of settlement was naïve in the least, and futile at best.

Given the flood of immigration flowing into the area, despair led to the violence of armed resistance.

The New York Iroquois could see how the Ohio dispute was evolving. They called a meeting with the Ohio tribes at Buffalo Creek in the spring of 1786. No one came. At first. However, in July of that year, representatives of the western alliance tribes arrived to ask the Iroquois Confederacy for help against the Americans.

In the meantime, in order to pay pressing American Revolutionary War debts, the United States Congress had sold land claim rights to a New Jersey syndicate and the Ohio Company. American settlers flooded into the Ohio territory. Native land was taken over by squatters. Treaty boundaries were ignored. Strength of arms was the rule of the day. Possession of land was nine-tenths of the law.

By 1785, there were an estimated 12,000 white settlers north of the Ohio. The only way the encroachment could be stopped would be if the government declared war on the frontiersmen. A bad idea. The dogs of an internal American Civil War would be unleashed.

Infuriated, the Shawnee and Mingo began raiding in the east Kentucky territory. Joseph Brant travelled to the region in November, 1786. He spoke eloquently and his inspirational speech enabled a consensus among the western alliance tribes that the Ohio River would be the boundary.

The reinvigorated alliance, instead of moving forward with force, agreed to a truce until the spring. The truce was intended to allow the word of the consensus on boundary to be spread and received by the American Congress. It is not known why, but the message did not reach the American Congress until July of the following year. In the meantime, fighting had resumed.

A final attempt to find a treaty resolution was made in December, 1787. American Governor Arthur St. Clair called for a meeting with the western alliance. The meeting would be held at Fort Harmar, built at the confluence of the Ohio and Muskingum Rivers. The meeting would not take place until January, 1789. The differences among the western alliance tribes on how to respond and what to ask for could not be hammered into a consensual bottom line. Without alliance consensus, it would be difficult to be forceful in terms of drawing lines of resistance in the sand or engaging in effective negotiation. This was a persistent and damaging challenge for the alliance.

At the alliance council meeting, Joseph Brant demanded the repudiation of all treaties that had ceded any part of the Ohio. The Wyandot proved troublesome for Brant. They wanted to negotiate. The Wyandot now had the support from the Delaware, Detroit Ottawa, Ojibwe and Potawatomi. Brant was disheartened when he could not find consensus among the parties. Frustrated, Brant transferred his role as mediator to the Shawnee and Miami. Brant packed his tent and returned to the Six Nations Reserve in Brantford, Ontario.

The 1789 meeting resulted in setting the Muskingum River as the frontier boundary. None of the participating parties were satisfied. The western alliance tribes continued raiding farms and settlements. Throughout the summer of 1789, the Americans struck back at the Kickapoo, Wea, and Piankashaw villages along the lower Wabash River. The western tribal alliance was now dominated by the Shawnee and Miami war chiefs.

Frustrated with the absence of a resolution satisfactory to all parties, and knowing the government had to be decisive, the Americans reached a decision that involved settling the dispute with force of arms. As the fighting intensified, the western tribal alliance again approached the New York Iroquois for help. Again, the Iroquois refused. As ineffective as it had been in recent times, the influence the New York Iroquois had managed to retain with the western alliance tribes was now lost.

The *Northwest Indian War* broke out and the Americans began to raid the Western Confederacy tribes. Western Confederacy tribes asked Joseph Brant to bring Iroquois warriors into the war as their allies. Brant refused to agree to this appeal. However, Brant did approach Lord Dorchester, the Governor of Quebec, for British aid. Dorchester also refused. Later, in 1794, Dorchester did authorize the supply of arms and provisions to the embattled Western Confederacy.

The *Northwest Indian War, 1785-1795,* is also known as *Little Turtle's War, 1790-94*. The war was fought between the United States and a confederation of 'Indian' tribes allied with Great Britain for control over a vast wilderness territory called the Northwest Territory. The territory included all of the lands of present-day Ohio; Michigan; Indiana; Illinois; and Wisconsin.

The allied 'Indian' confederation was known as the Western Alliance Tribes, or the Western Confederacy. The alliance included the following members: Huron-Wyandot; Shawnee; Council of the Three Fires made up of the Ojibwe, Odawa, Potawatomi; Lenape; Miami; Kickapoo; Kaskaskia; Chickamauga; Cherokee; and the Wabush Confederacy made up of the Wean and Piankashaw. This complex tribal alliance was led by Chief Little Turtle (Michikinikwa) of the Miami tribe. The ancestral lands of the Miami occupied much of present-day Ohio. (Sword, 1985)

American justification for the war was to gain control of the Northwest Territory and then open it for American settlement. The British, in accordance with the terms of the *1783 Treaty of Paris,* had ceded control of the Northwest Territory to the United States. However, the British continued to garrison their forts in the territory and attempted to enforce policies intended to support the Indigenous tribes living in the territory.

You may ask why *Little Turtle's War* and the Northwest Territory, far from the ancestral homeland of the Iroquois, had anything at all to do with the Iroquois Confederacy.

The Iroquois Confederacy continued to be seen by Great Britain and the United States as having a capability to impose their influence on other tribes. Although badly bruised and seriously weakened as a political and military entity, the Iroquois Confederacy had skilled ambassadors who could be used to influence reluctant parties. The Iroquois Confederacy continued to represent unity among allies. The Confederacy also retained potential strength through the Covenant Chain coalition. Both Great Britain and the United States continued to respect the Iroquois Confederacy. Accordingly, when matters were not proceeding well, both Britain and the United States would call upon the Iroquois Confederacy to intervene in disputes and participate in treaty discussions and negotiation. And so, it was that the Americans, after suffering two decisive defeats from the Western Alliance tribes, called upon the Iroquois Confederacy to talk peace with the Western Alliance.

Little Turtle's War resulted in treaties and surrenders of territory that, although distant from the Iroquois homeland, would have terrible repercussions for the Iroquois Confederacy.

Little Turtle's War

Enormous pressure was on the United States government to seize control of the Northwest Territory and open the lands for settlement. The United States government was being pummelled by the howling demands of politically influential land speculators seeking their fortunes in the disputed territory. Skirmishing between indigenous tribes and frontiersmen was frequent, brutal, and growing in both scale and scope. President George Washington ordered his Army to put an end to the hostilities and establish United States sovereignty over the Northwest Territory. The Presidential order brought about *Little Turtle's War, 1790-94*.

Little Turtle's War began very badly for the Americans. In 1790, General Josiah Harmar was ordered to begin an offensive into Shawnee and Miami territory. In October of that year, General Harmar's 1,453 soldiers assembled near present-day Fort Wayne, Indiana. Harmar committed 400 of his men to attack the alliance force estimated to be 1,100 warriors. The Harmar foray, commanded by Colonel John Hardin, was badly and decisively mauled by the alliance warriors. An estimated 129 soldiers were killed in the assault. General Harmar's campaign was a disaster. Chief Little Turtle, and the Shawnee Chief Blue Jacket, won two engagements against Harmar's soldiers. The victories convinced the Ottawa and Wyandot to join the Western Alliance fighting the expansion of American settlement. (Carter, 1987)

The next American military rout occurred on November 4th, 1791. Major General Arthur St. Clair led a force of 920 officers and men accompanied by a group of 200 camp followers. The camp followers would have been a mix of women, children, and travelling pedlars.

General St. Clair, similar to General Harmar, was hampered by the shortage of well trained and experienced professional soldiers. The Continental Army had experienced large scale demobilization after the cessation of *American Revolutionary War* hostilities. The western alliance tribes took full advantage of the opportunity to fight an army weakened by loss of veteran leadership and combatants.

General St. Clair established a badly defended bivouac near present-day Fort Recovery, Ohio. Chief little Turtle, leading a force of 2,000 warriors, using surprise to their advantage, quickly overwhelmed the bivouac perimeter defences. The new recruits who made up the bulk of General St. Clair's forces were cut down in a brutal and merciless fight. 632 of General St. Clair's officers and men were killed, another 264 were wounded. All of the estimated 200 camp followers were killed. The 1791 battle between Chief Little Turtle's Western Alliance and General St. Clair's American force resulted in the greatest number of United States casualties of any campaign ever, past and future, against tribes of North America. (Edel,1997. Roosevelt, 1896)

Historian Wiley Sword (2000, pg. 107) referred to Little Turtle as *"the most capable Indian leader in the old Northwest"*

The defeats of General Hamar in October, 1790, and General St. Clair in November, 1791, were devastating. But the Americans could not quit the campaign. They simply could not afford to lose. General George Washington, now President of the United States, ordered General 'Mad Anthony' Wayne to take command of the Ohio territory and settle the land disputes for once and all.

Wayne began to prepare his campaign. Over a two-year period, General Wayne trained a force of 5,000 recruits into a disciplined professional army. This army was called the *Legion of the United States*. This force would augment the undisciplined and inadequately trained militia that had performed poorly in early engagements with warriors of the Western Alliance tribes. (Nelson, 1985)

1792 was a busy year for the Americans. Mad Anthony was training his troops and pulling the undisciplined militias into some semblance of an effective fighting force. At the same time, the Americans continued to pressure the New York Iroquois to talk peace with the Western Alliance tribes. However, the alliance was celebrating their recent decisive victories over Generals Hamar and St. Clair. The victorious were on a roll. They were not in a mood to listen to talks of peace. When the Western Alliance tribes did show up to council, they listened, then threw the American treaty terms into the fire and called the Iroquois representatives 'coward red men'. The Iroquois representatives were lucky to leave the council alive. Iroquois Confederacy influence with the Western Alliance tribes had certainly reached rock bottom.

The New York Iroquois had lost favor, certainly, but Joseph Brant and his Canada Iroquois continued to carry some weight in the affairs of nations. The Western Alliance had been watching 'Mad Anthony' Wayne forge his army into a superior fighting force. The Ohio tribes now had cause to worry and began to wonder if they could win the war.

In the fall of 1793, General Wayne began his march into northern Ohio. The Western Alliance asked Brant to intercede and negotiate a peace with the Americans. The British had also begun to seriously doubt that they could come out of this pending firestorm with any gains at all. They were now ready to resolve their differences with the Americans.

Sadly, the messaging between the British and Americans about peaceful resolution was conducted in secret. Brant's understanding continued to be that the British would support the alliance if it decided to fight. Brant, thinking he had a world power behind him, urged war. Surprisingly, a good part of the Western Alliance supported Brant's call to war.

In August, 1794, 2,000 soldiers of Wayne's Legion, using Choctaw and Chickasaw scouts, were ready for battle with the 1,500 Western Alliance warriors and a 500-soldier company of regular British soldiers. The battle would be fought at a location then known as Fallen Timbers, not far from present-day Toledo, Ohio.

The *Battle of Fallen Timbers, 1794,* was a short, brutal and decisive affair. After several musket barrages, General Wayne followed up with a bayonet charge. A bayonet charge is a terrifying shock wave of violence when delivered by trained and disciplined regular troops. As the stab and cut carnage of bayonet work took its toll, General Wayne sent his cavalry to outflank Shawnee Chief Blue Jacket's warriors. Both of Wayne's advances met with quick success.

The alliance tribe warriors retreated to the British Fort Miami. They found the fort's gate blocked against them. The British commander, Major William Campbell, was unwilling to start a war with the United States by providing sanctuary to the defeated warriors of the Western Alliance. (Gaff, 2004. Winkler, 1794)

The butcher's bill was 33 of General Wayne's soldiers killed; and an estimated 19 to 40 of the opposing side killed.

After the battle, General Wayne's soldiers spent a few days destroying villages and burning crops. Then they retreated. The *Battle of Fallen Timbers* was the final battle for the Northwest Territory in the Ohio region.

Northwest Territory, 1785

Chapter 20

A Time for Treaties

Treaty of Canandaigua, 1794; Jay Treaty, 1794;
Greenville Treaty, 1795; Treaty of Big Tree, 1797

The *Treaty of Canandaigua (Konondaigua),1794*, is a treaty between the United States and the Iroquois Confederacy. The treaty was signed at Canandaigua, New York, on November 11, 1794.

The full Iroquois Confederacy Grand Council of fifty condoled royaner was present to sign the treaty. The fifty Haudenosaunee royaner represented the Five Nations of the Iroquois Confederacy: Mohawk, Oneida, Onondaga, Cayuga, and Seneca. Iroquois signatories included: *Kaiiontwa'kon* (Corn Planter); *Kon-ne-at-or-tee-ooh* (Handsome Lake); *Se-quid-ong-guee* (Little Beard); *Sog-goo-ya-waut-hau* (Red Jacket); and *Honayawus* (Farmer's Brother). Timothy Pickering signed the treaty as the official agent of President George Washington. (Jemison et al, 2009)

The intent of the treaty was to appease the Five Nations of the Iroquois Confederacy. The appeasement was intended by the United States to keep the

Iroquois Confederacy from aiding the tribal alliance being assembled to defend the Ohio Valley Region.

During the late 1780s and early 1790s, the Iroquois had lost much of their ancestral homeland in New York State. Land loss was directly related to fraudulent and illegal land transactions between land speculators and the Iroquois. During this time of land loss, treaty making and Iroquois land purchases were not in compliance with *Article 9 of the Articles of Confederation*. Neither were Iroquois land purchases in compliance with the *Commerce Clause of the United States Constitution*.

Despite the existing laws, New York State had secured 26 land leases from the Iroquois. Many of the leases were for 999 years. Leases to date had claimed huge parcels of the Iroquois ancestral homeland. Fearful that the Iroquois would aid the fight to defend the Ohio Valley Region from encroaching white settlers and unscrupulous land speculators, the United States federal government sent a delegation to Canandaigua, Seneca territory. (Jemison, 2000. Hauptman, 2001)

The *Treaty of Canandaigua* affirmed Haudenosaunee land rights in New York State. The Iroquois land boundaries established by the 1788 *Phelps and Gorham Purchase* were also affirmed. The treaty established friendship and peace between the Iroquois Confederacy and the United States. (ibid, 2000)

The *Treaty of Canandaigua* is also known as the *Pickering Treaty* and the *Calico Treaty*. Up until 1941, the Iroquois in New York State received calico cloth as treaty payment. Until 1941, the Oneida Nation in Wisconsin continued to receive an annuity payment of $1,800.00. (Houghton, 2009, pgs. 25-26)

The *Treaty of Canandaigua* was the second diplomatic agreement made by the new United States of America under its Constitution. The first agreement was with the Creek tribe in 1790.

Jay Treaty, 1794

On November 19, 1794, the *Jay Treaty* between Great Britain and the United States was signed. The British began to withdraw their garrisons from all

American territory. The Western Alliance, fighting to protect their ancestral homelands from American encroachment, was abandoned by their British allies.

The treaty is named for John Jay, the Chief Justice of the United States and a signatory of the treaty. The full name for the *Jay Treaty* is the *Treaty of Amity, Commerce, and Navigation, Between His Britannic Majesty and the United States of America*. Other names for the treaty include: *Jay's Treaty*; the *British Treaty*; and the *Treaty of London, 1794*. (Olson, 1991)

The *Jay Treaty* was not popular with the American people. However, President George Washington understood the *Jay Treaty* was the price for peace with Great Britain. Washington believed the treaty would give the United States valuable time to consolidate the new United States and rearm in the event of future conflict with Great Britain.

In numerous ways, the *Jay Treaty* has great significance for North America and the Iroquois Confederacy. First, the treaty was an instrument of diplomacy that avoided war between the United States and Great Britain. This was done, in part, by resolving issues that had remained as sore points since the *1783 Treaty of Paris* which had ended the *American Revolutionary War*.

The treaty was written by Secretary of the Treasury Alexander Hamilton; advised by President George Washington; and supported by John Jay, the lead treaty negotiator. The treaty accomplished pressing American objectives. The first objective was to secure the withdrawal of British army regiments from the pre-Revolutionary War forts in the Northwest Territory. Great Britain had resisted relinquishing the forts even though the *1783 Treaty of Paris* had recognized the territory as American. The treaty also set out an agreement that deciding the American and Canadian boundary description would be a matter for arbitration. The Jay Treaty provides an example of one of the first applications of the process of arbitration in diplomatic history. (Bemus, 1923)

The *Jay Treaty* includes content that is particular to 'Indian' rights that remain contentious for the Iroquois to this day.

Article III of the *Jay Treaty* states: *"It is agreed, that it shall at all times be free of His Majesty's subjects, and to the citizens of the United States, and also to the Indians dwelling on either side of the said boundary line, freely to pass and repass, by land or* inland navigation into the respective territories and countries of the two parties on the continent of America and freely carry on trade and commerce with each other." (ibid, 1923)

Article III of the *Jay Treaty* declares: 'the right of Indians as well as of American citizens and Canadian subjects to trade and travel between the United States and Canada.'

The *Jay Treaty* is specific that 'Native Indians born in Canada are therefore entitled to enter the United States for the purpose of employment, study, retirement, investing, and /or immigration.'

Article III of the Jay Treaty set out: "nor shall the Indians passing or repassing with their own proper Goods and Effects whatever nature, pay for the same any Impost or Duty whatever. But Goods in Bales or other large Packages unusual among Indians shall not be considered as Goods belonging bona fide to Indians."

When the *War of 1812* broke out, the United States declared the *Jay Treaty* abrogated.

An argument has been put forward that Article 9 of the *Treaty of Ghent*, 1815, restored the provisions of the *Jay Treaty*. Article 9 reads in part: "And His Britannic majesty engages, on his part, to forthwith restore to such Tribes or Nations, respectively, all the Possessions, Rights and Privileges, which they may have enjoyed or been entitled to in 1811, previous to such hostilities."

Although the matter of passage of Native goods across borders without payment of taxes and duties seems resolved for Canada, the Iroquois in general, and certainly the Mohawk in particular, have a very different view of the matter.

In the 1956 Supreme Court of Canada case of <u>Louis Francis vs Her Majesty the Queen,</u> the Supreme Court found that Article 3 of the *Jay Treaty* and Article 9 of the *Treaty of Ghent* are not applicable in Canada since they have not been implemented or sanctioned by Canadian legislation. Decisions of the Supreme Court of Canada are binding, conclusive, and final. Decisions are not subject to appeal by either judiciary or executive branches of government.

Today, the ongoing issue of movement of goods, such as tobacco, to Canada by the Mohawk without paying customs tax and duty remains contentious and often violent. The Mohawk consider free movement with goods between the United States and Canada to be their right as a sovereign Nation in accordance with the *Jay Treaty*. The Canadian government views this movement of undeclared goods as smuggling and a criminal offence.

> I recall visiting with an experienced smuggler and member of the Akwesasne warrior society, and listening as he justified his smuggling activity as his 'right.'

> He said: 'When George Washington supported the Jay Treaty he said that even an Indian on a horse would be able to freely pass under the rope separating the United States and Canada.'

Greenville Treaty, 1795

On August 3rd, 1795, the *Treaty of Greenville* was signed at Fort Greenville, present-day Greenville, Ohio. The treaty flowed from the defeat of the Western Alliance at the *Battle of Fallen Timbers* the previous year.

The treaty ended the *Northwest Indian War* in the Ohio Valley Region. The treaty signatories were the Native tribes of the *Western Confederacy (Alliance)* and the United States government. General Anthony Wayne signed for the United States government. The notable alliance signatories included: Chief Tarhe, Wyandot; Chief Leatherlips and Chief Roundhead, Delaware (Lenape); Chief Blue Jacket, Shawnee; Chief Little Turtle, Miami. Other signing tribes included the Ottawa; Chippewa; Potawatomi; Wea; Kickapoo and Kaskaskia. (Capitol Ohio: 113 - Treaty of Greenville)

The treaty established the *Greenville Treaty Line*, a boundary between 'Indian Territory' and lands open for American settlement. In a large part, the treaty line was ignored by frontiersmen as they aggressively pushed further west and continued to encroach on tribal lands.

The *Greenville Treaty* would also have a significant future effect on tribal and American relations. The treaty began an annuity payment system that consisted of federal money grants and supplies of calico cloth to the Western Confederacy tribes who had signed the treaty. This treaty provision enabled the government to seize greater influence in tribal affairs. The *Greenville Treaty* is also accepted as the *'beginning of modern Ohio history'*. (Kappler, 1904)

After forty years of war the ownership of the Ohio Region was settled. The Iroquois ancestral homeland was not protected by the *1784 Fort Stanwix Treaty* which had surrendered the Ohio Region a second time. Over the next 60 years, Ohio lands were gradually sold off to land speculators who came from most of the wealthy and politically powerful founding families of New York State.

The Oneida were among the first Iroquois to suffer. The Oneida had served the Americans during their rebellion against Britain. However, the honourable Oneida allegiance was not an American consideration in the frenzy of land acquisition. George Washington had promised the Oneida that they would 'be forever remembered' for their sacrifices and contributions during the *Revolutionary War*. The Oneida were given assurances that their sovereignty and land rights would be honored. For the Oneida, the promises were hollow. They would not be honored by the American government.

After the war the Oneida were living in poverty. They were pushed aside. The new United States did not get around to compensating the Oneida until 1795.

In the meantime, the Oneida had taken in the refugee Christian Stockbridge and Brotherton Natives from New England. The Oneida were desperate. They could not feed themselves let alone the refugees. Destitute and hopeless, the Oneida signed a treaty of land surrender with New York State Governor George Clinton. The Oneida surrendered claim to most of their six million acres in exchange for a small parcel of reservation lands.

The Onondaga were a defeated and humiliated people. New York State was able to convince the Onondaga to sign treaties in 1788 that were similar to the Oneida treaties.

The Cayuga, in no better shape than the Oneida and Onondaga, agreed to treaties with New York State in 1789. The treaties allowed New York State to buy the land from the Cayuga, set aside parcels of land as reservations, then confine the people to the reservation.

Iroquois land continued to be swallowed up by land speculators at an alarming rate. Congress passed the *Non-Intercourse Act in 1790*. This Act prohibited the sale of Iroquois lands to anyone except the federal government.

To be able to implement the *Non-Intercourse Act* effectively, the United States had previously signed the *Canandaigua (Pickering) Treaty, 1794*. The treaty established well defined boundaries for Iroquois land. The efforts of the United States to bring some order to land speculation and the erosion of the Iroquois land base failed to bring a stop to land loss. The political influence and power of prominent New York State families was sufficient to ignore legislation and treaties.

Treaty of Big Tree, 1797

In 1797, at a place called Big Tree, New York State, the Seneca relinquished their rights to nearly all of their ancestral homeland in New York State.

Prior to this, in the *1788 Phelps and Gorman Purchase*, the Seneca had sold their rights to their land between Seneca Lake and the Genesee River.

The 1797 *Treaty of Big Tree* was attended by an estimated 3,000 Seneca. Representing the Seneca were hereditary *royaner* and other Iroquois notables including: Cornplanter; Red Jacket; Young King; Little Billy; Farmer's Brother; Handsome Lake; Tall Chief; Little Beard; and many Clan Mothers of the Five Nations. The United States was represented by Colonel Jeremiah Wadsworth, assigned by President George Washington; Captain Charles Williamson and Thomas Morris; General William Shepherd representing Massachusetts; and William Bayard representing New York State.

After a month of sometimes heated negotiations, the *Treaty of Big Tree* was signed on September 15, 1797. The treaty opened all the country west of the Genesee River for settlement.

The *Treaty of Big Tree* established ten Seneca reservations; guaranteed perpetual annuities and hunting and fishing rights for the Seneca in western New York State. (Wilkinson, 1953)

Chapter 21

A Broken Chain

The Iroquois Confederacy and the War of 1812

In 1791, the British *Constitution Act* authorized the division of the Province of Quebec into Upper Canada (Ontario) and Lower Canada (Quebec).

As the inevitable war between Great Britain and the United States approached, the Iroquois Confederacy found themselves in disunity over matters of allegiance.

The Five Nations of the Iroquois Confederacy, scattered across their ancestral homeland, and beyond, and with the unity of the Confederacy fractured, were unable to come to one mind on what to do. The Haudenosaunee could not reach a unified response to how they would participate - if at all - in the coming war. Even more troublesome, divided loyalties festered within each of the Mohawk, Oneida, Onondaga, Cayuga, and Seneca Nations.

The Confederacy now recognized that there were two Covenant Chains, one with the British Crown and another with the American Congress.

The Haudenosaunee Confederacy royaner, for the most part, favored neutrality in the coming conflict. However, there was no consensus between the New York State Iroquois and the Upper Canada Iroquois of the Six Nations Territory. The Haudenosaunee royaner at Buffalo Creek in western new York State could not find a common ground with the Haudenosaunee royaner at the Six Nations of Grand River, Ontario.

Young warriors were impatient and angry. Many believed that perhaps a new war between Britain and the United States could bring back some of the lost glory of the Iroquois. The young men were reluctant to listen to arguments for Confederacy neutrality from old men.

Before the outbreak of war, in June of 1812, Seneca leaders and warriors accompanied by representatives of the Cayuga and Onondaga, went to the Six Nations of Grand River to talk about neutrality. Many of the leaders and warriors at Grand River remained furious over their losses resulting from the *American Revolutionary War*, and remained staunch allies of the British Crown. Given this environment, the Haudenosaunee royaner found it impossible to come to one mind on the matter of neutrality in the coming war.

Matters grew increasingly tense. The Grand River chiefs told British officials that friendship among the Haudenosaunee had ended. In an effort of appeasement, Seneca leader *Hure-hau-stock* (Captain Strong) made an effort to give the Grand River chief a wampum belt. The gesture was ignored, the wampum belt refused.

The revered and unifying Great Binding Law that had brought armistice and unity among the Five Nations of the Iroquois Confederacy since 1142 CE, was unravelling.

After the United States declared war on Great Britain on June 18, 1812, a second delegation of Onondaga and Seneca supporters of neutrality, travelled to Queenston, Ontario, to meet with the faction from Six Nations of Grand River who supported the British. Only a few of the Onondaga and Seneca delegates were allowed to cross the Niagara River to attend the meeting at Queenston. General Isaac Brock (1769-1812), administrator of Upper Canada, accompanied by the Mohawk leader John *Teyoninhokovrawen* Norton, dominated the meeting and presented strong arguments for supporting the British Crown. The few Onondaga and Seneca who attended were given very little time to present their position.

Seneca speaker *Arosa* (Silver Heels), stood before the delegates with wampum belt in hand, and spoke of the miseries and destruction that was the nature of war. *Arosa* spoke of Iroquois unity of the Great Binding Law and the tragedy that would unfold if old friends fought themselves in war.

" Brothers, the people of the Great King are our old friends, and the Americans are our neighbours. We have determined not to interfere, for how could we spill the blood of the English or of our Brethren? We entreat you therefore to imitate our determination.

Listen to the words of our mothers, they are particularly addressed to the War Chiefs, they entreat them to be united with the village chiefs, and to have a tender regard for the happiness of their women and children and not allow their minds to be too much elated or misled by sentiments of vanity or pride."

And still the Grand River delegates would not listen to the plea for neutrality. Seeing this, Arosa said:

" Let the warrior's rage only be felt in combat, by his armed opponents; let the unoffending Cultivator of the Ground, and his helpless family, never be alarmed by your onset, nor injured by your depredation." (Klinck et al, 1970, pgs. 289-292)

The Americans continued to negotiate to keep the Six Nations of Grand River out of the war. At the beginning of the July 12, 1812, invasion of Upper Canada, Brigadier General William Hull, Governor of the Territory of Michigan, and Commander of the Northwest Army of the United States, sent a message to the Grand River Iroquois that their settlements and families would not be troubled if their warriors remained home.

In a counter threat, General Isaac Brock, furious by the lack of support from the Grand River Iroquois in Britain's time of need, told the leaders that if they did not join with the British they would be removed from Grand River to other lands in the west.

John *Teyoninhokovrawen* Norton made a decision. Refusing to comply with the Grand River Council of Chiefs decision to remain neutral, he would enter the war as allies of the British. John Norton, the adopted nephew of Mohawk leader Joseph Brant, was of Scottish and Cherokee ancestry. Norton may have been made a Pine Tree Chief by the Grand River Council of Chiefs. This was a temporary appointment usually given to War Chiefs. Norton had a history as a staunch activist in his Uncle Joseph Brant's quest for justice from the Crown in matters associated with land rights and the Grand River Iroquois territory.

On September 6, 1812, fearing that American invasion was imminent, Norton sent word to Grand River that all warriors and leaders should assemble at Fort George, without delay. Once assembled, Norton struck his hatchet into a war pole, and accepted from the attending warriors a piece of red painted wood, a symbol of commitment to the coming battle.

Battle of Queenston Heights

The first major battle of the *War of 1812*, was the *Battle of Queenston Heights*. Fought on October 13, 1812, the battle was a humiliating defeat for the Americans. The American forces were pummelled by British artillery while attempting to cross the Niagara River.

The American militia, handicapped by inadequate training and no combat experience, was unable to provide adequate support for the regular force soldiers, and the Americans failed to secure the advantage. The British forces were able to fend off the attackers until reinforcements arrived from their Lake Erie garrisons. The American defeat was enormous in terms of losses. Out of a combined force of 900 regulars, and 2,650 militia, they suffered 100 killed, 170 wounded, and 835 captured. The British butcher's bill was less. Out of a combined force of 1,300 regulars, militia, and Iroquois, they suffered 21 killed, 85 wounded, and 22 captured.

Major General Isaac Brock was wounded, and then killed during the battle. His first wound was a musket ball to the wrist. He continued to fight and press his advantage over the Americans. He had adorned his already bright uniform with a colorful sash given to him eight weeks earlier by the Shawnee war chief Tecumseh after the siege of Detroit. He was an outstanding target on the battlefield. The fatal wound came when he was shot in the chest by an unknown American from a distance of some fifty yards. The musket ball killed General

Brock instantly. Brock, 'the saviour of Upper Canada,' was dead on the field of battle. (Cruikshank, 1964, pg. 36)

John Norton and his 160 Iroquois warriors fought with distinction during the *Battle of Queenston Heights*. Eyewitness accounts, supported by the research of historians, credit the Iroquois for slowing the American advance in the thick of battle. Their efforts gave the British defenders the time needed for reinforcements to arrive from their Lake Erie garrisons.

The Six Nations of Grand River war chiefs and leaders who fought in the *Battle of Queenston Heights* included: John *Ah'you'wa'eghs* Brant, son of Joseph Brant; John *Teyoninhokarawen* Norton; Thomas *Toowaghwenkaraghkwen* Davis; Aaron *Kenwendeshon* Hill; and David *Karaghkohtye* Davids. Killed in action during the battle were the Cyauga war chiefs *Ayanete* and *Kayentaterhon*. Also, an Onondaga warrior named *Ta Kanentye*; and two Oneida warriors named *Kayarawagor* and *Sakangongu'quate*. (Compiled by Rick Hill, Chairman, Six Nations Legacy Consortium)

The Iroquois conducted a General Council of Condolence at the Council House at Fort George on November 6th, 1812. The Council of Condolence was attended by Six Nations of Grand River, Wendat, Chippewa, Potawatomie, and others.

Kodeaneyonte (Little Cayuga) condoled the British for the death of Major General Brock at Queenston.

Standing and holding a wampum belt, Kodeaneyonte said:

"Brother, we, therefore, now seeing you darkened with grief, your eyes dim with tears and your throat stopped with the force of your affliction, with these strings of wampum we wipe away your tears, that you may view clearly the surrounding objects. We clear the passage in your throats that you may have free utterance for your thoughts, and we wipe clear from blood the place of your abode, that you may sit there in comfort without having renewed the remembrance of your loss by the remaining stains of blood."

Bringing forth a white wampum belt, Kodeaneyonte continued to speak.

"Brother, that the remains of your late beloved friend and commander, General Brock, shall receive no injury we cover it with this belt of wampum, which we do from the grateful sensations which his friendship towards us continually inspired us with, as also in conformity to the customs of our ancestors, and we therefore now express with unanimous voice of the chiefs and warriors of our respective bands the great respect in which we hold his memory, and the sorrow and deep regret with which his loss has tilled our hearts, although he has taken his departure for a better abode, where his many virtues will be rewarded by the great dispenser of good, who has led us on the road to victory."

Kodeaneyonte finished his address.

" We assure him [Brock's successor] of our readiness to support him to the last, and therefore take the liberty to exhort him to speak strong to all his people to co-operate with vigor, and trusting in the powerful arm of God not to doubt of victory. Although our numbers are small, yet counting Him on our side how ever decided on the day of battle, we look for victory whenever we shall come in contact with the enemy." (Canadian Archives, C. 256, Pg. 194)

Battle of Fort George and the Battle of Beaver Dams

The *Battle of Fort George*, at present-day Niagara-on-the-Lake, Ontario, near Queenston Heights, was fought May 25 -27, 1813. The battle was an American victory and Fort George, in Upper Canada was captured. The engagement included regular infantry; militia; Iroquois warriors, and armed vessels of the America navy.

The battle started with an amphibious assault by 14 armed American vessels. The British forces were able to avoid encirclement, and escaped capture. The Americans captured the fort. British forces consisted of 1,355 combatants. The British butcher's bill was 52 dead, 306 wounded or deserted, 276 captured. American forces included 4,000 regular infantry plus the support of 14 armed vessels. Their butcher's bill was 40 dead and 113 wounded. (Cruikshank, 1990)

After the battle, the Americans, due to war pressures on other fronts, maintained only a small defensive enclave at Fort George. A disaster for the occupying force was a failed sortie against a British outpost at a place called Beaver Dams, present-day Thorold, Ontario. The day before the battle, the advancing American troops had billeted in the village of Queenston, Ontario. A resident of Queenston, Laura Secord, learned of the American plans and embarked on a long and perilous journey to warn the British at a place called Decous, a stone house near present-day Brock University. The warning allowed the British and their Iroquois allies to organize an ambush.

The Iroquois contingent of the British force consisted of 300 warriors, mostly Mohawk, from Kahnawake, also known as Caughnawaga. The Native force was commanded by Captain Dominique Ducharme of the Indian Department. Another 100 Mohawk were commanded by Captain William Johnson. A force of 46 men of the 49th Regiment were held in reserve.

The *Battle of Beaver Dams* was fought on June 24, 1813. The Americans were forced to surrender. The butcher's bill for the Americans was 25 killed; 50 wounded and taken prisoner; and another 462 captured. The British causalities were 5 to 15 killed; and 20 to 25 wounded. The Americans abandoned Fort George in December, 1813. (Elting,1991, pgs. 139-140)

The force of British allied Mohawk from the Lower Canada settlement of Kahnawake, located on the St. Lawrence River adjacent to the City of Montreal, represents a Quebec contribution to the *War of 1812* and the defense of Canada from American invasion.

The tide of battle changed, as it always does in war. The July 5th, 1814, *Battle of Chippewa*, followed by the *Battle of Lundy's Lane*, were victories for the Americans. For the Iroquois, the aftermath of the *Battle of Chippewa* would provide a critical opportunity for peacemaking internal to the Iroquois.

Seneca leader Red Jacket, who was then in his 60s, had allied with the Americans. Red Jacket led Seneca warriors against 200 warriors from Six Nations of Grand River and other Native allies led by British leader John Norton. Red Jacket was a Seneca Wolf Clan Chief [in his youth known as *Otetiani*, and later in life, due to his oratory skills, *Sagoyewatha* - Keeper Awake]. An example of his oratory skills can be found in his 1805 speech *'Religion for the White and the Red'*.

The *Battle of Chippewa* battle casualty list was brutal. The British butcher's bill was 108 dead; 319 wounded; 75 wounded and taken prisoner; 15 captured; and 18 missing. The American battle causality list included: 60 dead; 249 wounded; and 19 missing. (Cruikshank, 1997, pg. 43)

In the immediate aftermath of the battle, Norton and his warriors found the bodies of 87 of their kinsmen allied with the Americans and killed in the battle. The American Seneca later found 25 of their own dead and many wounded. Oneida Chief Cornelius Doxtator was also killed in the skirmishing.

The *Battle of Chippewa* was traumatic for the Iroquois, who now found themselves killing and maiming each other. Grieving what amounted to large scale fratricide, the Iroquois realized something had to be done about disengaging from the horror and tragedy of the war.

In 1813, American ally Red Jacket gave two young chiefs a mission. They were to go to the British encampment at Burlington and arrange to meet with the Six Nations of the Grand River leaders and any others allied with them. Their mission was to offer a proposal for a mutual withdrawal from the war. Red Jacket's emissaries, known as Buffalo Creek Chiefs, were able to meet with their kinfolk. Together, they talked for three days. Returning to Red Jacket's camp, the young chiefs told Red Jacket his idea was acceptable.

This was a crucial moment for the Five Nations of the Iroquois Confederacy. Two weeks after the *Battle of Chippawa*, the opposing warriors met in council and agreed to end the fratricide. The warriors withdrew from their respective allies and returned to their homes.

But the peace was temporary. As the war ebbed and flowed, rebellious Iroquois warriors fought as 'unofficial' allies of both the British and the Americans. After a long procrastination, the New York State Iroquois were forced to abandon their hope of remaining neutral. On August 24, 1813, the Six Nations Haudenosaunee Council at Buffalo Creek, New York State, declared allegiance to the Americans.

As the war wound down, the Seneca attacked the British after the British attacked and occupied Grand Island in the Niagara River. The Seneca claimed the island as their land. The leaders of the Seneca warriors were: Farmers

Brother, Red Jacket, Little Billy, Pollard, Black Snake, John Silver Heels, Captain Half Town, Major Henry O'Bail, and Captain Cold. The British responded by attacking and burning a Tuscarora village near Niagara Falls, New York State. (Edmunds, 2006)

In 1814, American General Jacob Brown led a force that included 500 Buffalo Creek Haudenosaunee made up of Seneca, Onondaga, Oneida, and Tuscarora warriors commanded by Red Jacket and General Porter. This force captured Fort Erie from the British. (From the compilation by Rick Hill, Chairman, Six Nations Legacy Consortium)

Tecumseh's Confederacy

The continuing loss of Native land to American settlers provided the bitterness that became the foundation for the resistance movement led by the Shawnee leader *Tecumseh* and his brother *Tenskwatawa*, known as the 'Prophet'.

During the *War of 1812*, some Mingo, under the leadership of Tecumseh, allied with the British. In the beginning, most of the Mingo - by now an integrated community of Seneca, Cayuga, Shawnee, Delaware, and Susquehannock - with the Iroquois in New York State, tried to remain neutral. But there were exceptions. After the War of 1812, alliances changed. Many of the Mingo allied themselves with the Shawnee leader Tecumseh until his death in 1813.

Tecumseh gathered an alliance of tribes into a confederacy. Tecumseh had stoked the fires of discontent by reviving the idea first advocated years before by the Shawnee leader Blue Jacket and the Mohawk leader Joseph Brant that *'Native American land was owned in common by all tribes and land could not be sold without agreement of all tribes.'*

Tecumseh won a following of Fox, Sauk, Piankeshaw, Kickapoo, and many militant members of the Shawnee, Chickamauga, Ojibwe, Mascouten, Potawatomi and a scattering of rebellious Iroquois warriors eager to attempt to recover something of which they had lost in the *American Revolutionary War*. Tecumseh now had as many as 5,000 warriors under his command. The United States began to consider Tecumseh as a threat that would have to be dealt with. The sooner the better.

On November 7th, 1811, American forces under the command of William Henry Harrison, attacked Tecumseh's confederacy forces in a pre-emptive strike at present-day Battle Ground, Indiana. The battle became known as the *Battle of Tippecanoe*.

Tecumseh's brother Tenskwatawa (the Prophet), a spiritual leader but not a military man, led 500 to 700 warriors in Tecumseh's absence. Tenskwatawa was defeated by Harrison's forces. Tecumseh's coalition of tribes never recovered from the defeat.

Tecumseh attempted to rebuild his confederacy which had been smashed by Harrison in 1811. At the outbreak of the *War of 1812*, Tecumseh allied himself with the British in Canada and declared war on the United States.

He planned and implemented a series of raids to attack American forts in the Indian Territories. Tecumseh played an important part in the war of 1812. Tecumseh's warriors assisted a small force of 700 British regulars and Canadian militia to capture Fort Detroit in August, 1812, forcing the surrender of 2,500 American soldiers.

The guerilla war fought by Tecumseh forced the Americans to fight rear-guard actions. The guerilla strategy divided the American forces, subsequently denying them sufficient capability and coordination needed to invade and occupy Lower Canada (Quebec).

Tecumseh was killed in 1813, at the *Battle of the Thames*, near present-day Chatham, Ontario. Tecumseh was fighting to turn back American forces attempting to retake Fort Detroit, Ontario. Retreating British forces had abandoned Tecumseh's 500 warriors to face, alone without British support, an advancing American army of 3,000 infantry and cavalry. Tecumseh's death had a deep and demoralizing affect on his followers. Tecumseh's confederacy dissolved.

Representatives of Tecumseh's warriors signed the *1815 Treaty of Indian Springs*. This treaty allowed them to return to the United States. Two years later, overseen by US representatives Lewis Cass and Duncan McArthur, the Ohio tribes surrendered their last remaining Ohio lands in the *1817 Treaty of Fort Meigs*, at Maumee Rapids, Ohio. This treaty is also known as the *'Foot of the Rapids*

Treaty.' The Ohio tribes represented at the treaty included: Wyandot, Seneca, Delaware, Potawatomi, Ottawa, and Chippewa.

In exchange for peace with the United States, the tribes received parcels of reservation land. Very soon after the treaty, the land surrendered in the treaty by the tribes was auctioned off to white settlers. (Cave, 2002)

There were two Seneca groups represented by the *1817 Treaty of Fort Meigs*. The first group, a mixed Seneca and Shawnee community, were given reserve lands at Lewiston, Ohio. The second Seneca group received a 30,000-acre reserve on the Sandusky River north of the Wyandot Reservation. This group of Seneca became known as the Seneca of Sandusky. Treaties signed at St. Marys the next year added more land to both Seneca reservations.

Chapter 22

Haudenosaunee Reconciliation

William Claus Wampum Belt

In August, 1815, a Council of Reconciliation was held at Niagara. On the American side of the fire sat Seneca, Onondaga, and Cayuga from Buffalo Creek, Tonawanda, and Allegheny. The Canadian side of the fire was represented by warriors from the Six Nations of the Grand River. The first day the Grand River chiefs made presentation. On the second day, the American chiefs had the floor. And so it went, back and forth.

By the end of the Council of Reconciliation, the Haudenosaunee had 'mixed together' and become 'one people' again.

The Council of Reconciliation, known as the *King's Council Fire*, provides an excellent example of the internal reconciliation process.

Echo, an Onondaga Chief said: " *To make our Friendship lasting, we put the Hatchet the depth of a pine tree underground; and that it may not be removed we place over it a Tree that the roots may so cover it that it cannot be found again. We condole with you from the bottom of our hearts for the loss of your friends, and wipe the tears from your eyes, we open your throats so no obstruction shall remain, that you may speak your mind freely and with the same friendship which formerly existed between us, as we now in the name of the Nations already mentioned address you as friends."*

Following is the response was given by Seneca war leader Red Jacket:

" We are not of the same Nations only, but of the same Families also. We therefore ought to be united and become one Body. We seriously recommend that your people will now attend to your usual occupations of hunting and agriculture and that you pay due attention to your women, who by our ancient customs have a voice in bringing up your Young people to the practice of truth and industry." (DCB vol. VI: 759-760; MPHSC vol. XVI: 263-265; PSWJ vol. XII: 628)

William Claus Wampum Belt

At the cessation of hostilities of the *War of 1812*, the British were eager to secure, and in some formal manner, reinforce the loyalty of the Iroquois. It was decided that a great council would be hosted by the British and a wampum belt would be given to the Iroquois.

The presenter would be Deputy Superintendent General, Colonel William Claus (1765-1826). Colonel Claus had a long family history in Native affairs. He was the grandson of Sir William Johnson; the son of Colonel Daniel Claus; and nephew of Sir John Johnson the Superintendent of Indian Affairs. This was some pedigree. Indeed, the Imperial Indian Department had been administered by the Johnson family since 1755 and would continue to do so until 1830.

The wampum belt, also known as the *Pledge of the Crown Wampum Belt*, was designed to represent an ongoing friendship between the British and the Haudenosaunee. The wampum bead pattern might have been borrowed from an ancient design called the *meander*, or *Greek Key*. The pattern was common in representing bonds of love and friendship.

Colonel Claus commenced the Great Council at Burlington on April 15, 1815. The council was attended by delegates from the Six Nations of the Iroquois (Mohawk, Oneida, Onondaga, Cayuga, Seneca, Tuscarora). Also attending were representation from the Wendat, Shawnee, Lenape-Delaware, Kickapoo,

Chippewa (Ojibwe), Ottawa, Sauk, Mequakie(Fox), Creek, Munsey Delaware, Moravian, and Nanticoke.

Colonel Claus opened the council with the traditional condolence of wiping the tears of those who had lost comrades during the war.

"The ceremony of condolence for the loss of our near and dearest relations and friends, now must be performed, which I do very sincerely. I now gather together the bones of those dear Friends and relations whom it pleased the Great Spirit to remove from this world. I place them all in one Grave, and to prevent all briars and rubbish from collecting thereon, I cover it with this belt."

Holding the wampum belt, Claus spoke:

"To inform you that Peace has been concluded, and that all hostilities are to cease between your Great Father's children and the Americans, and it is his earnest wish for the sake of your Women and Children that you join sincerely in this Peace. It is therefore my duty to inform all the Nations here assembled, that the Hatchet which you so readily took up to assist your Great father, should now be laid down and buried, that it may not be seen. You have fought and bled in the cause which you espoused and your Father is sensible of the value of your friendship and services. This belt which I now hand to you I ask in compliance with your Customs be sent by you with these my words in his behalf to all the Nations in friendship with your Great father the king of England.

I am further instructed to inform you that in making Peace with the Government of the United States of America, your interests were not neglected, nor would Peace have been made with them had they not consented to include you in the Treaty, which they at first refused to listen to. I will now repeat to you one of the Articles of the Treaty of Peace which secures you to the Peaceable Possession of all the Country which you possessed before the late War, and the Road is now open for you to pass and repass without interruption.

I now look towards the Sachems and principal chiefs, who after the Hatchet is laid down by the War Chiefs and Warriors, will again take their seats in front of the Warriors and resume their duties whilst the others return to their hunting and other occupations. Your Great Father's Council Fire will again be kindled at the usual posts, the smoke from which will be seen by all Nations around you." (NAC RG8 C Series Vol. 258 pt. 1 pp. 60-70a)

This is the verse of honest and honorable intentions. But could such words of promise and hope spoken with such passion by Echo, the Onondaga chief; by the Seneca war chief Red Jacket; and Colonel Claus; withstand the coming tests of greed for land and the sham of politics.

We shall see.

Pledge of the Crown Wampum

Chapter 23

A Defeated People
From Princes of Empire to Refugee

The Winter of an Empire
From Princes of Wilderness Empire to Refugee

All things have a beginning and an end. Time and again throughout history empires rise, celebrate their strength and achievement, then weaken and fall. This is the cycle of history.

The wilderness empire of the Haudenosaunee Confederacy was built on the belief they needed to dominate the economic power of the fur trade. For a time, the Iroquois were the political and military equal of the European imperial powers wrestling for control of eastern North America.

For the Iroquois, the loss of their wilderness empire was inevitable. The deck was stacked against them from the beginning. It was only a matter of time before the Iroquois would be overwhelmed by the flood of European population onto ancestral lands and the vast wilderness territory claimed by the Iroquois through conquest.

In the beginning, the North American population of Swedish, Dutch, French, and English traders and colonists was insignificant. The European populations were weak and vulnerable. The survival of the first Europeans to North America was perilous at best. European survival, or not, was entirely dependant on the good will, support, and alliances of the Indigenous people they first encountered.

To sustain their meager footprint in the wilderness, Europeans required effective alliances with the indigenous tribes on whose ancestral lands they trespassed.

The Haudenosaunee Confederacy, grown dependant on European trade goods, was introduced to the alien concepts of economic power and expansionist policies.

Believing that their military power could seize and sustain economic dominance and territorial expansion, the Haudenosaunee Confederacy engaged in intelligent strategies of alliance building. They established coalitions of Nations using the Covenant Chain treaty framework of coexistence introduced by the Dutch.

Inevitably, European immigration increased to levels of population that broke their dependence on the Indigenous tribes and confederacies. In time, strong self-sustaining European populations boldened European behaviour and policy towards their tribal hosts. European policies of coexistence evolved into policies of subjugation.

The Haudenosaunee Confederacy transitioned from political and military equality with the eastern North America Dutch, French, and English, to a proxy military asset. European imperialism pulled and pushed the Haudenosaunee Confederacy in directions that, ultimately, were not in the interest of a sustainable Confederacy.

Imperial European ambitions to secure territory and win economic dominance erased any compunction to refrain from acts of betrayal and treachery towards tribal allies. Fraudulent treaties and the duplicity of European allies prevailed in the face of overwhelming pressure to neutralize tribal resistance and secure land for settlement.

France, England, and the United States used the Iroquois Confederacy and their Covenant Chain coalition as a proxy military asset. England and the United

States also used the Iroquois Confederacy as a proxy enforcement agent to threaten regional tribes to bend to the will of British or American policy particular to treaty compliance and land settlement.

Forced to decide on alliances in the French and English struggles for economic dominance, and the increasing belligerence of the Thirteen Colonies against Britain, the Iroquois found themselves fractured and allied with opposing sides. This situation was untenable in terms of the Five Nations unity of the Great Binding Law. Iroquois were killing Iroquois. A civil war among the Iroquois was in progress.

The flood of Europeans onto wilderness lands of eastern North America was unmanageable and unstoppable. Enforcing any regulation particular to the sale of 'Indian' lands and migration of settlers onto tribal land would be a doomed government endeavour. The affluence and political influence of land speculators combined with the unrelenting demands of migrating settlers made for an intense and volatile environment. Any attempt to impede or halt expansion would kick the hornet's nest of civil disobedience. Governments had no hope of regulating the encroachment of settlers trespassing on ancestral lands. Settler migration was a dark tide of greed and violence that crept further and further west from the original Atlantic seaboard colonies.

The inability of government to regulate migration, driven in a large part by the greed of land speculators, meant the Iroquois were overwhelmed. Their capacity to influence any sort of restraint on settler invasion was exhausted. Short of offering hollow threat and the inevitable hopelessness of armed conflict, there was little the Iroquois Confederacy could do.

In time, the Covenant Chain coalition began to weaken. Covenant Chain members no longer considered the Iroquois Confederacy capable of managing their petitions. They did not see the Confederacy having the strength to enforce treaty articles for the benefit and security of members. The Iroquois Confederacy had also lost much of its credibility with the tribal alliances resisting settler expansion into the Ohio Valley Region and the Northwest Territory. The Confederacy was seen to be increasingly irrelevant as an influencing agent in matters of treaty and land negotiation.

The immense scale and intensity of world, regional, and territorial events had simply overwhelmed the political and military capability of the Iroquois Confederacy.

Hostilities between Britain and the rebellious Thirteen Colonies intensified. The Iroquois found themselves in a position of having to chose whether to ally with the British Crown or the rebellious colonists. The hereditary royaner of the Iroquois Confederacy preferred to remain neutral. A position of neutrality in the approaching revolutionary war did not sit well with the hot-blooded young warriors who eagerly longed for the opportunity to fight, mostly as allies of the British.

The young men turned aside from the traditional leadership of their hereditary royaner and responded to war cries howling from the wilderness. The young charismatic Mohawk, Joseph *Thayendanegea* Brant, gathered together Iroquois warriors, and in defiance of the Iroquois Confederacy royaner, declared alliance with the British.

The unity of the Iroquois Confederacy was shattered. Now it would be Iroquois fighting Iroquois. The Confederacy fire at Onondaga was extinguished by the Haudenosaunee Firekeepers. The unity the Peacemaker had forged among the Five Tribes of the Haudenosaunee was shattered. The Great Binding Law of the Haudenosaunee Confederacy was in tatters.

The beginning of the *American Revolutionary War, 1775-1783,* was also the beginning of the end for the Iroquois Confederacy as an influential entity. By the end of the war, the Five Nations of the Iroquois Confederacy had been devastated. The people had fallen from princes of empire to refugees in their own ancestral lands.

Near the end of the *American Revolutionary War,* relentlessly harassed by local militias and the Continental Army of the new United States, many Iroquois left their ancestral lands and fled to British Upper Canada. There, as a reward for being loyal allies, and in *Honour of the Crown,* land grants were awarded to the Iroquois refugees. One of the land grants is known today as the Six Nations of Grand River located near present-day Brantford, Ontario. A second land grant is the Tyendinaga Mohawk Territory, near present-day Deseronto on the Bay of Quinte, Lake Ontario.

Some historians believe the lowest point in the history of the Iroquois people probably occurred during the ten-year period between the *1784 Fort Stanwix Treaty*, which surrendered the Ohio Region for the second time, and the *1794 Canandaigua Treaty*, which designated specific boundaries for the Iroquois Confederacy people.

Lands Lost to Treaty

Large parcels of ancestral Seneca land were sold in 1802 and 1823. By 1807, the Cayuga had sold the last of their New York lands. Many of the now dispossessed Cayuga went west to the Ohio Region to take up residence with the Mingo who were now known as the Seneca of the Sandusky. Other groups of Cayuga joined the Mohawk in New York State, or crossed the border to join the Iroquois in Canada.

The Mohawk story is similar in many ways to other Iroquois Confederacy Nations. Only two Mohawk leaders signed the *1784 Fort Stanwix Treaty*. Most of the Mohawk leaders were with Joseph Brant in Canada. The Mohawk were still at war with the Americans in the Ohio Region. During the years following the *Fort Stanwix Treaty*, the Mohawk homeland in upper New York State was overrun by settlers. It was now apparent to the Mohawk that they had lost their New York State ancestral homeland.

Joseph Brant, found himself in the awkward position of having to sell parcels of the Grand River land grant to secure necessary funds to feed the people. Brant also ceded a good amount of New York State Mohawk land in a treaty signed at Albany, New York, in 1797. The Onondaga sold much of their reservation land to New York State in 1822.

The same year, the tension between the Quaker missions and the Oneida over Haudenosaunee spirituality began to flare. In 1822, the Oneida sold their land. An estimated half of the Oneida population decided to move to Wisconsin. The Christian Stockbridge and Brotherton Natives decided they would leave with the Oneida. The move was delayed when the United States government ran into problems with the purchase of land from the Menominee. However, by 1838, more than 600 Oneida had settled near Green Bay, Wisconsin. The Tuscarora also agreed to move, but in the end, most stayed in New York State or moved to Canada.

The Seven Nations of Canada Relinquished Land Claims in New York State

The *Iroquois of Caughnawaga [Kahnawake]* signed one treaty with the United States. The treaty was signed in 1796, at present-day New York City, on behalf of the *Seven Nations of Canada [League of Seven Nations]*.

The treaty relinquished Caughnawaga land claims in New York State except for a 36-square mile territory on the New York State and Quebec, Canada, border. This small territory was called the St. Regis Reservation, and is located on the St. Lawrence River in present-day Quebec Province. Their Canadian residence excluded the St. Regis Mohawk from the removal provisions of the American *Indian Removal Act.*

The Caughnawaga and other groups of Canadian Iroquois were active throughout the mid and late 1800s as participants in western Canada exploration, survey expeditions, and the fur trade. Canadian Iroquois worked for both the Hudson Bay Company and the Northwest Company. Mohawk from the Montreal area were sought after as voyageurs on the long and arduous canoe routes to the Mackenzie Delta and the Pacific Coast. The rugged Iroquois voyageurs gave a competitive edge to the company for whom they worked.

Due to their occupations in the fur trade, the Caughnawaga Mohawk had frequent contact with western Canada tribes. Intermarriage was common. In 1840, a Caughnawaga Mohawk, Ignace Lamoose, brought the Jesuit missionaries to the Flathead and Kalispel tribes of Montana.

During the 1840s, Mohawk families working for the Hudson Bay Company settled in the Willamette Valley of Oregon. As early as 1800, the Northwest company had encouraged Caughnawaga families to move west and settle in Alberta. In 1877, the Canadian government established a reserve for the Iroquois band of Chief Michel Calihoo near Villeneuve, Alberta. Today, Villeneuve is the home of the Michel First Nation.

The Indian Removal Act, 1830

The final blow to the Iroquois arrived with the enactment of the *Indian Removal Act, 1830*. Pressure from settlers had been growing to remove the remaining Iroquois from upper New York State. The *Treaty of Buffalo Creek, 1838*, resulted in an Iroquois concession they would move to southeastern Kansas. Much of the agreement was never implemented. Politically influential Quakers stepped up to defend the Iroquois and succeeded in blocking the intent of the *Treaty of Buffalo Creek*.

By 1846, one group of 210 New York Seneca had moved to Kansas. In 1873, the Kansas Iroquois lands were declared forfeit and the land rights of the 32 Iroquois still living there were repurchased by the government. Groups of Seneca and Onondaga who had fought the Americans in the *Revolutionary War*, remained in New York.

The Oneida had a difficult time. In 1839, after the *Buffalo Creek Treaty*, some 250 New York Oneida purchased land near London, Ontario, Canada. By 1845 there were more than 400 Oneida living there. Another 200 Oneida continued to live near Oneida, New York, or moved to live with the Onondaga. Today, there are 5,209 band members of the *Oneida Nation of the Thames*, living near London, Ontario. An estimated 2,030 of these Oneida live on the land known to the Oneida who live there as the Oneida Community. The Canadian Federal government lists the Oneida community as *Oneida 41 Indian Reservation*.

Despite Federal laws to protect Iroquois land in New York State, the Seneca continued to see their land base diminish with sales to settlers. The sale of land was the result, in a large part, of incompetent and corrupt Seneca leadership. The Seneca, having lost their trust in their traditional leadership, ended the Haudenosaunee tradition of governance through hereditary Confederacy royaner. Demoralized and fractured from within, the Seneca separated from the Iroquois Confederacy in 1838.

The Mingo in Ohio fought as part of the Western Tribal Alliance until their defeat at the *Battle of Fallen Timbers, 1794*. In 1795, the Mingo had made a peace with the Americans at Fort Greenville.

The name *Mingo* is a Delaware word *Minqua* meaning *treacherous*. The Delaware called the Susquehannock and other Iroquoian speaking tribes Minqua. By 1830, the Mingo had become a mixed group of Seneca, Cayuga, some Shawnee, Delaware and Susquehannock, with descendants of Neutrals, Wendat, and Erie who had been adopted by the Iroquois during the 1650's. The British and Americans recognized the Mingo as a distinct tribe. In the early 1700s the Mingo settled in Ohio and western Pennsylvania. The Mingo established villages with the Delaware and Shawnee who arrived in the area after the Mingo settlement.

In 1805, the Wyandot signed the *Treaty of Fort Industry*. This treaty ceded the eastern part of northern Ohio forcing the remaining Mingo villages to relocate to northwest Ohio. In 1807, the Mingo were joined by a large group of Cayuga from New York State. In 1830, with the passage of the *Indian Removal Act*, the century long residence of the Mingo in Ohio came to an end.

In February, 1831, the Seneca of the Sandusky signed a treaty agreeing to their removal to the northeast part of Indian Territory, the lands west of the Mississippi River and adjacent to the western Cherokee. In July, the Seneca and Shawnee group at Lewiston also agreed to move to the Indian Territory.

In 1857, some 200 Kansas Wyandot moved to the same area as the Seneca and Shawnee.

The *American Civil War* was now being fought. Unfortunately, the group of Kansas Wyandot who had settled with the Seneca had declared themselves to be pro-Union. In June, 1862, soldiers of the *Confederate States of America* moved onto the Seneca Reserve, forcing the Wyandot, and many of the Seneca, to leave. The Seneca spent the civil war in refugee camps on the Marais des Cygnes River in eastern Kansas.

After the Civil War ended, Kansas demanded the removal of all 'Indians' from inside its borders. In 1867, the Federal government negotiated a treaty with the eastern tribes who had been removed to Kansas during the 1830s. Most of the people moved to Oklahoma. This included the 200 Seneca who had arrived from New York State in 1846. The mixed Seneca and Shawnee group, along with the Seneca of Sandusky group, joined together to form the present-day *Seneca Cayuga Tribe of Oklahoma*.

Iroquois Communities (Cdn.) and Reservations (U.S.), 2016

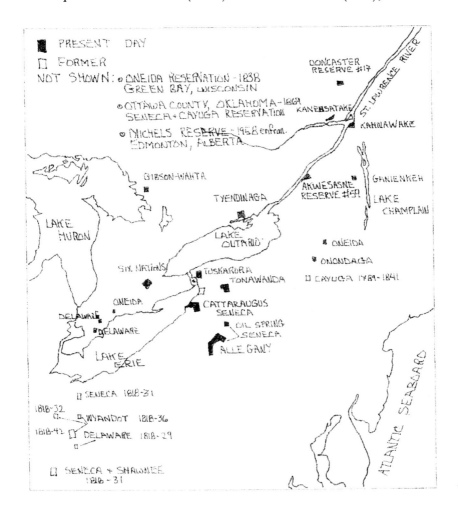

The Iroquois in Recent Times

Chapter 24

The Iroquois in Recent Times

The influence of the Seneca prophet Handsome Ganiodaiio Lake and the Good Message; Suppression of Traditional Governance

Many Iroquois believe the teachings of Handsome *Ganiodaiio* Lake are an important part in the cultural recovery of the Iroquois. The teachings are attributed to protecting much of the traditional culture, ceremonies, and civil governance of the Iroquois.

In 1799, the Seneca prophet Handsome *Ganiodaiio* Lake, received a spiritual vision that would change his life. *Ganiodaiio's* vision would also alter the spiritual belief and lives of many Iroquois. Handsome Lake preached the Good Message, known as the *Gai'wiio*. The *Gai'wiio* is the foundation of the *Longhouse Religion*.

The *Longhouse Religion* is a blend of Haudenosaunee values captured in the *Great Binding Law* and Christian bible messages. The religious teaching that Handsome Lake shared are accepted as universal and commendable by many Iroquois.

Handsome Lake's teaching held an element of accommodation with the white man. Many American leaders viewed the *Longhouse Religion* as an indication that the Iroquois were becoming more accepting and comfortable with the white man's way of thinking. President Thomas Jefferson sent Handsome Lake a letter commending him on his vision and efforts to share his world view.

However, Handsome Lake was not in the business of appeasement or surrendering ancestral beliefs. Handsome Lake's time and energy were dedicated to finding a way to adopt the messages of the Great Binding Law to the new world of the Iroquois. Handsome Lake was in the business of ensuring cultural survival. His passion was the preservation of as much Haudenosaunee culture as possible in his lifetime, certainly a time of rapid cultural transmission.

Handsome Lake's teaching contains a message tone that encourages the people to adapt a code of personal discipline to meet the physical and spiritual dangers of their time. The Good Message recognized the traumatic change the Iroquois had experienced in a very brief time period. As a society, the Iroquois, and certainly Handsome Lake himself, suffered trans-generational trauma. The people needed all the encouragement they could find to survive this chaotic period of devastating cultural change.

Handsome Lake's *Longhouse Religion* is a traditional Native religion that has ensured the preservation and practice of the messages of the *Great Binding Law*. The *Good Message* gives great importance to the purpose and observance of traditional cultural ceremonies. Handsome Lake recognized that the ceremonies are the core of Iroquois culture.

Handsome Lake opposed, with vigor, Christian missionaries competing for Native converts. The various Christian religions considered Native settlements a gold mine for souls for conversion. The missionaries, from every Christian denomination, could not build their reservation churches fast enough.

Besides the choice of either the traditional Haudenosaunee spirituality or the *Good Message* teachings of Handsome Lake, other societal divisions remain among the Iroquois. The matter of the Iroquois Confederacy 'fire' remains contentious. Does the true council fire rest with the Six Nations in Canada; or with the Onondaga in New York State? After all, the Peacemaker designated the Onondaga and their leader Tadodaho to be *Keepers of the Fire*, responsible for its safekeeping. Certainly, the internal dispute particular to the Confederacy fire will find satisfactory resolution in the years ahead.

Suppression of Traditional Governance

In 1924, Canada involuntarily imposed band government on the Canadian Iroquois. Rather then the traditional system of consensual acceptance of clan sponsored hereditary royaner, the Canadian band system was based on an election system to select 'council chiefs.' Elected chiefs would serve the community for a two-year period, unless otherwise specified in regulation made pursuant to the *Indian Act, 1876*.

In the United States, the Iroquois opposed American citizenship when it was extended to the American Iroquois in 1924. The American Iroquois also fought against the *1934 Wheeler-Howard Indian Reorganization Act*. This legislation would a have introduced a mandatory legislated process requiring federal approval for tribal government structure and process.

Today, the traditional civil governance system of hereditary royaner is experiencing recovery in some Iroquois communities. Among the Five Nations of the Iroquois, a current challenge is to bring forth the full slate of fifty hereditary royaner. Condoling hereditary Lords must involve the traditional Haudenosaunee practice of consensual nomination and selection process initiated by Clan Mothers.

None of the Five Nations have yet to assemble the full roster of condoled hereditary royaner originally negotiated by the Peacemaker. In many Nations, sub-chiefs are acting as intermediaries until condoled hereditary chiefs are in place. The process of restoring longhouse government is dependant on the availability of applied traditional knowledge particular to governance. The political will of the people, or its absence, and presence of traditional leadership is also a factor for some Iroquois communities. These matters require time.

The elected band councils, brought in to satisfy the Federal governments on both the United States and Canadian sides of the border, are tolerated by the Haudenosaunee. The Haudenosaunee view of elected council is that they serve a municipal government function - filling potholes and snowplowing roads. Perhaps, from time to time, the elected councils conduct some affairs whose dealings with provincial, state, and federal governments are viewed as *memorandums of understanding without precedent or prejudice*. At the same time, the shadow government of traditional Haudenosaunee condoled hereditary royaner conducts the function of a federal government in matters of national policy, treaty negotiation and interpretation, land claim settlement, and inter-government conflict resolution.

> *A few years ago, during the hostile Six Nations occupation of lands adjacent to the Six Nations Territory, at Grand River, Brantford, Ontario, several publicly and politically notable persons were appointed to negotiate a settlement with the Six Nations at Brantford.*
>
> *At the time, I was the Native Affairs Specialist, Ontario Ministry of Natural Resources, Eastern Region. As such, I was well informed concerning the interaction between Native and Non-native communities and governments across southern Ontario.*
>
> *The Six Nations land issue, instigated by land speculators and residential developers, had moved from dispute to open conflict. Events had escalated and turned ugly. A heavy police presence was required to keep the peace between the Six Nation occupiers and local non-Native residents.*
>
> *The negotiation was arranged to be a tripartite endeavour. The Federal government, the Ontario government, and the Six Nations Reserve Band Council would sit together to find a resolution.*
>
> *Where, at the invited table, was the traditional Haudenosaunee government – the condoled hereditary royaner who represent the national interests of their people and community? They were not – officially by invitation – at the table. There was turbulence on the horizon.*
>
> *Looking at news photographs of the attendees, wanted or not, invited or not, there sat men wearing the traditional kahstowa headdress with small deer antlers attached. The deer antlers told those who knew, that the wearer was a condoled hereditary royaner of one of the Five Nations of the Iroquois Confederacy. The position of the feathers on the kahstowa identified which one of the Five Nations the wearer belonged to.*

Not a good start to restoring peace and harmony among cultures and community. After all, it is the hereditary condoled royaner of the Iroquois Confederacy who – still today, supported by a significant part of the Iroquois population - represent the real negotiating and decision making capacity for the Iroquois Confederacy. They are the 'federal' government of the Iroquois. Although Canada struggles with this concept, the federal and state governments of the United States have, for some time, acknowledged the participation and counsel of the hereditary Haudenosaunee condoled royaner

The Canadian government, many years previously, imposed the Band Council electoral system on the Canadian Iroquois. This was done in accordance with the <u>Indian Act, 1876,</u> as amended. This arbitrary ruling essentially cast aside the six centuries old traditional Haudenosaunee system of government. The <u>Indian Act</u> forcibly replaced the government of life-time hereditary condoled royaner with Band Council government made up of elected chiefs to serve a two-year term unless otherwise specified in regulation made pursuant to the <u>Indian Act.</u>

The <u>Indian Act, 1876</u>, as amended, is a consolidation of legislation applicable to Indigenous persons in Canada and legislated prior to July 1, 1867, the date of Canadian Confederation. The most notable legislation consolidated into the <u>Indian Act</u> are the <u>Gradual Civilization Act of 1857;</u> and the <u>Gradual Enfranchisement Act of 1869.</u> Both pieces of legislature were passed by the Upper Canada legislature.

So here they all were at the negotiating table – municipal government, provincial government, and federal government - ready to find a resolution. Unfortunately for the negotiation, the historically authentic Iroquois Confederacy leadership had not been officially invited to participate. The traditional Haudenosaunee government had been sidelined by Canada.

I recall hearing that in the beginning of talks, a federal negotiator asked 'who are those guys with the feathered hats and deer antlers.' I am quite sure that, at the time, his/her provincial counterparts

> were no better educated. Such an absence of cultural knowledge can bring no good. The Federal and Provincial government negotiators did not know who they were talking to. To make matters more awkward, neither did they know how to talk to them.
>
> Sir William Johnson (1715-1774), British agent to the Iroquois and British Superintendent of Indian Affairs, would have been aghast at such ignorance for the culture and history of those about to be negotiated with.
>
> It would seem that little has changed in matters of national interest between the Iroquois and the Canadian government. The Honour of the Crown continues to be tested. Sadly, it is too often found lacking.
>
> It is little wonder that the Six Nations land dispute negotiations foundered, and still lingers today, largely unresolved.

In 1989, the State of New York returned Iroquois Confederacy wampum belts to the Onondaga.

In recent years, the Iroquois have succeeded in some land claim action in both Canada and the United States.

There are many more land claims on file. There is much more to come.

Chapter 25

The Great Binding Law in Contemporary Times

The Mohawk community of Akwesasne has suffered more than her share of internal social conflict and fractured community unity.

Raynald Harvey Lemelin writes: " *By 1980, many of the unifying ideals on the longhouse were shown to be irrelevant when pertaining to the Band Council supporters. The supporter's identification with Christian religions, American culture, and a high level of acculturation into the larger society that surrounded the Akwesasne territory rekindled factions and social conflicts in Akwesasne. While such concepts as sovereignty, nationhood, and power gained significance, concepts such as solidarity, sharing, and rational decision making were uprooted or discarded.*" (1996. Social Movements and the Great Law of Peace in Akwesasne. Thesis. School of Graduate Studies, University of Ottawa)

The heart and soul of *Kaianerenko:wa* [*The Great Binding Law*] is a simple message. Peace and harmony will flow from goodness of the mind; goodness of the heart; and goodness of the soul.

However, there is a sadness here. In recent decades, the history of social upheaval in Akwesasne may suggest that a fragmented *Great Binding Law* exacerbated social dissension in Akwesasne rather than serving to alleviate a leaning towards social dysfunction.

The *Code of Handsome Lake* mixed Christian concepts and interpretations with traditional Haudenosaunee messages of the *Great Binding Law*. The *Good Word* teaching of the Seneca prophet Handsome Lake caused confusion and dissent among some Haudenosaunee longhouse followers across Iroquoia.

Like many communities of the Five Nations, Akwesasne has a strong connection with the message of *Kaianerenko:wa*, the *Great Binding Law*. The messages are recognized and accepted as *the good teachings of the clear minded*.

Beginning in the 1930's, the Longhouse experienced a revival in Akwesasne. For many residents of the community, there was a concern for what they believed to be a weakening of values underpinning the contemporary formal structures of the Iroquois Confederacy. Concerned parties began to develop an ideology which attempted to replicate the authentic Confederacy before it had been altered by the influence of Handsome Lake. (Alfred, 1995, pg. 69)

In the 1950s and 1960s the popularity for the *Great Binding Law* gradually increased. During this time, many Christian Mohawk returned to the Longhouse. Many of those returning to the Longhouse wanted to distance themselves from Christianity. Gradually, the *Gai'wiio*, Handsome Lake's *Good Word Message*, became a source for healing and for controversy. The *Good Word* messages were rejected by some. (Paul Wallace - The Great White Roots of Peace)

The choice of religion is sometimes not either one or the other. Of course not. It is not uncommon for a Christian Mohawk to also accept the message of the Great Binding Law and participate in the Longhouse ceremonies. After all, as a good Mohawk friend said to me: "*Mike, when it comes to my soul I want to have all the bases covered.*" Fair enough.

Today, the teaching of the *Great Binding Law* is being revived across many Iroquois communities. The *Great Binding Law* provides a catalyst for rejuvenating the relationship among the Five Nations. The Peacemaker's message is also the undisputed foundation for Iroquois sovereignty and the Mohawk view of *Kashwentha* [nationhood].

The *Great Binding Law* is the cultural cornerstone of Haudenosaunee communities and Iroquois nationalism. The *Great Binding Law* continues to be the socio-political and spiritual foundation of the Iroquois Confederacy. The Peacemaker's message is the Constitution of the Iroquois.

Interpretation of the Great Binding Law
Differences and Division

The role of the *Kaianerenko:wa* [*Great Binding Law*] in Iroquois Confederacy matters in contemporary times can be complicated. In some matters, interpretations of the role of the *Great Binding Law* have divided the Iroquois Confederacy. Some believe that the Handsome Lake's *Kaiwiio*, the *Good Word* message, has a fundamental role in matters particular to the healing of pain experienced by the Haudenosaunee and the preservation of Haudenosaunee culture. Others believe that the *Kaiwiio* is no longer valid for contemporary Haudenosaunee society.

Similar for all oral histories and stories, with each telling there can be changes in words, emphasis, and interpretation. This is integral to oral transmission of information. Some within the Haudenosaunee community are anxious that the Longhouse has been weakened by an absence of true interpretation of the *Great Binding Law* and the intent of the *Kaiwiio*. This uncertainty provides an opening for various interpretations of intent and application of the *Great Binding Law* and the *Good Word*.

There is an oversite mechanism in place which is intended as a safeguard for interpretation and application of the *Great Binding Law* and the *Good Word*. When interpretation of intent wanders from the original intended message, the Grand Council of the Iroquois Confederacy attempts to rectify this at their annual meeting.

Disputes and conflict can be a consequence of different Longhouse interpretations of the *Great Binding Law*. While some Longhouse followers accept the *Good Word* as an extension of the *Great Binding Law*; other Longhouse followers reject the *Good Word* and use only the *Great Binding Law* for guidance. So, now different groups use different interpretations of the *Great Binding Law*. Each group believes their interpretation is the authentic one. This division does not complement the unity and harmony that was the original strength of the Five Nations.

In contemporary terms, the influence of the *Great Binding Law* can be divided into two principal categories:

- spiritual holistic philosophy
- political interpretation of the *Great Binding Law*.

Each category has a different group of supporters. The spiritual holistic philosophy is supported by the *longhouse proponents* and the *traditionalists*. This group is generally opposed to gambling. The *progressives* support the political interpretation and are supporters of the gambling and contraband industries. The political interpretation is used to justify the *progressive* group's activities in terms of their view of sovereignty and the integral rights of a Nation.

Each group's interpretation of the *Great Binding Law* offers different meanings to matters associated with defense, nationality, and sovereignty. These issues have led to conflict between parties culminating in the vicious 1990 civil conflict in Akwesasne. The conflict raged between the group that supported gambling business entrepreneurs; and the group drawn largely from the traditional Longhouse people who opposed on-reserve gambling enterprises.

The reason why there are different renditions of the *Great Binding Law* may be found within the *Great Binding Law* itself.

Lemelin (1966) writes: *"The Great Law of Peace is a complex adaptive system with a dynamic flexibility that allows it to be open to interpretations that either emphasize or minimize the reciprocal roles of the individual's responsibility toward the nation / community and the nation / communities' responsibility toward the individual. The dynamic flexibility of the Great Law of Peace allows it to be used as a political construction to serve the needs of various, and sometimes opposing Mohawk political groups."*

Akwesasne politics are often contentious. There is seldom a shortage of lively issues. The people of the community are informed, involved, and participate actively in matters of community governance. Indeed, it is safe to suggest that interest and participation in Akwesasne community politics is much higher than in many Canadian communities.

The dynamics of Akwesasne politics have given rise to three distinct parties:

i) The *traditionalists* resist what they see as a gradual erosion of both individual and community values. Needless to say, they promote increased support for past Mohawk values such as sharing and service to the community.

ii) The *progressives* argue for more individual choice and support individual initiatives that can provide individual prosperity.

iii) The *longhouse proponents* are identified as those who are faithful to Longhouse ceremonies and follow the teaching of the Great Binding Law. The *Longhouse proponents* believe in the sovereignty of Kashwentha (nationhood). Supporters will not accept; indeed, they reject, any form of foreign interference whether in local or national politics. Longhouse supporters refuse to participate in band council elections and promote the traditional clan based system of condoled life-time royaner as prescribed in the Great Binding Law.

In the Mohawk community of Akwesasne, Longhouse proponents are divided. In accordance with their nationalist interpretation of the *Jay Treaty*, some support the contraband trade involving cross border transport and sale of tobacco products as an expression of their rights associated with sovereignty and nationalism. Any external government interference to impede free passage of goods or interference with Mohawk entrepreneurship is seen as a violation of Mohawk sovereignty.

The emergence of the controversial Warrior Society was largely due to divisions in the Akwesasne community particular to building and operating casinos within the Mohawk territory. On the United States side of the Mohawk territory, the elected chiefs and the Warrior Society wanted gambling. The revenues from gambling were accepted as a way to ensure self-sufficiency, not only for the US part of Akwesasne, but on all Iroquois reservations in upper New York State. The traditional Haudenosaunee leadership opposed casinos on both moral grounds and their fear that corruption and organized crime would become rooted in the community.

The controversial Warrior Society introduced great dissension among groups. The Warrior Society had been paid by entrepreneurs engaged in the contraband and casino industry to provide security on their behalf. The warrior Society was alienated from the Haudenosaunee leadership. The traditional chiefs, associated with the Longhouse religion, represented consensus-democratic values. The Warrior Society ideology was critical of the Longhouse traditions and promoted independence from any external government interference or internal interference from any group opposed to the idea of individual prosperity.

The *traditionalist group* was opposed to the Warrior Society. After a time, the *Longhouse proponents* distanced themselves from the ideology and actions of the Warrior Society.

The contemporary concept of the Warrior Society, culturally and in the wampum of the *Great Binding Law*, is foreign to traditional belief. For traditionalists, a militia of young men ready to protect the community in time of need and placed under the leadership of a Pine Tree chief appointed by the hereditary royaner of the Iroquois Confederacy is the true concept.

The emergence of the contemporary Warrior Society during the civil unrest in the Mohawk communities of Akwesasne, Kanesatake and Kahnawake during the turbulent years 1990 and 1991, was traumatic. As a result of their protectionist stance, the Warrior Society adopted a rigid militant ideology which frightened and threatened citizens.

The seeds for internal conflict were sown. The Warrior Society considers any position taken by opponents or interference from opponents as an infringement and threat to their particular idea of sovereignty.

At the same time, the *Longhouse proponents* oppose the casino industry on Mohawk territory. This group advocates a peaceful co-existence and tolerance both within and outside the community. The Warrior Society has expressed the same interest, but only on their own rigid terms.

So, the fracturing of the Akwesasne Longhouse is due, in a large part, to differences in interpretation of the *Kaianerenko:wa*. This situation has resulted in community division and conflict.

The traditional people in Akwesasne began to shun the pro-gambling group and its spokespersons. They were no longer welcome in the Longhouse. So, the shunned group built their own Longhouse, not so far from the old one.

> *I recall having a discussion with a warrior Society member about Mohawk sovereignty and issues of jurisdiction on St. Lawrence River waters adjacent to the Mohawk Territory of Akwesasne.*
>
> *At some point, the discussion came around to the confrontational and combative stance of some Mohawk in their dealings with government. Mention was made that a combative approach to problem solving involving threat was never productive.*
>
> *Comment was offered that although the Akwesasne conflict had resulted in loss of life and great grief within the community, some things were achieved. The speaker believed, that after a calm had returned to Akwesasne, the community had received funding for much of the infrastructure the Mohawk Council of Akwesasne had been badgering the Canadian government for. Shortly after the Akwesasne turmoil had burned itself out, the foundations were laid for a new arena, a senior's residence, and a medical center.*
>
> *The message was clear. At times, conflict can get you what you want.*

Louis Karoniaktajeh Hall and the Warrior Society

Perhaps this is the appropriate place to share a little about Louis *Karoniaktajeh* Hall (1918-1993). A fervent Haudenosaunee nationalist, Karoniaktajeh is considered by many to be the Mohawk responsible for rejuvenating, and activating, the contemporary Iroquois Warrior Society.

Karoniaktajeh was born in the Kahnawake Mohawk Territory, Quebec. He was educated by Catholic priests. He wanted to be a priest himself, although he was never ordained into the priesthood. A weight lifter who loved wrestling, he said he could never have been a priest because there wasn't a priest's collar big enough to fit his very large and muscular neck.

Karoniaktajeh was an author, a painter, and a politician. He was outspoken and dedicated his writing to Iroquois issues and the importance of maintaining and protecting strong communities without compromising sovereign rights.

In the best of times, Louis Hall was viewed as a controversial figure. In the worst of times, he was seen by many as an intimidating influence and threat to the authority of the Grand Council of the Iroquois Confederacy.

Louis Hall was a committed follower of the Peacemaker and the teachings of the Great Binding Law. He was in conflict with many Iroquois who had accepted and followed the message of the Code of Handsome Lake. Louis believed that Handsome Lake's interpretations of the Great Binding Law were unacceptable in terms of the true message of the Peacemaker.

The Code of Handsome Lake promoted the ideas of peace and harmony in human relations. Louis Hall had no trouble with this concept as long as Iroquois traditional government, communities, and people were not threatened. Louis Hall's belief was that a Mohawk should always be ready and willing to pick up a weapon to defend the rights of the people. His actions and writings promoting this belief made him a controversial figure criticised by other Mohawk.

In 1974, Louis Hall was the principle player in establishing the traditional settlement of *Ganienkeh* in upper state New York. The settlement was located on the 612 acres of land near Moss Lake. In negotiating the land deal with New York State, Louis Hall told the State negotiator, Raymond B. Harding: *"What we seek to build is a self-sufficient agricultural community run by and for native people according to our own laws, customs and traditions. Only by re-establishing our own independent nation can we build such a community."* (Akwesasne Notes: Summer 1975).

Like Louis Karoniaktajeh Hall himself, the traditional Mohawk settlement of *Ganienkeh* is controversial and has a history of intolerance and violence against New York State authorities.

Louis Hall wrote two unpublished books that focused on a somewhat radical approach to securing and protecting the sovereignty of the Iroquois Confederacy. His writing encouraged application of the principles of the Confederacy to grow 'Indian' power, not only within the Five Nations of the Confederacy, but across all Indigenous Nations.

In his book *Rebuilding the Iroquois Confederacy*, Louis Hall writes:

"The Five Nations had joined in an alliance under the guidance of the great Founder Deganawida who wanted all the native nations in America to be members of the alliance which became known as the Iroquois Confederacy. He wanted all the nations to be equal in power, influence, and legal authority. He had no plans for a super nation or nations to lord it over other nations. Deganawida wanted all the Rotiyaner (Chiefs) to be equal in power. He had no wishes to see a single individual elected as a grand or supreme chief as such a position only leads to errors and corruptions. He got the original Five Nations of the Confederacy to offer up the position of 'Grand Chief' to the Creator who does not err, cannot be corrupted and does not die.

Gayanerekows, the Great Law, began with thirty articles or wampum formulated by Deganawida himself. Other laws were added 'to the rafters' by the Grand Councils in the following centuries as needed. It took five years for Deganawida and Ayonwatha - a transplanted Onondaga who left his nation because of persecutions suffered by his family and joined the Mohawk who recognized his special abilities and made him one of the Turtle Clan Chiefs - to gather and join into an alliance, the first Five Nations. Convinced they'll do fine, Deganawida set out to gather more nations to join his great alliance. He was never seen again. It is believed that he came upon evil people and got killed. Deprived of his counsel and sound guidance, the people of the original Five Nations were not ready to act with good judgement when the outside nations came to join the Alliance. Instead of making them equals, they put them in a subordinate state without a voice in the Grand Council. They came in 'on the cradleboard', meaning they were treated like children and not allowed to develop their potential. In time, there were 28 of these dependant nations in the Iroquois Protectorate of Indian Nations. The Five Nations became overlords of the 28 subordinate nations, not what Deganawida had in mind at all. The Five Nations Grand Council even added 'a law to the rafters' that any adoption of nations shall be temporary only, subject to certain conditions and they shall have no voice in Grand Councils or have any authority. When Deganawida left to gather in more nations, he certainly did not want to bring them in 'on the cradleboard' but as equals.

Indians all over America can do wonders by following the Great Plan of Deganawida, by joining all American Indian nations to be equal in power, influence and legal authority. Had the original Five Nation Iroquois Confederacy followed Deganawida's Great Plan, there would now be a 200 Nations or more Confederacy. What kept the Iroquois down was their elitist chiefs who wanted equality for only five nations and subjection for all others." (Hall, 19___, pgs. 1-3).

Louis Hall laments the failure of the Five Nation leaders to move beyond their own Confederacy and recruit more Nations to be a part of the grander picture. After all, the Haudenosaunee Confederacy had historically demonstrated their ability to effectively wage war and overwhelm enemies, even when outnumbered and fighting on several fronts. Knowing this, Louis Hall would have seen a confederacy of two hundred Nations as a very well organized, motivated, and impressive foe for any repressive regime. After all, the Five Nations of the Iroquois, after the armistice that created the Haudenosaunee Confederacy had implemented a successful expansionist policy. The Confederacy had absorbed many tribes and huge swaths of territory under the umbrella of the Haudenosaunee Confederacy.

According to Louis Hall, none of the Confederacy allies were given any official place or process in Confederacy governance. Even the officially adopted Tuscarora, who have a seat in the Longhouse, came in 'on the cradleboard'. In the Longhouse, the Tuscarora listen but do not speak unless they have an issue specific only to the Tuscarora. Their issue must be presented to the Grand Council through the Cayuga.

In summary, given the Iroquois Confederacy's history of military prowess, subjugation of tribes, assimilation of other peoples, and expansionist policies, it was well for the newly arriving Europeans that they were not facing a Confederacy of two hundred Nations. It was tough and challenging enough for the Swedes, Dutch, French, and English arrivals to deal with the Five Nations.

In 1990, Louis Hall publicly declared himself a spiritual general of the warrior movement (Toronto Sun. July 26, 1990). Although Louis Hall had a small and somewhat supportive audience in the beginning, his warrior policy was extreme for many. Hall's threatening and intimidating behaviour, seen as anti-sovereignty actions, began to frighten both elected and traditional leaders of the Iroquois Confederacy.

Chapter 26

Political Positions of the Mohawk Haudenosaunee; a Contemporary View

Tragedy of Societal Dilution;
Language – the Keeper of Culture;
Steadfast Iroquois Nationalism

In November, 1994, I had the good fortune to meet and talk with a member of the Mohawk Nation Council of Chiefs (MNCC). The MNCC is the traditional Longhouse government of the Mohawk Nation. Members and supporters are Haudenosaunee. Members of the MNCC are not elected by their community. They are *put up* by Clan Mothers and approved by the Mohawk Haudenosaunee.

Think about the MNCC as the equivalence of provincial or state government of the Mohawk Nation. It falls to the MNCC to deal with Mohawk Nation matters particular to interprovincial and state relations. In this context, the Grand Council of the Iroquois Confederacy is the federal equivalent of government. This level of governance is concerned with national policy, treaty, rights, sovereignty and self-determination. The Mohawk Council of Akwesasne (MCA) is the municipal level of community government. This system was explained to me in precise terms - the MCA fill potholes, the MNCC makes policy.

During our friendly and informative meeting, information was shared that was, at the time, not encouraging with regard to the state of affairs particular to political positions and the Mohawk Haudenosaunee.

My companion had invested a great deal of time and energy to researching the clan system and the political positions that made up the Haudenosaunee Longhouse government. He had established that a sub-chief would be *put up* at the same time as a life-time Chief through the condolence process of confirmation for a life-time hereditary royaner. Apparently, at the time, this procedure was not being followed. He believed that in 1994, there were only two condoled royaner for the Mohawk Nation, Chief Ross David in Akwesasne and a second condoled chief residing on the Six Nations Reserve,

My companion also believed that no sub-chiefs had been *put up* in the traditional sense. Persons were sitting in these positions in an acting capacity. There were plenty of Faith Keepers but none had been *put up*. Putting up Faith Keepers for the process of clan approval was difficult because there were so few condoled Mohawk royaner. There has to be the properly approved line-up of Clan Mother, Condoled Chief, Sub-chief, and Faith Keeper to approve and sanction official positions in the proper manner. This proper manner is laid out in Great Binding Law wampum particular to civil process. It was the belief of my lunch companion that if the required line-up of official positions is not available, then the *real positions* could not be brought forward. There would only be acting positions.

That was 1994. Little in the way of Haudenosaunee political title approvals occurred in Akwesasne from 1994 until 1997. I do know that since 1997, there has been Clan activity in terms of putting forward nominees for condoled chief positions and the acceptance of those nominees as hereditary royaner in the traditional manner.

Within some Clans, things are growing stronger in terms of bringing forward positions in accordance with Haudenosaunee traditions of governance. Recovery has been slow. But recovery is ongoing and that it is what is important.

Tragedy of Societal Dilution

Societal Dilution. Such a harsh term. The words convey a callous tone. There is a sense of something that is irreversible.

In a sense, the term societal dilution should be no stranger to the Haudenosaunee. Indeed, the mourning-war cultural practice of securing captives for adoption was in itself societal dilution.

Since the arrival of the Swedes, Dutch, French, and English to the regions the imperial powers called New Sweden, New Amsterdam, New France, and New England, there have been extinctions of societies and loss of cultures.

Starting then, and continuing to now, a process social sciences call *societal dilution*, has been ongoing.

Perhaps, in a way, this entire story has been about societal dilution of the Indigenous people of eastern North America.

Societal dilution of Indigenous cultures involves the following process:

1. Tribes are pushed out of ancestral homelands and find sanctuary; are adopted; or resettle. The people are assimilated by another society and gradually acculturated into the larger, dominant society. The people's language is gradually lost. When their language is gone, so to is much of their distinct culture.

2. Traditional spirituality is marginalized by imported religion. The most intimidating and aggressive religion wins converts. Abandoning traditional spirituality in favor of conversion to a new religion brings social dysfunction.

3. Transfer from a sharing society whose concept of 'ownership' is absent, to an ownership economy involving land and articles is dysfunctional for that society.

4. The ceding of land and resources through treaty creates competition which stimulates greed for wealth. The politics and civil governance system of clans and the strengths of traditional leadership are weakened, corrupted, and legislated against by the dominant society.

The process of societal dilution ensures that the skills, the stories, the ceremonies, the people's strength of independence, their spirituality - all of it fades away. And after a time, the language fades away. With the loss of language comes the loss of the people's culture. Acculturation of a people into the larger society, for better or worse, is only a matter of time.

We might muse and say: *Well, yes, but the great majority of us now live where and how we do because at some point in the past, we were forced out of our former habitats and ways of living by economics or a more aggressive, and perhaps, better adapted tribe.*

This may be true. But certainly, the social harm and tragic personal consequences of trans-generational trauma of the transition experience by tribes who inhabited the St. Lawrence River Region, the Great Lakes Region, the Hudson Valley Region, and the Ohio Valley Region, should not be so easily cast aside.

And what has all of this meant for the Iroquois Confederacy? It all started with competition between Nations - Native and European - for the wealth of the fur trade and the building of empire. It finished with the fall of the Iroquois Confederacy empire and loss of territory and ancestral lands to European settlement. In a few centuries, the once politically and militarily influential Haudenosaunee transitioned from rulers of an empire to refugees in their own ancestral lands.

Language - the Keeper of Culture

The loss of language is an immense concern for all the Iroquois. Fewer and fewer of the new generations speak their mother tongue. There are some parts of some communities where the traditional language is spoken on a daily basis. In the marshland part of Akwesasne known as *Tsi:snaihene,* Mohawk continues to be the working language of grandmothers and grandfathers.

The Mohawk have had some success in keeping their mother tongue a working language within their communities. The Akwesasne community is working hard to keep their language alive. The Akwesasne Freedom School is using curriculum that includes both Mohawk and English. The Iroquois are fully aware that after losing so much in the last several centuries, the loss of their language will also mean the loss of more of their culture.

It is difficult to have an accurate count for the number of fluent language speakers in any of the Iroquois communities. Canadian Iroquois communities are strong supporters of their sovereignty - the Mohawk in particular - and many residents of the Mohawk territories do not respond to census taking by the federal government. Knowing the number of fluent speakers for any of the Six Nations is never a true count. It is always a weak estimate at best. The fear is, unless there is real change, the numbers of Iroquois with Native language fluency will not likely be sufficient to sustain the language in the long term.

All of the Five Nations languages are classified as 'at risk'. Recognizing this, the majority of communities of the Iroquois Confederacy have school programs and language programs in place to address the challenge of language loss.

The Canadian government, encouraged by the Assembly of First Nations, has introduced a government Bill particular to indigenous languages. If passed into legislation, funding will be made available for the teaching of Indigenous languages in schools.

Some communities, such as the Mohawk community of Akwesasne, are applying innovative ways to keep their language active. On a recent visit to Akwesasne I noticed that street stop signs no longer show *stop*. Now, the sign says *testa'n*, the Mohawk language word for stop.

Mohawk Council of Akwesasne departments have adopted Mohawk language titles. The Department of Environment is now called Tehotiiennawakon. By themselves, these may be small things. Together across the community, these things share a message that the Mohawk language is alive and being used.

A conservative estimate of the current state of Iroquois languages follows:

Mohawk: an estimated 3,433 fluent speakers.

Oneida: an estimated 190 fluent language speakers (2011 survey).

Onondaga: an estimated 50 fluent language speakers.

Cayuga: an estimated 100 fluent language speakers.

Seneca: an estimated 100 fluent language speakers in 2007; An estimated 50 fluent speakers in 2012.

Tuscarora: in the mid- 1970s, an estimated 52 fluent language speakers.

Some of the tribal languages of the old Algonquin and Wendat-Huron alliances are now classified as extinct. The Petun; Neutral; Wenro; Erie; Susquehannock; Nottaway; and Meherrin languages are now extinct. These are only a few of the many.

It is a sad matter when a language is lost for all time. Language is irrevocably attached to the speaker's culture. Loss of language means the loss of social culture. In so brief a time; barely a few centuries; entire cultures have been extinguished. The loss of such vibrant and sophisticated peoples; the loss of so much culture; all of this must certainly convey a profound sadness.

Steadfast Iroquois Nationalism

In the hearts of many Haudenosaunee rests a zealous nationalist fervor. Haudenosaunee accept and actively promote their view that they are neither American nor Canadian. Their political and cultural position is that they are a sovereign Nation.

Indeed, many Canadian Iroquois do not participate as voters in provincial or federal elections. Akwesasne is certainly a champion of Iroquois nationalism. Reserve residents, for the most part, do not respond to Canada census request for population information.

The Haudenosaunee issue their own national passport. The Haudenosaunee, from time to time, issue national position papers.

An example is the Haudenosaunee submission to the United Nations particular to the state of the environment and environmental protection. The Haudenosaunee paper is a chilling harbinger of warnings associated with climate change. The paper was presented to the United Nations by the Haudenosaunee before the words *climate change* became the controversial issue they are today.

Iroquois nationalism is very much alive in Canadian Mohawk communities. The Mohawk approach to Canadian provincial and federal government is on a Nation to Nation basis. This is complicated by the fact that the Canadian federal government does not recognize the traditional hereditary Haudenosaunee royaner as the legitimate government of the Iroquois. The elected Band Councils pursuant to the administrative sections of the *Indian Act* is the only governing body accepted by the Canadian government.

A combative attitude and confrontational process has, from time to time, complicated intercommunity and intergovernmental relationships. This seems an incongruity. The process of traditional Longhouse governance was built on the teaching of the Great Binding Law with a foundation of unity and consensual decision making using the tools of compromise and negotiation. This similarity to modern democracy is profound.

Perhaps the rub is that Haudenosaunee decision making must involve consensus. Consensus can be explained as *'although I don't agree with you on all matters, I can accept the decision that has been presented.'* Canadian law requires decision making to involve thorough and inclusive consultation. However, the requirement for universal consensus is not a mandatory obligation before implementing a decision for action - or not.

Regardless, Haudenosaunee politics, like the politics of democratic governments today, rely on statesmanship and skills of negotiation and compromise. Agreement with the implicit rules of due process and seeking ways to bridge disagreements are the essence of modern governance.

Considering this for a moment, we can recognize, as did the fathers of the Constitution of the new United States of America, that the centuries old Great Binding Law of the Haudenosaunee Confederacy is, in many ways – subtle and not so subtle - a play book for present-day participatory democratic process.

Chapter 27

Wandering from the Path

And now, this story of the building of a wilderness empire by the Haudenosaunee has come to an end. I am reluctant to leave. So, before I put my pen down, I feel there are a few more stories that are worth the telling. Wandering from the path can be good for the soul.

Perhaps this is the appropriate place to tell about an experience at the Canadian Police College, Ottawa, Ontario.

In 1992, I had just started my new job as Native Liaison Specialist, Eastern Region, Ontario Ministry of Natural Resources. The liaison positions were new government jobs. So new that, in the beginning, there was no job description available for reference and guidance. This was not a problem. It was a blessing. Our single guiding rule was 'do no harm.'

I was anxious. After twenty-five years in natural resources law enforcement, my experience with Indigenous people had, on occasion, been confrontational. I had no idea about how to begin to work to build relationships with First Nation persons, communities, and governments.

I placed a call to RCMP Inspector Jim Potts. Inspector Potts was the RCMP liaison in Akwesasne. His focus was mostly with the Warrior Society. Inspector Potts and I had a long discussion during which I probably, and unintentionally, conveyed my anxiety about the expectations of my new position. We arranged to meet.

A week after talking with Inspector Potts, I received a phone call from the Canadian Police College, Ottawa. I was offered a seat on the upcoming Native Liaison Officers Course. The course was starting in two weeks. I asked 'when do you need to know if I will attend?' The reply was a terse 'today.' I took the seat.

The five-week course was a gift from heaven. Course candidates came from across Canada. Students came from various municipal and federal police forces. Half the candidates were Indigenous. By the end of the course, I was feeling confident and eager to get started. I may not have been ready, but I was certainly eager.

During the course, we benefited from guest speakers from First Nation and Inuit communities across Canada. Some speakers were angry, many were sad, all provided great learning experiences.

There are several stories from the Police College course that I want to share.

> When asked to share something about his residential school experience, an Ojibwe RCMP Constable came to the front of the class and said:
>
> *"Okay. My residential school number was 649. I guess I got lucky.*
>
> *There was an invitation to a school reunion last year. No one showed up."*
>
> Then he returned to his seat.

> A guest speaker from an Inuit village was angry. The Inuit women said:
>
> *"The RCMP came to our communities and told us we are all the same. That they were there to be our friends and to help us. That*

they were not separate from us, that there should be no barriers between us."

Looking at an RCMP Sergeant, she asked:

"If that is true, why do you build white picket fences around the places where you live and work in our community. Before you came to our community, we had no fences. We didn't know what they were. We didn't need them then, and we don't need them now."

A guest speaker from a Manitoba First Nation was sad. She said:

"Much is said and written about physical and sexual abuse among our people.

Before the white man arrived to live among us, brought his religion, his justice, and his gifts of alcohol and disease, physical and sexual abuse was a rare occurrence in our communities. When it did happen, we looked after it ourselves. The abuse stopped.

Today, you take away our offenders. Your justice puts them in jail.

There is no healing of the hurter or the hurt. The abuse does not stop. It is getting worse."

An RCMP constable, member of a Mi'kmaq First Nation, spoke to the class. The constable's first name is Michael.

"You know, sometimes it is very difficult to be an Indian. At my detachment, in the locker room before and after a shift, there is a lot of racial comment against the Mi'kmaq. Drunken Indians, lots of bad stuff.

The guys I work with call me Chief and Tonto. I do not find that amusing and I told them so. One of them said 'well, what do you want us to call you?'

I replied 'Why don't you call me Michael?' "

One weekend at the Police College, Michael showed me how to make *dreamcatchers* the Mi'Kmaq way. He told me that I could show anyone I wanted to how to make a Mi'kmaq dreamcatcher. This was his gift to me.

Years later, I spent time in Kabakaburri, an Arawak village in Guyana, South America. One afternoon I sat with village ladies weaving baskets for market that was many canoe paddling hours away.

The Arawak ladies asked me if I knew any Indians where I lived. Yes I did. They asked if I knew how to make anything that the Indians at home made. Yes I did.

We spent a wonderful afternoon making Mi'kmaq dreamcatchers. Now, all the huts in the Arawak village of Kakakaburri, on an island of high ground on the banks of a black water Amazon River, have dreamcatchers hanging near their children's hammocks.

Arawak mothers know the dreamcatchers will catch their children's bad dreams in the web and keep them locked away in the tips of the feathers and pieces of clam shell.

My friend Michael would be happy and proud to know how his gift to me had been shared.

Epilogue

The grand story of the Haudenosaunee Confederacy is fraught with political intrigue, military victory and defeat, greed, religious tension, civil war, and both terrible vengeance and great humanity to others.

The Haudenosaunee were coerced to serve as proxy policemen and soldiers for the imperial European powers. In doing so, the Iroquois Confederacy sacrificed their own influence and power for the benefit of the opposing regional geopolitical aspirations of rebellious Americans and British colonists.

The culminating events that brought about the ruin of the Haudenosaunee Confederacy began with the treachery and brutality of the *American Revolutionary War, 1765-1783*. The American scorched earth policy of the Iroquois homeland, transformed the Iroquois from a politically influential and agriculturally wealthy people to refugees in their own land.

This social and economic tragedy for the Iroquois brought about by the *American Revolutionary War* was soon followed by the Covenant Chain failures during the Ohio Valley settlement wars. The unmanageable, irreversible, and overwhelming flood of American settlers onto lands protected for the various tribes of the Covenant Chain alliance further eroded what little political influence the Iroquois Confederacy had left.

The final blow for the Iroquois was the civil war within the Confederacy. This internal war was brought about the Iroquois Confederacy allying themselves with opposing forces in the War of 1812. Iroquois fighting Iroquois, brethren against brethren. The Great Binding Law of armistice, unity, and justice that bound together the Iroquois Confederacy was broken. The Longhouse Fire of the Iroquois Confederacy, first lit all those centuries ago by the Peacemaker, had been extinguished.

The crumbling of the Iroquois Confederacy, the loss of ancestral homelands, and the fall from princes of the land to refugee, was due, in the largest part, to one irrevocable cause. That cause was an unquenchable European greed for land.

In the beginning the greed was limited to acquiring wealth from the fur trade. The fur trade wreaked havoc on the cultures and societies of Indigenous tribes throughout the fur trading territories, but this was not the defining cause of collapse. In the end, the Iroquois Confederacy empire, and the Confederacy itself, was overwhelmed by the consequences arising from the unstoppable flood of European immigration scrambling for land to settle.

The fall of the Iroquois Confederacy and empire was always about the land. Land that no amount of faithful alliance; treaty; or hopeful promise could protect from the ever-growing tide of white settlers, timber cutters, and unscrupulous land speculators. In the end, the supplication of the governments of Great Britain and the new United States of America could no more slow the flood of immigrant settlers onto Indigenous ancestral lands than could a decayed dike hold back flood waters.

The quest for ownership of land was a journey of treachery, greed, war, broken treaties, and the tragedy of extinction of many distinct tribes and the loss, forever, of sophisticated and dynamic Indigenous cultures.

The collapse of the Iroquois Confederacy, the transition of the people of the Five Nations from successful and influential societies to refugees in their ancestral lands, is a tragic example of a consequence of European settlement and plunder of eastern North America.

The Indigenous people of Canada are inherently tough, physically and mentally.

How else could they have made successful societies in a harsh wilderness. How else could they have developed wonderful cultures, amazing spirituality, and impressive social and civil systems of governance.

Without integral characteristics of courage and generosity, the Iroquois, Huron, Susquehannock, Algonquin, Mahican, and Anishinaabe, among many others, could not have been the intelligent strategists competing with the imperial European powers who sought dominance and empire in eastern North America.

Perhaps the stories shared in this book will help provide an understanding and appreciation for the amazing history and achievements of the Indigenous Nations, confederacies, and alliances that played a crucial role in shaping eastern North America.

It is difficult to know where we are going if we don't know where we came from.

Acknowledgements

During my time working with the Mohawk and Algonquin people and communities, I made many good friends. Much was shared with me about Mohawk culture and history and Algonquin vision and hope for their future.

The wisdom, kindness, patience and quiet teaching of my good friend Ernie Kaientaronkwen Benedict (1918-2011), one of the last of the Rotinonkwisere Longhair Chiefs, and Mohawk Elder, educator and writer, kept me out of harm's way on many occasions.

Thank you, Salli Kawennotakie Benedict (1954-2011), full of unquenchable curiosity, for always being willing to make time for unannounced visits.

Lloyd Skaroniati Benedict, politician, and entrepreneur, is acknowledged for his tenacious defence of what is right. Thank you, Lloyd, for your friendship and trust.

The knowledge, energy, and great humour of Tom Sakokwenionkwas Porter, Mohawk Elder and educator, is always remembered. Mohawk Nation Chief Jake Tekaronianeken Swamp (1940-2010) is acknowledged for his cultural teaching and the visionary work of his Tree of Peace Society.

Thank you, Joyce Tekahnawaiiks King for your patience, counsel, and generosity in sharing traditional cultural knowledge with me.

Michael L. Hart

The friendship shared with Henry Lickers, Seneca Nation, has always brought wisdom and humour into my life. Thank you, Jim Potts, for your wise counsel and wonderful stories.

Thank you, Kirby Whiteduck for your courtesy and steadfastness as you juggled much responsibility during the Algonquin of Golden Lake First Nation land claim process.

Thank you, Darren Akiatonharonkwen Bonaparte for your research and writing and your dedication to sharing Haudenosaunee culture and history. The history and stories of wampum belts shared in your many presentations to students at St. Lawrence College is particularly appreciated.

My sincere appreciation and respect belongs to all the people who I began to know during my relationship with the communities of Akwesasne and Golden Lake. Thank you for your kindness and for sharing with me a part of your culture and history.

Book Cover Art

Sincere thanks is extended to artist Doug Hall, eastern woodland historical artist, for permission to use his painting 'Battle Ready.' Mr. Hall lives and paints in Missouri, U.S.A.

About the Author

The author of this book is not Aboriginal. A fifth generation Canadian, the author's ancestors sailed from England to begin a new life in Canada.

Michael Hart was a Conservation Officer, serving in postings throughout eastern Ontario. On January 7th, 1968, after graduation from the Ontario Forest Technical School, he began his service in Moosonee, James Bay Region. He retired in 1997 as the Native Liaison Specialist, Southeastern Region, Ministry of Natural Resources, Ontario

The author is a graduate of Queens University; Ontario Police College, and the Canadian Police College. After retirement from the Ministry of Natural Resources, Michael taught in the Police Foundations Program, St. Lawrence College, Brockville Campus. He retired from the college in 2013.

During his years with the Ontario government, and later, during several consulting opportunities, the author enjoyed experiences and adventures working with a number of Indigenous communities. Communities include the Mohawk of Akwesasne and Tyendinaga; the Algonquin of Golden Lake First Nation; James Bay Cree, and Ojibwe of Northeastern Ontario. Outside of Ontario, Michael enjoyed opportunities to work on various projects with the Arawak of Kabakukirri, Guyana; the Caribe on the island of Commonwealth of Dominica; and with Mayan villagers in Chapas Region of Mexico.

Michael has been fortunate in his many cultural experiences. At Six Nations of Grand River, he has listened to condoled hereditary Cayuga Chief Jacob Hadajihgre:ta Thomas recite the Great Binding Law of the Haudenosaunee. He has danced Mohawk traditional social dances at the Wahta Mohawk First Nation longhouse; and learned to weave black ash baskets with Akwesasne Clan Mothers. In a ceremony, the author has received medicine from an Ojibwe Faithkeeper of the Midewiwin Medicine Society. It was the author's honor and privilege to be invited to participate in a traditional sweat lodge with men of the Dakota Nation, Saskatchewan.

Michael has received two eagle feathers. One from a member of a Haida Nation, and a second from a Cree Elder. Much to his amazement and immense pleasure, upon his retirement the Chiefs of the Mohawk Council of Akwesasne presented Michael with a lifetime fishing and hunting license for the Mohawk Territory of Akwesasne.

Bibliography

Primary Sources

Adams, Nick. 1986. *Iroquois Settlement at Fort Frontenac in the Seventeenth and Early Eighteenth Centuries.* **Ontario Archeology.**

Akwesasne Notes. **1975. Summer Edition.**

Alfred, Gerald R. **1995.** Heeding the Voices of Our Ancestors: Kahnawake Mohawk Politics and the Rise of Native Nationalism. **Oxford University Press, Toronto, Ontario.**

Anderson, Fred. **2000.** The Crucible of War: The Seven Years War and the Fate of Empire in British North America, 1754-1766. **Vintage Books, New York.**

Barr, Daniel P. **2006.** Unconquered: The Iroquois League at War in Colonial America. **Greenwood Publishing Group. Pgs. 9-13.**

Beardsley, Levi. **1852.** Reminiscences: Personal and Other Incidents; Early Settlement of Otsego County. **Charles Vinton Publishing, New York.**

Bemus, Samuel Flagg. **1923.** Jay's Treaty: A Study in Commerce and Diplomacy.

http://hdl.handle.net/2027/hvd.32044020001764

Bigger, H.P. **1922-36.** The Works of Samuel de Champlain. 6 vols. **The Champlain Society, Toronto, Ontario, Canada**

Black, Jeremy. **2009.** The Three Sieges of Quebec. *History Today.* **History Today Ltd.**

Bonaparte, Darren. 2013. Presentation, Haudenosaunee culture and history; St. Lawrence College, Brockville Campus, march, 2013. **Personal communication.**

Brasser, T.J. **1978.** *Mahican in B.G. Trigger (Ed.), Northeast Handbook of North American Indian Languages (Vol. 15).* **Smithsonian Institution, Washington, D.C. Pgs. 198-212.**

Burrage, Richard (ed.) **1906.** *Early English and French Voyages: Chiefly from Hakluyt, 1534-1608.* **C. Scribners & Sons, New York.**

Billington, Ray A. **1944.** *The Fort Stanwix Treaty of 1768.* **New York History, JSTOR 25#2. Pgs. 182-194.**

Brinton, Daniel G., Anthony, Albert S. **1888.** *A Lenape-English Dictionary; from an Anonymous Manuscript in the Archives of the Moravian Church at Bethlehem, Pennsylvania.* **Historical Society of Pennsylvania. Philapelphia.**

Calloway, Colin G. **2006.** *The Scratch of a Pen: 1763 and the Transformation of North America.* **Oxford Press.**

Campbell, William W. **1831. Annals** *of Tryon County; or, the Border Warfare of New York During the Revolution.* **J & J Harper Publishing, New York. OCLC**

Canadian Archives _____. **C 256, pg. 194**

Carter, Harvey Lewis. **1987.** *The Life and Times of Little Turtle: First Sagamore of the Wabush.* **University of Illinois Press.**

Cave, Alfred. **2001.** *Blue Jacket: Warrior of the Shawnees.* **Journal of the Illinois State Historical Society.**

Cave, Alfred A. **2004.** *The French and Indian War.* **Greenwood Press.**

Chartrand, Rene. **2000.** *Ticonderoga 1758: Montcalm's Victory Against All Odds.* **Osprey Publishing.**

Commager, H.; Morris, R. **1958.** *The Spirit of Seventy-Six, Vol. II.*

Convention on the Prevention and Punishment of Genocide, **1948. United Nations.**

Cruickshank, Ernest A. **1964.** *The Battle of Queenston Heights.* **In Zaslow, Morris (Ed.) The Defended Border. Macmillan of Canada.**

Cruickshank, Ernest. **1971.** *The Documentary History of the Campaigns Upon the Niagara Frontier in 1812-14. Volume XI: December, 1813, to May, 1814.* **Arno press Inc. New York. (First Published in 1908)**

Cruikshank, Ernest. **1990.** *The Battle of Fort George. Niagara on the Lake, Ontario.* **Niagara Historical Society.**

Cruickshank, Ernest. **1893.** *Butler's Rangers and the Settlement of Niagara.*

Day, Gordon M. Foster, Michael K, and Cowan, William (eds.) **1970.** *In Search of New England's Native Past.* **University of Massachusetts Press.**

DCB. _____ Vol. 759-760. NAC RG8 C Series.

Demos, John. **1994.** *The Unredeemed Captive: A Family Story from Early America.* **Vintage Books, New York.**

Dunnigan, Brian Leigh. **1996.** *Siege-1759, The Campaign Against Niagara.*

Eckert, Allan W. **1978 (2003).** *The Wilderness War.* **Little Brown & Company, New York.**

Edel, Wilbur. **1997.** *Kekionga! The Worst Defeat in the History of the U.S. Army.* **Praeger Publishers.** *Edmunds, David.* **2006. Tecumseh and the Quest for Indian Leadership. Library of American Biography Series. 2nd edition.**

Elting, John R. **1991.** *Amateurs to Arms. A Military History of the War of 1812.* **Da Capo Press, New York.**

Eshleman, H.F. **1909.** *Lancaster County Indians: Annals of the Susquehannock and Other Indian Tribes of the Susquehanna Territory from About the Year 1500 to 1763, the Date of Their Extinction. An Exhaustive and Interesting Series of Historical Papers Descriptive of Lancaster County's Indians.* **Princeton University Press.**

Fenn, Elisabeth A. **2000.** *Biological Warfare in Eighteenth Century North America: Beyond Jeffrey Amherst.*

Foote, Allan D. **1998.** *Liberty March, The Battle of Oriskany.* **North Country Books.**

Fraser, Alexander. **1907.** *Fourth Report of the Bureau of Archives,1906.* **Toronto: Ontario Bureau of Archives, Dept. of Public Records and Archives. OCLC 1773270**

Gaff, Allan D. **2004.** *Bayonets in the Wilderness: Anthony Wayne's Legion in the Old Northwest.* **University of Oklahoma Press.**

Gipson, Lawrence Henry. **1965.** *The British Empire before the American Revolution.* **Vol. 7. Knopf Publishing, New York.**

Glatthaar, Joseph T.; Martin, Joseph Kirby. **2006.** *Forgotten Allies: The Oneida Indians and the American Revolution.* **Hill and Wang Publishers, New York.**

Goodnough, David. **1968.** *The Cherry Valley Massacre, November 11, 1778, The Frontier Massacre that Shocked a Young Nation.* **Franklin Watts Publishing, New York. OCLC**

Granger, Erastus. _____ *Treaty of Big Tree (1794).* **The Erastus Granger Papers. State University of New York, Syracuse, New York.**

Graymont, Barabara. 1972. *The Iroquois in the American Revolution*. **Syracuse University Press, Syracuse, New York.**

Graymont, Barbara. 1983. *Thayendanega (Joseph Brant)*. **In Halpenny, Francess G., Dictionary of Canadian Biography. V (1801-1820). University of Toronto Press, Toronto, Ontario.**

Hahn, Henry George; Towson, Carl Behm. 1997. *A Pictorial History of Maryland Town*. **Pgs. 12-13. Donning Co., Baltimore, Maryland.**

Hakluyt, Richard. 1600. *The Principal Navigations, Voyages, Traffiques and Discoveries of the English Nation.*

Hall, Louis Karoniaktajeh. _____*Rebuilding the Iroquois Confederacy*. **Self Published**

Hall, Louis Karoniaktajeh _____*Biography*. http://www.louishall.com/bio/hisstory.html

Hall, Louis Karoniaktajeh. _____*The Iroquois Confederacy*. **Self Published**

Halsey, Francis Whiting. 1902. *The Old New York Frontier*. **C. Scribner's Sons, New York. OCLC**

Hamilton, Milton W. 1976. *Sir William Johnson: Colonial American, 1715-1763*. **Kennikat Press, Port Washington, New York.**

Harstead, Peter T. 1959. Sickness and Disease on the Wisconsin Frontier: Malaria, 1820-1850. Wisconsin Magazine of History. Vol. 43 No. 2. Wisconsin Historical Society.

Hauptman, Laurence M. 2001. *Conspiracy of Interests: Iroquois Dispossession and the Rise of New York State.*

Hessel, Peter. 1993. *The Algonquin Nation*. **Kichesippi Books, Arnprior, Ontario, Canada.**

Hewitt, J.N.B. 1907. *Conestoga. Handbook of American Indians North of Mexico. Bureau of American Ethnology Bulletin 30*. **Smithsonian Institution, Washington, D.C.**

Houghton, Gillian. 2009. *The Oneida of Wisconsin*. **The Rosen Publishing Group.**

Hunt, G.T. 1940. *The Wars of the Iroquois*. **University of Wisconsin Press, Madison, Wisconsin.**
Jemison, G. Peter (Ed.); Schein, Anna M. (Ed.); Powless Jr., Irving (ed.) 2000. *Treaty of Canandaigua 1794: 200 Years of Treaty Relations Between the Iroquois Confederacy and the United States*. **Clear light Publishing.**

Jennings, Francis. 1984. *The Ambiguous Iroquois Empire: The Covenant Chain Confederation of Indian Tribes with English Colonies*. **W.W. Norton and Company, New York.**

Jennings, Francis (ed.) 1985. *The History and Culture of Iroquois Diplomacy: An Interdisciplinary Guide to the Treaties of the Six Nations and Their League.*

Jesuit Relations. **1896-1901.** *The Jesuit Relations and Allied Documents: Travels and Explorations of the Jesuit Missionaries in New France.* **73 vols. R.G. Thwaites Ed. Barrows Brothers, Cleveland.**

Jesuit Relations. Vol 22, Vol 28; Vol 30

Johansen, Bruce E. **1995.** *Dating the Iroquois Confederacy.* **Akwesasne Notes New Series 01 (03-04) Pgs. 62-63.**

Johansen, Bruce E. **2006.** *The Native Peoples of North America.* **Rutgers University Press.**

Jones, Charles Henry. **1882.** *History of the Campaign for the Conquest of Canada in 1776: from the Death of Montgomery to the Retreat of the British Army Under Sir Guy Carleton.* **Philedelphia: Porter and Coates. OCLC 2110167.**

Jordan, Kurt A. **2013. Incorporation and Colonialization: Post Columbian Iroquois Satellite Communities and Processes of Indigenous Autonomy. American Anthropologist 115(1).**

Josephy, Alvin M. **(ed.) 1961.** *The American Heritage Book of Indians.* **American Heritage Publishing Co. Pgs. 188-189.**

Kapler, Charles J. **1904.** *United States Government Treaties with American Indian Tribes: Treaty with the Wyandot, 1795.* **Oklahoma State University Library.**

Karr, William J. **1970.** *Explorers, soldiers and statesmen: a history of Canada through biography.* **Ayer Publishing.**

Kelsay, Isabel Thompson. **1984.** *Joseph Brant, 1743-1807, Man of Two Worlds.* **Syracuse University Press, Syracuse, New York.**

Klinck, Carl F.; Talman, James J. **1970.** *The Journal of Major John Norton, 1816.* **Champlain Society Publications, Toronto, Ontario, Canada.**

Konrad, Victor. **2013.** *An Iroquois Frontier: The North Shore of Lake Ontario During the Late Seventeenth Century.* **Journal of Historical Geography.**

Lahontan, Baron. **1703.** *New Voyages to North America.* **London**

Lanctot, Gustave. **1967.** *Canada and the American Revolution 1774-1783.* **Cameron, Margaret M. (translator). Cambridge, MA: Harvard University Press. OCLC 2468989.**

Lemelin, Raynald Harvey. **1996.** *Social Movements and the Great law of peace in Akwesasne.* **Thesis. School of Graduate Studies, University of Ottawa, Ottawa, Ontario**

Marcel, **C.M.W. 2014.** *Iroquois Origins of Modern Toronto.* **Counterweights.**

MacLeod, Peter. **1992.** *Notes on 'The Treaty of Kahnawake, 1760.'* **Ottawa Legal History Group, Ottawa, Ontario. http://www3.sympatico.ca/donald.macleod2/border.html**

MacLeod, Peter. **1996.** *The Canadian Iroquois and the Seven Year's War.* **The Canadian War Museum, Ottawa, Ontario.**

Marshall, Peter. **1967.** *Sir William Johnson and the Treaty of Fort Stanwix, 1768.* **Journal of American studies 1#2. Pgs. 149-179.**

Marston, Daniel. **2002.** *The French-Indian War 1754-1760.* **Osprey Publishing**

Mathieu, Jacques (ed.) **1992.** *The Plains of Abraham. The Culture of an Ideal.*
Dundurn Press. Canadian War Museum Historical Publication No. 29.

Mithun, Marianne. **1981.** *Stalking the Susquehannock.* **International Journal of American Linguistics. 47:1-26.**

Moogk, Peter. **2007.** *Adam Dollard des Ormeaux.* **The Canadian Encyclopedia.**

Murray, Stuart A. P. **2006.** *Smithsonian Q & A: The American Revolution.* **Harper Collins Publishing, New York. OCLC**

Myrvold, Barbara. **1997.** *The People of Scarborough: A History.* **City of Scarborough Public Library Board.**

National Archives of Canada, **1822Record Group 10, Indian Affairs Paper. Vol. 1822, pp. 22, 35..**

Nelson, Paul David. **1985.** *Anthony Wayne: Soldier of the Early Republic.* **Indiana University Press, Bloomington, Indiana.**

New York Colonial Documents. Part V, pgs. 724-725

Olsen, James S. **1991.** Historical *Dictionary of European Imperialism.* **Greenwood Publishing Group.** *O'Toole, Fintan.* **2005.** *White Savage: William Johnson and the Invention of America.* **Farrer, Straus and Giroux Publishing, New York.**

Pargellis, S. **1935.** *Braddock's Defeat.* **American Historical review, 41 (1935-6). Pgs. 253-69**

Parker, Arthur C. **1916.** *The Constitution of the Five Nations – or – The Iroquois Book of the Great Law.* **University of the State of New York, Bulletin 184.**

Parker, Arthur C. **1922.** *The Archeological History of New York.* **New York State Museum bulletin 235-238.**

Parker, Arthur C. **1968.** *Parker on the Iroquois.* **Syracuse University Press, Syracuse, New York.**

Little, Brown and Company, Ninth Edition. Pgs. 34-42.

Parkman, Francis. **1867.** *Jesuits in North America in the Seventeenth Century.*

Parkman, Francis. 1877. *Count Frontenac and New France under Louis XIV.* **Pgs. 140-143. Published in 2005 by Hayes Barton Press; A Division of Vital Source Technologies Inc., Raleigh, North Carolina.**

Peckham, Howard H. 1947. *Pontiac and the Indian Uprising.* **University of Chicago Press. Pgs. 170; 226.**

Pound, Arthur. 1930. *Johnson of the Mohawks.* **Macmillan Publishing, New York.**

Randall, E.O. 1902. *The Dunmore War.* **Heer Publishing, Columbus, Ohio.**

Roosevelt, Theodore. 1896. *St. Clair's Defeat, 1791.* **Fort Wayne Convention Bureau.**

Schoolcraft, Henry Rowe. 1856. *The Myth of Hiawatha, and the Other Oral Legends, Mythological and Allegoric, of the North American Indians.*

Skidmore, Warren; Kaminsky, Donna. 2002. *Lord Dunmore's Little War of 1774: His Captains and Their Men Who Opened Up Kentucky & the West to American Settlement.* **Heritage Books Inc., Bowie, Maryland, U.S.A.**

Sioui, Georges E. 1999. *Huron-Wendat: The Heritage of the Circle.* **University of British Columbia Press.**

Smith, Justin H. 1907. *Our Struggle for the Fourteenth Colony, Volumes 1 and 2.* **New York: G.P. Putnam and Sons. OCLC 259236**

Starna, William A. 2013. *From Homeland to New Land: A History of the Mahican Indians, 1600-1830.* **University of Nebraska Press, Nebraska, U.S.A.**

Sultzman, Lee. 2014. *First Nations Histories. Iroquois History.* **http://www.tolatsga.org/iro.html** *Swinnerton, Henry.* 1906. *The Story of Cherry Valley.* **New York State Historical Museum, Cherry Valley, New York.**

Sword, Wiley. 1985. *President Washington's Indian War: The Struggle for the Old Northwest, 1790-1795.* **University of Oklahoma Press.**

Taylor, Alan. 2006. *The Divided Ground: Indians, Settlers, and the Divided Borderland of the American Revolution.* **Alfred A. Knopf Publishing, New York.**

Trigger, Bruce. 1976. *The Disappearance of the St.*

Tooker, Elisabeth. 1991. *An Ethnography of the Huron Indians, 1615-1649.* **Syracuse University Press.** *Lawrence Iroquoians* **from** *The Children of Aataenstic: A History of the Huron People to 1660, Vol. 2.* **McGill-Queens University Press, Kingston and Montreal.**

Toporoski, Richard. 1998. *The Invisible Crown.* **Monarchist League of Canada, Toronto.**

Treaty Minutes. 1774. Pennsylvania Council Minutes, June 16. 4:706-09

Trigger, Bruce (ed.) 1978. *Handbook of American Indians;* **Volume 15. Pgs. 287-288. Northeast Publishing.**

Trudel, Marcel. **1979** (1966) *Donnacona.* **In Brown, George Williams. Dictionary of Canadian Biography. University of Toronto Press, Toronto.**

Tyler, Lyon Gardiner. 1907. *Narratives of Early Virginia 1606-1625.* **Barnes & Noble Publishers.**

Waddell, Louis M.; Bomberger, Bruce D. 1996. *The French and Indian War in Pennsylvania: Fortification and Struggle During the War for Empire.* **Pennsylvania Historical and Museum Commission, Harrisburg, Pennsylvania.**

Wallace, Paul. 1946. *White Roots of Peace.* **University of Pennsylvania Press, Philadelphia.**

Warrick, Gary. 2003. *European Infectious Disease and Depopulation of the Wendat-Tionontate (Huron-Petun).* **World Archeology 35. Pgs. 258-275.**

Watt, Gavin. 2002. *Rebellion in the Mohawk Valley: The St. Leger Expedition of 1777.* **Dundurn Press, Toronto, Ontario.**

Wilkonson, Norman B. 1953. *Robert Morris and the Treaty of Big Tree.* **Organization of American Historians.**

Williams, Paul. 1993. *The Covenant Chain.* **North American Indian Travelling College, Cornwall Island, Akwesasne, Ontario.**

Winkler, John F. 2013. *Fallen Timbers, 1794: The U.S. Army's First Victory.* **Osprey Publishing.**

Wood, William. 1911. *Tercentennial Quebec.* **In Doughty, A.G.; Wood, William.** *The King's Book of Quebec.* **The Mortimer Co. Ltd.; Ottawa, Ontario, Canada**

Wrong, George; Langton, H. H. 2009. *The Chronicles of Canada: Volume IV - The Beginnings of British Canada.* **Fireship Press, Tucson, Arizona, U.S.A.**

Secondary Sources

Abler, Thomas S. 1980. *Iroquois Cannibalism: Fact not Fiction.* **Ethnohistory, Vol. 27, No. 4. Special Iroquois Issue, Autumn 1980. Pp.309-316. Duke University Press.**

Abler, Thomas S. 2001. *Cornplanter: Chief Warrior of the Allegany Seneca.* **Syracuse University Press, Syracuse, New York.**

Allen, Robert S. 1992. *His Majesty's Indian Allies: British Indian Policy in the Defenses of Canada.* **Dundurn Press, Toronto.**

Allen, Thomas B. 2010. *Tories: Fighting for the King in America's First Civil War.* **Harper Collins Publishing, New York.**

Bailyn, Bernard. _____ *The Barbarous Years: The Peopling of British North America: The Conflict of Civilizations, 1600-1675.*

Beauchamp, William Martin. **1905.** *A History of New York Iroquois: Now Commonly Called the Six Nations.* **Bulletin 78, Archeology 9, University of the State of New York Press. Pgs. 156-157.**

Bemus, Samuel Flagg. **1935.** *The Diplomacy of the American Revolution.*

Betts, William W. **2010.** *The Hatchet and the Plow: The Life and Times of Chief Cornplanter.*

Bonaparte, Darren. **2006.** *Creation and Confederation. The Living History of the Iroquois.* **Published by The Wampum Chronicles, The Mohawk Territory of Akwesasne.**

Bonaparte, Darren. _____ **The** *Seven Nations of Canada. The Other Iroquois Confederacy.* http://www.wampumchronicles.com.sevennations.html. Published by The Wampum Chronicles, Mohawk Territory of Akwesasne.

Bonaparte, Darren. **2009.** *A Lily Among the Thorns. The Mohawk Repatriation of Kateri Tekahkwi:tha.*

Published by The Wampum Chronicles, The Mohawk Territory of Akwesasne.

Bonvillian, Nancy. **2005.** *Hiawatha: Founder of the Iroquois Confederacy.*

Boyd, Julian P. (ed.) *Indian Treaties Printed by Benjamin Franklin, 1736-1762*

Boyce, Douglas W. **1973.** *A Glimpse of Iroquois Culture History through the Eyes of Joseph Brant and John Norton. Proceedings of the American Philosophical Society,* **117(4): pgs. 286-294.**

Brandao, J.A. **1997.** *Your Fyre Shall Burn No More: Iroquois Policy Toward New France and Its Native Allies to 1701.*

Brandon, William. Josephy, Alvin M. (ed.) **1961.** *American Heritage Book of Indians.* **American Heritage Publishing Company.**

Cadwallader, Colden. **1958.** *The History of the Five Indian Nations: Depending on the Province of New York in America.* **Cornell University Press, Ithaca, New York, U.S.A.**

Calloway, Colin G. **1995.** *The American Revolution in Indian Country: Crisis and Diversity in Native American Communities.* **Cambridge University Press, Cambridge, England.**

Campisi, Jack; Starna, William. **1995.** *On the Road to Canandaigua: The Treaty of 1794.* **American Indian Quarterly, Vol. 19, No. 4.**

_____ *Treaty of Grenville,* **Capital Ohio:113**

Canadian Archives _____ **C. 256. Pg.194**

Cappel, Constance. **2007.** *The Smallpox Genocide of the Odawa Tribe at L'Arbre Croche, 1763: The History of a Native American People.* **Edwin Mellon Press, Lewiston, NY.**

Carus, Paul. **1902.** from *Hiawatha and the Onondaga Indians,* **by Charles l. Henning, The Open Court, A Monthly Magazine, XVI. The Open Court Publishing Company, Chicago, Illinois, U.S.A. Pgs. 461, 550, 561.**

Coleman, Margaret. **1977.** *The American Capture of Fort Orange.* **Parks Canada Bulletin.**

Corbett, Theodore. **2012.** *No Turning Point: The Saratoga Campaign in Perspective.* **University of Oklahoma Press.**

_____ **2001.** *Iroquois Democracy.* **Portland State University.** http://www.iroquoisdemocracy.pdx.edu/html/covenantchain.htm

Clement, Daniel. **1996.** *The Algonquin.* **Canadian Museum of Civilization, Hull, Quebec.**

Covenant Chain. **2001.** *Iroquois Democracy.* **Portland State University**

Craven, Wesley Frank. **1968.** *The Colonies in Transition: 1610-1713.* **Harper & Row, New York.**

Densmore, Christopher. **1999.** *Red Jacket: Iroquois Diplomat and Orator.* **Syracuse University Press, Syracuse, New York.**

Dickason, Olive Patricia. **1992.** Canada's First Nations. A History of the Founding Peoples from Earliest Times. McClelland & Stewart Inc., Toronto, Ontario, Canada.

Dickason, Olive Patricia. **1996.** *Huron/Wyandot.* **Encyclopedia of North American Indians. Pgs. 263-65. Hoxie, Frederick E. (Ed.). Houghton Mifflin Publishing, Boston, Massachusetts.**

Dixon, David. **2005.** *Never Come to Peace Again: Pontiac's Uprising and the Fate of the British Empire in North America.* **University of Oklahoma Press. Pgs. 152-155.**

Dowd, Gregory Evans. **1992.** *A Spirited Resistance: The North American Indian Struggle for Unity, 1745-1815.* **Johns Hopkins University Press, Baltimore and London.**

Dowd, Gregory Evans. **2002.** *War Under Heaven. Pontiac, the Indian Nations, and the British Empire.* **Johns Hopkins University Press. Pgs. 144-7; 190.**

Drake, Samuel Adams. **1901.** *The Making of the Ohio Valley States, 1660-1837.*

Drake, Samuel Adams. **1910.** *The Border Wars of New England.* **C. Scribner's Sons Publishing.**

Dull, Jonathan R. **1987.** *A Diplomatic History of the American Revolution.* **Yale University Press**

Eccles, William J. **1955.** *Frontenac and New France, 1672-1698.* **McGill University Press, Montreal, Quebec.**

Eccles, William J. 1959. *Frontenac: The Courtier Governor*. **McClelland & Stuart, Toronto, Ontario.**

Eccles, William J. 1983. *The Canadian Frontier, 1534-1760*. **University of New Mexico Press, Albuquerque, New Mexico.**

Eccles, William J. 2000. *Brisay de Denonville, Jacques-Rene de, Marquis de Denonville*. **Dictionary of Canadian Biography. University of Toronto Press, Toronto.**

Edmunds, David R. 1984. *Tecumseh and the Quest for Indian Leadership*. **Little Brown, Boston.**

Edmunds, Walter D. 1997. *Drums Along the Mohawk*. **Syracuse university Press, Syracuse, New York.**

Eid, Leroy V. 1979. *The Ojibway-Iroquois War: The War the Five Nations did not Win.*

Favor, Leslie J. 2003. *The Iroquois Constitution: A primary Source Investigation of the Law of the Iroquois.* **The Rozen Publishing Group.**

Fenton, William N. 1941a. *Masked Medicine Societies of the Iroquois.* **In the annual report of the Smithsonian institution for 1940. Pgs. 397-430. Washington, D.C.**

Fenton, William N. 1944. *The Requickening Address of the Iroquois Condolence Council* **by JNB Hewitt. Journal of the Washington Academy of Sciences 34.3. Pgs. 65-85.**

Fenton, William N. 1985. *Structure, Continuity and Change in the Process of Iroquois Treaty Making in the History of Culture of Iroquois Diplomacy.* **Syracuse university Press, Syracuse, New York.**

Fenton, William N. 1998. *The Great Law and the Longhouse: A Political History of the Iroquois Confederacy.* **Norman University of Oklahoma Press.**

Fischer, Joseph R. 2007. *A Well-Executed Failure: The Sullivan Campaign Against the Iroquois, July -September 1779.* **University of South Carolina Press, Columbia, South Carolina.**

Flexner, James T. 1959. *Mohawk Baronet: A Biography of Sir William Johnson.* **Syracuse University Press. Also published in 1979 as** *Lord of the Mohawks*.

Foster, Michael K.; Campisi, Jack; Mithun, Marianne. 1984. *Extending the Rafters.* **State University of New York Press.**

Gayanashagowa (a) – http://www.indigenouspeople.net/iroqcon.htm

Gayanashagowa (b) - **different translation of** *Kaianerekowa Hotinonsionne, The Great Law of Peace of the Longhouse People.* http://www.manataka.org/page135.html

Gayanashagowa c) - **another rendition of the** *Constitution,* **displaying sections 1-28. http:// magic .education2020.com/Websites/Literature/Constitution_of_the_Iroquois_ Nations.htm**

Garrad and Heidenreich. _____ *Handbook of North American Indians; Khionontateronon (Petun).* **Smithsonian Institution.**

George-Kanentiio, Doug. **2000.** *Iroquois Culture and Commentary.* **Clear light Publishing, Santa Fe, New Mexico.**

George-Kanentiio, Doug. **2006.** *Iroquois on Fire. A Voice from the Mohawk Nation.* **Greenwood Publishing Group.**

Greene, Nelson. **1925.** *History of the Mohawk Valley, Gateway to the West, 1614-1925.* **Reprint Services Corp.**

Grenier, John. **2005.** *The Far Reaches of Empire: War in Nova Scotia; 1710-1760.* **Oklahoma University Press.**

Gus, A.L. **1883.** *Early Indian History on the Susquehanna: Based on Rare and Original documents.* **L.S. Hart printer (Harvard Reprint).**

Grumet, Robert S. **1991.** *The Minnisink Settlements: Native American Identity and Society in the Munsee Heartland, 1650-1778.* **In** *The People of Minnisink,* **David Orr and Douglas Campana, (Eds.) Philadelphia National Park Service. Pg. 236.**

Graves, Donald E. *Red Coats and Grey Jackets: The Battle of Chippawa.* **Dundurn Press, Toronto, Ontario, Canada.**

Greene, Nelson (ed.). **1925.** *History of the Mohawk Valley. Gateway to the West 1614-1925.* **Dekanawida and Hiawatha, Chapter Nine. The S.J. Clarke Publishing Company, 1925, at Schenectady Digital History Archive.**

Haan, Richard. **1980. The Problem of Iroquois Neutrality: Suggestions for Revision.**

Harris, Marvin. **1977.** *Cannibals and Kings: The origins of Cultures.* **Random house, New York.**

Harris, R. Cole; Mathews, Geoffrey J. **1987.** *Historical Affairs of Canada: From the Beginning to 1800.* **University of Toronto Press, Toronto.**

Hauptman, Lawrence M. **1988.** *Formulating American Indian Policy in New York State, 1970-1986.* **State University of New York Press.**

Hauptman, Laurence M. **2008.** *Seven Generations of Iroquois Leadership: The Six Nations Since 1800.* **Syracuse University Press, Syracuse, New York, U.S.A.**

Heidenreich, Conrad E. *1978.* Huron. **Handbook of North American Indians. Trigger, Bruce (Ed.). Vol 15, Northeastern Indians. Smithsonian Institution.**

Henning, Charles L. **1902.** *Hiawatha and the Onondaga Indians.* **Open Court periodical.**

Hewitt, J.N.B. **1894.** *Era of the formation of the Historic League of the Iroquois.* **Judith Detweiter printers, Washington, D.C.**

Hewitt, J.N.B. 1920. *A Constitutional League of Peace in the Stone Age of America. The League of the Iroquois and Its Constitution.* **Smithsonian Institute Series. Pgs. 527-545.**

Hintzen, William. 2001. *The Border Wars of the Upper Ohio Valley (1769-1794).* **Manchester CT: Precision Shooting Inc.**

Hodge, F.W. 2009. *Tuscarora. Handbook of American Indians.*

http://www.accessgeneology.com/native/tribes/tuscarora/tuscarorahist.htm.

Smithsonian Institution, Washington, D.C.

Hale, Horatio. 1881. *Hiawatha and the Iroquois Confederacy: A Study in Anthropology.*

Hatzan, A. Leon. 1925. *The True Story of Hiawatha, and History of the Six Nation Indians.*

Heidenreich, C.E. 2001. *Huron-Wendat.* **The Canadian Encyclopedia.**

Henning, Charles L. 1902. *Hiawatha and the Onondaga Indians.* **The Open Court Publishing Company.**

Hitsman, J. MacKay; Graves, Donald E. 1999. *The Incredible War of 1812.* **Robin Bass Studio, Toronto.**

Houston, Jean; Rubin, Margaret. 1997. *Manual for the Peacemaker: An Iroquois Legend to Heal Self and Society.* **Quest books.**

Innis, H.A. 2001 [1930]. *The Fur Trade in Canada. An Introduction to Canadian Economic History.* **University of Toronto Press, Toronto**

Jaenen, Cornelius J. 1973. *Friend or Foe; Aspects of French Amerindian Culture Contact in the 16th and 17th Centuries.* **McClelland & Stuart, Toronto.**

Jennings, Francis. 1988. *Empire of Fortune: Crowns, Colonies, and Tribes in the Seven Years War in America.* **Norton Publishing, New York.**

Johansen, Bruce E.; Mann, Barbara Alice. 2010. *Ganondagan.* **Encyclopedia of the Haundenosaunee (Iroquois Confederacy). Greenwood Publishing Group.**

Jortner, Adam. 2011. *The Gods of Prophetstown: The Battle of Tippecanoe and the Holy War of the American Frontier.* **Oxford University Press.**

_____. 1982. *Forgotten Founders. Benjamin Franklin, the Iroquois, and the Rationale for the American Revolution.* **Chapter Five "The Philosopher as Savage." Gambit Publishing, Ipswich, Massachusetts, U.S.A.**

_____. *The Onondaga Nation.* http://www.onondaganation.org/aboutus/history.html

_____ *Iroquois Great Law of Peace.* http://www.history and the headlines.abc-clio.com/ContentPages/ContentPage.aspx?entryId=117174&currentS.

_____ *King William's War: 1689-1697.* h ttp://www.usahistory.info/colonial-wars/King-Williams-War.html

Kirke, Henry. 1908. *The First English Conquest of Canada with some account of the earliest settlements in Nova Scotia and Newfoundland.* Sampson, Low, Marsten & Compnay Ltd., London.

King, Thomas. 2012. *The Inconvenient Indian.* Doubleday Publishers; Canada.

Knowles, Nathaniel. 1940. *The Torture of Captives by the Indians of Eastern North America.* Proceedings of the American Philosophical Society 82:151-225.

Knopf, Richard C. 1960. *Anthony Wayne: A Name in Arms.* University of Pittsburgh Press, Pittsburgh, Pennsylvania.

Kooperman, Paul. 1977. *Braddock at the Monongahela.* University of Pittsburgh Press, Pittsburgh, Pennsylvania.

Kurt, Jordan A. 2013. *Incorporation and Colonization: Post Columbian Iroquois Satellite Communities and Processes of Indigenous Autonomy.* American Anthropologist 115(1)

Keith, Patrick. 2005. *Through Colonialism and Imperialism: The Struggle for Tuscarora Nationhood in Southeastern North Carolina.* http://www.ais.arizona.edu/people/patrick-keith. M.A. Thesis, University of Arizona.

Kent, Barry. 1984. *Susquehanna's Indians.* The Pennsylvania Historical and Museum Commission, Harrisburg, Pennsylvania.

Laing, Mary E. 1920. *The Hero of the Longhouse.*

Langguth, A.J. 2006. *Union 1812: The Americans Who Fought the Second War of Independence.* Simon & Schuster, New York.

Lancaster, Bruce. 1971. *The American Revolution.* American Heritage Books, New York.

Latimer, John. 1812. *War with America.* Howard University Press, Cambridge, Massachusetts, U.S.A.

Leckie, Robert. 1999. *A Few Acres of Snow: The Saga of the French and Indian Wars.* John Wiley Publishing, New York.

Leder. (ed) 1747. *Livingston Indian Records,* 136-137; 172-174.

Levinson, David. 1976. *An Explanation for the Oneida-Colonist Alliance in the American revolution.* Ethnohistory 23, no.3. Pgs. 265-289.

Litabien, Raymond; Vaugeois, Denis (eds.) **Translated by Kathe Roth. 2004.** *Champlain. The Birth of French America.* **McGill-Queens University Press, Montreal and Kingston.**

Lucas, Charles Prestwood. **1901.** *History of Canada: Part 1, New France.* **Clarendon Press**

Mann, Charles C. **2005.** *New Revelations of the Americas Before Columbus.* **Alfred A. Knopf Publishing, New York.**

McCardell, Lee. **1958.** *Ill-Starred General: Braddock of the Coldstream Guards.* **University of Pittsburgh Press, Pittsburgh, Pennsylvania.**

MacLeod, Peter. **2008.** *Northern Armageddon: The Battle of the Plains of Abraham.* **Douglas & McIntyre, Vancouver, British Columbia.**

Middleton, Richard. **2007.** *Pontiac's War: Its Causes, Course and Consequences.* **Pgs. 83-91.**

Hamilton, Milton W. **1976.** *Sir William Johnson: Colonial America, 1715-1763.* **Kennikat Press, Port Washington, New York.**

Mintz, Max M. **1999.** *Seeds of Empire: The American Revolutionary War Conquest of the Iroquois.* **New York university Press, New York. OCLC**

Morgan, Lewis Henry. **1877.** *Ancient Society.* **Pg. 97.**

Morgan, Lewis Henry. **1995.** *The League of the Iroquois.* **J.G. Press**

Morrissey, Brendan. **2000.** *Saratoga, 1777: Turning Point of a Revolution.* **Osprey Publishing**

Morrison, Kenneth. **1984.** *The Embattled Northeast: The Elusive Ideal of Alliance in Abenaki -Euroamerican Relations.* **University of California Press.**

Moulton, G. (ed.) _____ *Journals of the Lewis and Clark Expedition. Vol. 2.*

Nester, William. **2000.** *The First Global War: Britain, France, and the Fate of North America, 1756-1775.* **Greenwood Publishing Group.**

Nester, William. **2004.** *The Frontier War for American Independence.* **Stackpole Books.**

Nester, William. **2008.** *The Epic Battles of Ticonderoga, 1758.* **State University New York Press, Albany, New York.**

O'Callaghan, E.B. (ed). **1853-1887.** *Documents Relative to the Colonial History of the State of New York.*

New York Colonial Documents. 15 vols. Weed Parsons, Albany, New York.

New York Colonial Documents. IV, 337, 768

New York Colonial Documents. IX, 281,725

Orr, Charles (ed.) 1897. *History of the Pequot War. The Contemporary Accounts of Mason, Underhill, Vincent and Gardner.*

Parkman, Francis. 1898. *The Conspiracy of Pontiac and the Indian War After the Conquest of Canada.*

Parkman, Francis. 1897. *Montcalm and Wolfe, Volume 1.* **Little, Brown, and Company.**

Parkman, Francis. 1877. **Count Frontenac and New France under Louis XIV. Boston.**

Paul, Daniel N. 2006. *First Nations History: We Were Not Savages.* **Fernwood Publishing, Nova Scotia, Canada.**

Peckham, Howard. 1964. *The Colonial Wars, 1689-1762.* **University of Chicago Press.**

Pendergast, James F. 1998. *The Confusing Identities Attributed to Stadacona and Hochelaga.* **Journal of Canadian Studies 32(4).**

Perkins, Bradford. 1955. *The First Rapprochement: England and the United States, 1795-1805.*

Plank, Geoffrey. 2001. *An Unsettled Conquest: The British Campaign Against the Peoples of Acadia.* **University of Pennsylvania Press.**

Preston, Richard A. Trans., Lamontagne, Leopold, (ed.) 1958. *Royal Fort Frontenac.* **Toronto**

Radisson, Peter Esprit. 1885. *Voyages of Peter Esprit Radisson.* **The Prince Society, Boston, Massachusetts,**

Ranlet, Philip. 2000. *The British, the Indians, and Smallpox: What Actually Happened at Fort Pitt in 1763.* **Pennsylvania History in JSTOR. Pgs. 427-441.**

Government of Canada. 1996. *Looking Forward, Looking Back. Report of the Royal Commission on Aboriginal Peoples.* **Volume 1. Canada Communication Group Publishing, Ottawa, Ontario, Canada.**

Richardson, Boyce. 1993. *People of Terra Nullius.* **Douglas & McIntyre Publishing, Vancouver & Toronto, Canada.**

Richter, Daniel K.; Merrell, James H. (eds.) 1987. *Beyond the Covenant Chain: The Iroquois and their Neighbours in Indian North America, 1600-1800.* **Syracuse university Press, Syracuse, New York.**

Richter, Daniel K. 1992. *The Ordeal of the Longhouse: The Peoples of the Iroquois League in the Era of European Colonization.* **University of North Carolina Press, Chapel Hill, North Carolina, U.S.A.**

Sanday, Peggy Reeves. 1986. *Divine Hunger. Cannibalism as a Cultural System.* **Cambridge University Press, Cambridge, Massachusetts.**

Salvucci, Claudio R.; Schiavo Jr., Anthony P. 2003. *Iroquois Wars ll: Excerpts from the Jesuit Relations and Other Primary Sources.* **Evolution Publishing, Bristol, Pennsylvania.**

Saraydarian, Torkom; and Alesch, Joann L. 1984. *Hiawatha and the Great Peace.*

Sargent, W. 1855. *The History of an Expedition Against Fort Duquesne in 1775: Under Major-General Edward Braddock (1855).*

Schiavo Jr., Anthony P.; Salvucci, Claudio R. 2003. *Iroquois Wars l: Excerpts from the Jesuit Relations and Primary Sources 1535-1650.* **Evolution Publishing, Bristol Pennsylvania.**

Shannon, Timothy J. 2000. *Indians and Colonists at the Crossroads of Empire. The Albany Congress of 1754.* **Cornell University Press. Pgs. 6-8.**

Shannon, Timothy J. 2008. *Iroquois Diplomacy on the Early American Frontier.* **Viking Publishers, New York.**

Simonson, Lee. 2010. *Tuscarora Heroes.* **Historical Association of Lewiston, Lewiston, New York.**

Sipe, C. Hale. 1929. *The Indian Wars of Pennsylvania: An Account of the Indian Events, in Pennsylvania, of the French and Indian War, Pontiac's War, Lord Dunmore's War, the Revolutionary War, and the Indian Uprising from 1789 to 1795. Tragedies of the Pennsylvania Frontier.* **Telegraph Express, OCLC 2678875, Harrisburg, Pennsylvania.**

Sipe, C.H. 1931. *The Indian Wars of Pennsylvania.*

Skaggs, David Curtis (ed.) 1977. *The Old Northwest in the American Revolution.* **The State Historical society of Wisconsin, Madison, Wisconsin.**

Snow, Dean R. 1996. *The Iroquois.* **Blackwell Publishers, Boston, Massachusetts.**

Snow, Dean R. 2008. *Archeology of Native North America.* **Prentice Hall, New York.**

Spigelman, Robert. _____ How *the Sullivan-Clinton Campaign Dispossessed the Cayuga.* **http://www.sullivanclinton.com.** *Sullivan-Clinton Campaign. Then and Now.*

Stanley, G.F.G. 1963. *The Significance of the Six Nations Participation in the War of 1812.* **Ontario History LV (4).**

Starna, William A. 2004. *The Diplomatic Career of Canasatego.* **In William A. Pencak and Daniel K. Richter (Eds.)** *Friends and Enemies in Penn's Woods: Indians, Colonists, and the Racial Construction of Pennsylvania.* **University Park Press, Pennsylvania, U.S.A**

Steckley, John. _____ Wendat *Dialects and the Development of the Huron Alliance.* **http://www.wyandot.org/wendat.htm**

Stone, William L. 1841. *Life and Times of Red Jacket, or, Sa-go-ye-wat-ha: Being the Sequel to the History of the Six Nations.* **Wiley and Putnam, New York.**

Sugden, John. 2000. *Blue Jacket: Warrior of the Shawnee*. **University of Nebraska Press.**

Sugden, John. 1997. *Tecumseh: A Life*. **Holt Publishing, New York.**

Steckley, J. L. 2007. *Words of the Huron*.

Swanton, John Reed. 1906. *The Indian Tribes of North America*. **Pg. 74.**

Tannahill, R. 1975. *Flesh and Blood: A History of the Cannibal Complex*. **Stein and Day Publishing, New York.**

Thwaites, Ruben Gold. Compiled and Edited: 1896-1901. *The Jesuit Relations and Allied Documents: Travels and Explorations of the Jesuit Missionaries in New France, 1610 to 1791.* **Burrows Brothers Company, Cleveland, Ohio.**

Thwaites, Reuben Gold; Kellog, Louise Phelps (eds.). 2002. *Documentary History of Dunmore's War. 1774.* **Wisconsin Historical Society, Madison, Wisconsin.**

Tooker, Elizabeth. 1964. *An Ethnography of the Huron Indians*. **1615-1649. Bureau of American Ethnology Bulletin 190.**

Tooker, Elisabeth. 1990. *The United States Constitution and the Iroquois League*. **In Clifton, J.A. The Invented Indian: Cultural Fictions and Government policies. Transaction Publishers, New Brunswick, N.J., U.S.A. Pgs. 107-128.**

Tuck, James A. 1971a. *The Iroquois Confederacy*. Scientific American. 224(2):32-49.

Tuck, James A. 1971b. *Onondaga Iroquois Prehistory: A Study in Settlement Archeology*. **Syracuse University Press, Syracuse.**

Tuck, James A. 1990. *Onondaga Iroquois Prehistory. A Study in Settlement Archeology*. **Syracuse University Press, Syracuse, New York State, U.S.A.**

Trigger, Bruce. 1969. *The Huron: Farmers of the North*. **Holt Publishing, New York.**

Trigger, Bruce. 1976. *The Children of Aataentsic: A History of the Huron People to 1660*. **McGill-Queens University Press, Kingston and Montreal.**

_____ 2006. **Letters of Chief Samuel Johns to Frank G. Speck; reference to the Tutelo Indians.**

Wallace, Anthony F.C. 1957. **Origins of Iroquois Neutrality: The Grand Settlement of 1701.**

Wallace, Anthony F.C. 1969. *The Death and Rebirth of the Seneca*. **Vintage Books. New York.**

Warren, William W. Ed. Schenck, Theresa. 2009. *History of the Ojibway.* (**Second ed.**) **St. Paul Minnesota Historical Society press.**

Wheelock, Mathew. 1770. *Reflections, Moral and Political on Great Britain and Her Colonies.*

White, Richard. 2011 [1991]. *The Middle Ground: Indians, Empires, and Republics in the Great Lakes Region, 1650-1815.* **Cambridge University Press.**

Williams, Glenn F. 2005. *Year of the Hangman: George Washington's Campaign Against the Iroquois.* **Westholme Publishing.**

Witthoft, John. 1959. *Susquehannock Miscellany.* **Pennsylvania Historical and Museum Commission.**

Wright, Robert K. Jr. 1989. *The Continental Army.* **U.S. Army Center of Military History, Washington, D.C.**

Wright, James V. 1966. *The Ontario Iroquois Tradition.* **National Museum of Canada. Bulletin 210.**

Zaslow, Morris. 1964. *The Defended Border.* **MacMillan of Canada, Toronto.**

_____ *Cayuga Nation.* **http://tuscaroras.com/cayuganation/**

_____ **Haudenosaunee Grand Council.** *The Anti-Sovereignty Actions of the Warrior Society.* **http://www.sixnations.org/Threats_to_Traditional_Governments/**

CPSIA information can be obtained
at www.ICGtesting.com
Printed in the USA
LVOW12s1001070917
547862LV00001B/2/P